Indian Critiques of Gandhi

SUNY series in Religious Studies
Harold Coward, editor

Indian Critiques of Gandhi

Edited by
Harold Coward

State University of New York Press

Published by
State University of New York Press, Albany

For information, address State University of New York Press,
90 State Street, Suite 700, Albany, NY 12207

Production by Judith Block
Marketing by Anne Valentine

Library of Congress Cataloging-in-Publication Data

Indian critiques of Gandhi/edited by Harold Coward.
     p. cm. — (SUNY series in Religious Studies)
    ISBN 0-7914-5909-8 (alk. paper) — ISBN 0-7914-5910-1 (pbk. : alk. paper)
      1. Gandhi, Mahatma, 1869–1948—Political and social views. 2. India—
History—Autonomy and independence movements. 3. India—Politics and
Government—1919–1947. 4. Series.

DS481.G3153 2003
954.03'5'092—dc22
                                                      2003059082
          10 9 8 7 6 5 4 3 2 1

Contents

Acknowledgments

This book could not have appeared without the financial support of the Social Sciences and Humanities Research Council of Canada. Thanks are also due to the President, Vice President Research, the Deans of Humanities and Social Science, the Centre for Global Studies and the Centre for Asia Pacific Initiatives of the University of Victoria—all of whom provided financial help.

This book is a research project of the Centre for Studies in Religion and Society, University of Victoria, British Columbia, Canada. Special thanks are due to Moira Hill for arranging the meetings of the research team and to Connie Carter for preparing the manuscript for publication.

Introduction

Since his death in 1948 Gandhi's life has been the subject of more than one thousand books and and Sir Richard Attenborough's Oscar-winning film. Is another book needed? Surprisingly, an important aspect of Gandhi's life that has not been given sustained study is his engagement of other major figures in the Indian Independence movement who were often his critics during the years 1920–1940. This book aims to fill that gap. We will examine the strengths and weaknesses of his contribution to India as evidenced in the letters, speeches, and newspaper articles focused on the dialogue/debate between Gandhi and his major Indian critics. We have included within the term *Indian* not only obvious Indian colleagues who critically engaged Gandhi (e.g., Nehru, Tagore, and Ambedkar) but also two voices of British ancestry, Annie Besant and C. F. Andrews. Both had left England, made India their homeland, and debated with Gandhi the best course to take in achieving independence for India. Indeed it was the Home Rule movement of Besant that Gandhi had to displace in getting his Non-Cooperation, or Swaraj, movement adopted by the Indian National Congress at Calcutta in 1920.[1] Through letters, Andrews gave Gandhi critical counsel as an intimate friend throughout the 1920–1948 period. Included in our study are those who we felt were important leaders or groups within India from the perspective of Gandhi's focus on the achievement of Independence. While his power base was rural village India (and those alienated from their ancestral villages), Gandhi also sought to incorporate minority groups such as the Muslims, Sikhs, and Untouchables within his Non-Cooperation movement. Thus we have featured groups as well as individuals in our analysis. Due to limitations of space and time, however, not everyone who critically engaged Gandhi has been included. Among those deserving of discussion, but whom we were unable to include, are individuals such as Subhas Bose and groups such as the Indian Marxists. They are deserving of separate treatments elsewhere.

To his peers (both supporters and opponents) within the Indian Independence movements, Gandhi was a charismatic and frustratingly unpredictable colleague. He was the bane of orthodox Hindus who were infuriated
by his denunciation of caste and untouchability, and by his advocacy of secular politics. The Britisher, Lord Wavell, wrote in his journal in 1946 that
Gandhi was an "exceedingly shrewd, obstinate, double-tongued, single-
minded politician."[2] He was viewed as an enemy by supporters of both the
Hindu and the Muslim cause. Even within the Congress Party Gandhi faced
constant discontent. As B. R. Nanda notes,

> During the 1920's and 1930's young radicals like Jawaharlal Nehru, Sub-
> has Bose and Jayaprakash Narayan were straining at the leash: they fretted
> at the patient and peaceful methods of the Mahatma. The Indian commu-
> nists dubbed him a charismatic but calculating leader who knew how to
> rouse the masses but deliberately contained and diverted their revolution-
> ary ardour so as not to hurt the interests of British imperialists and Indian
> capitalists.[3]

Gandhi's response to his critics was one of patient engagement through letters and comment in his weekly journals (now published in his ninety volumes
of *Collected Works*). These writings, together with the responses of his critics,
form the primary source material analyzed by the writers of this volume.
Gandhi's attitude to his critics was evidenced in his comment to Nehru, "Resist me always when my suggestion does not appeal to your head or heart. I
shall not love you the less for that resistance."[4]

The Indian scene of Gandhi's day, says Eleanor Zelliot, "was marked by
a society-wide hierarchical system of social groups justified by religion; by the
presence of other vocal minorities especially that of the Muslims; and by the
administrative power of still another group, the British government in
India."[5] As a religiously based politician, Gandhi was well suited to work
within this pluralistic religious context. Perhaps his most unique contribution
was to attempt "the purification of political life through the introduction of
the *ashrama* or monastic ideal into politics."[6] Based on his experiments in
South Africa Gandhi saw himself as a renouncer and ashram dweller, a servant
of the people for whom the political fight for freedom was a sacred duty, a religious calling—even to the point of realizing the highest Hindu goal of release or *mokṣa* through political action. For his critics and colleagues, this
meant that Gandhi had to be engaged as a religiously motivated politician,
whom the masses regarded as a saint, a Mahatma, and who saw himself in a
monastic sense as being above the fray. Thus his practice of living simply in an

ashram withdrawn from worldly values, and following the guidance of his "higher inner voice."

As Judith Brown notes, such an approach generated

> misunderstanding and scepticism, hostility as well as love and loyalty. Few men have elicited such vitriolic opposition or such devoted service. Churchill's ignorant jibe at Gandhi as a half-naked, seditious fakir, Muslim distrust of this Hindu holy man who purported to speak for an Indian nation, the fanatical anger of the young Hindu who killed him for "appeasing" Muslims, were paralleled by crowds who flocked to venerate this frail, toothless man in loincloth and steel-rimmed spectacles with a commanding presence and magnetic voice.[7]

People from widely varying backgrounds were attracted to Gandhi and became followers or admirers, even though they would at times doubt his political principles or priorities that were often very opposed to those of today's world.

As a politician Gandhi was deeply engaged with the significant figures and movements within India's struggle for Independence. As Zelliot puts it, "Gandhi sought to weave the divergent interests in India into a unified opposition to the British, at the same time trying to pursue a course of reform without rending the social fabric of Indian society."[8] Many in India saw Gandhi, and Gandhi saw himself, as somehow through his monastic lifestyle standing above the discord around him and yet being able to unify it in the drive for Independence. This unique complexity that characterized Gandhi's life is reflected in the critiques of Gandhi contained in this volume. These chapters are written from the point of view of Gandhi's focus on Independence and his engagement with other important leaders of groups in that process.[9] For the timeline involved, see the chronology in the appendix.

Before Gandhi returned to India the stirrings of the Independence movement had already begun. The Theosophical Society led by the Englishwoman Annie Besant had established its headquarters in Adyar on the outskirts of Madras. In 1885 the Indian National Congress first convened under the direction of A. O. Hume, a former Indian civil servant and Theosophist. In 1891 Gandhi left India to study law in Britain. While studying in London Sir Aurobindo Ghose (see chapter 4) joined the student society Lotus and Dagger Indian for the overthrow of British rule in India. In 1893 Aurobindo returned to India to work in the Baroda civil service. He studied Sanskrit, Indian religion, the Upanisads and began writing a series in the Bombay paper *Indu Prakash* attacking the Congress's leadership. Having completed his studies and having returned to India for a brief period,

Gandhi left for South Africa where he led protests against discrimination toward Indians and developed the experimental Phoenix ashram refining his ideas on nonviolent resistance.

While Gandhi experimented in Africa, revolutionary fervor mounted in India. In 1899 V. D. Savarkar, the founding father of the Hindu Nationalist movement (see chapter 6) established the revolutionary organization Mitra Mela. In 1902 Aurobindo attended the Indian National Congress meeting for the first time. He aligned himself with the Extremists who advocated armed revolution and guerrilla warfare against the British using the Hindu scripture *Bhagavad Gita* to justify violence. Aurobindo moved to Calcutta in 1906 and helped form, with Congress, the group of Indian Nationalists who favor Indian self-reliance and British boycott. That same year Savarkar went to England to train young Indians in the theory of violent revolution. Living in London at India House he initiated the Free India Society. In 1908 Aurobindo was imprisoned for one year and while in jail immersed himself in the study and practice of Yoga. In 1909 Savarkar and Gandhi shared a public platform where they disagreed over interpreting the *Gita* as supporting armed struggle. On release from prison in 1910 Aurobindo withdrew from Indian politics and retired to Pondicherry to pursue Yoga but continued to disagree with Gandhi over the use of violence. Aurobindo refused repeated requests to lead Congress. Also in 1910 Savarkar was arrested in London and imprisoned in Bombay for participating in revolutionary activities. In 1914 World War I began and Besant launched her movement for Hindu reform and Indian self-government under British rule with better British–Indian understanding.

When Gandhi returned to India in 1915 after more than twenty years in South Africa, he did not immediately become engaged in Indian politics. In South Africa Gandhi's experiments in applying monastic value and practices to the achievement of political goals had evolved into his satyagraha, or nonviolent noncooperation technique, and his ashram style of life. However he did not see any prospect of launching a satyagraha in India for at least five years. He initially sought out a more obscure life, devoting himself to the problems of the masses of India in their local village settings. To identify with them he dressed in simple Gujarati clothes and spent a year with his wife, Kasturbhai, touring India, traveling third class on the train. Thus he saw India through the eyes of the poor and was shocked by the rough way they were treated by railway officials. But he was equally upset by the rude and dirty habits of the poor people who traveled third class and made the whole experience almost unbearable for Gandhi and Kasturbhai. Judith Brown comments, "The dirt, the numbers and the lack of facilities made third-class carriages little better than cattle trucks."[10] During his travels Gandhi spent some time at Shatiniketan, the new university community begun by Rabindranath Tagore, the Bengali writer and reformer who received the Nobel Prize for literature. While he was there Gandhi urged the teachers and students to do their own cleaning and cooking—something quite foreign to educated Indians—and to improve the hygiene in the kitchen area. Brown observes that "wherever Gandhi went, even when he was most welcome and at home, his critical eye was on people's habits and relationships, and he could not rest content without attempting reform according to his own ideals."[11]

These ideals of a simple ascetic life led Gandhi to oppose many aspects of modernity that had been adopted by some orthodox Hindus and especially by rising young leaders such as Jawaharlal Nehru. Gandhi described his monastic-based ideals of simplicity and self-discipline to satyagraha as follows: "[E]ven one truth-seeker by self-sacrifice could begin to cleanse the surrounding atmosphere and start the process of personal and social renewal."[12] Gandhi's unique insight was to apply these Hindu monastic ideals to the process of achieving political change. As a base for this activity he established the Satyagraha ashram on the outskirts of Ahmedabad in 1915 based on the model of his Phoenix ashram in South Africa. Vows of truth, nonviolence, celibacy (even between married couples), physical work, long hours, and simplicity in material possessions were required from all. In addition untouchables were included as full members; however, caste (as determined by birth) was followed as a social discipline but with no high or low status distinctions. Handweaving, work on the land, and helping with the routine household jobs of cleaning, cooking, and carrying water was expected from all. The inclusion of an untouchable couple and their child in the ashram cost Gandhi the loss of much orthodox Hindu support and, for a time, even that of his wife.

During this period Gandhi's concern was focused on the sanitation practices at pilgrimage sites such as Hardwar, acceptance of untouchables into Hindu society as servants *(shudras)* and the fostering of spinning wheels and handweaving as a way for village India to recover its self-sufficiency in the face of British-introduced industrialization. However, in 1915 Gandhi did involve himself in Indian politics to the extent of challenging Besant's agenda for "home rule" when he was on the platform with her at the opening ceremonies of the Banaras Hindu University. In 1916 Nehru first met Gandhi at the Lucknow meetings of Congress. It was at these same meetings that M. A. Jinnah, who later became the founding father of Pakistan, helped to develop the Lucknow Pact, which tentatively integrated the Hindu-dominated

Congress and the Muslim League by agreeing on separate electorates and Muslim representation—a high point in Hindu–Muslim political unity.

Despite his commitment to nonviolence, Gandhi supported the British war effort in World War I, but remained on the periphery of Indian politics. However, he would take a stand for prominent individuals or organizations if he thought that a moral issue was involved. For example, in 1917 Annie Besant was put in prison by the British for her leadership in the Home Rule for India campaign. Gandhi was tempted to engage in some sort of satyagraha campaign in Besant's support but in the end did not. Besant's Home Rule vision of self-rule *(Saraj)* for India did not square with Gandhi's—nor did he like her identification with the Theosophist movement of which she was president. Gandhi rejected the Theosophist notion of esoteric knowledge given by "Mahatmas" or great souls, and kept his distance from the Home Rule movement Besant was leading with Congress approval. Theosophists had for some thirty years been involved in the Indian nationalist movement. But it was Besant's Home Rule League initiative, begun in 1915, and her development of two newspapers *New India* and *Young India* that put her among the leaders of the Independence movement of the day. Because of her ideas and widespread popularity she was imprisoned by the British government in 1917, and while in prison was elected president of the Indian National Congress. As Joy Dixon shows in chapter 3, it was Besant's opposition to Gandhi's concept of satyagraha that led to a major falling out between them.

In 1919 the All-India Khilafat Committee was formed, with Gandhi's backing, to call for support of the Ottoman caliphate. During World War I, the Muslim Ottoman government of Turkey had aligned itself with Germany and opposed the British. The Khilafat agitation within the Muslim community in India was meant to support the Muslim cause in the old Ottoman Empire post World War I. Gandhi presided over the All-India Khilafat conference in Delhi and called on Hindus to support their fellow Muslims in this cause. His actions here exhibited the pattern he followed for the remainder of his life. If he thought the cause was morally right according to his own "inner voice" he would decide to support it even if he was alone and often without consulting colleagues. Thus, he announced his support of the Indian Muslim Khilafat movement before Congress. When the Indian National Congress formally met in 1920, Gandhi had already seized the initiative and was riding high in public opinion. Thus he was well positioned to introduce his noncooperation program, which Congress accepted making Gandhi the effective leader of both the Congress Nationalist initiative and the Khilafat struggles. He toured India with Muslim leaders, and Muslim–Hindu unity reached a high point. The

Muslim *ulama* endorsed a *fatwa* enjoining Muslim participation in Gandhi's Noncooperation movement as a religious duty. Jinnah, however, privately criticized Gandhi. It was also during this period that Gandhi proposed Hindustani as a national language—a suggestion that as Daud Rahbar shows in chapter 10 became a bone of contention with the Muslims.

In reaction to this Muslim–Hindu agitation, the government's passage of the Rowlatt Acts, which extended wartime restrictions on civil liberties into the post–World War I period, provoked Gandhi to launch a satyagraha campaign against the Rowlatt bills. With this move Gandhi and his nonviolent, noncooperation methods wrested leadership from Besant and her Home Rule idea. Gandhi also became editor of *Young India*, one of the papers started under Besant's initiative. In addition, the Jallianwala Bagh massacre of 1919 in Amritsar, where General Dyer ordered his troops to fire on an unarmed crowd gathered for a peaceful protest of the Rowlatt Acts, led Gandhi to reconsider his satyagraha strategy against the British. But in 1920 Gandhi launched a full noncooperation campaign. As T. S. Rukmani shows in chapter 5, this led to strong differences of opinion between Gandhi and Tagore. Tagore joined Gandhi in protesting against the Amritsar atrocities by renouncing his knighthood from England, while Gandhi returned his Boer War medals, but they parted company over issues such as the burning of British-made clothing and the withdrawal of students from government schools. Tagore, who saw clothes needed by the poor being burned as a protest against the British, was appalled and spoke out against such forms of Gandhi's noncooperation. Andrews also questioned Gandhi's tactics in the burning of clothes. Yet through all their disagreements these two men remained friends with Gandhi.

Also, soon after World War I commenced, the British government had imprisoned the Muslim brothers Shaukat and Mahomed Ali for their Pan Islamic and pro-Turkish Khalifat sympathies and journalism activities. Gandhi took up their cause both because of the injustice involved and because it offered an opportunity to work at improving Muslim–Hindu cooperation, which he judged essential to the achievement of independence in India. Gandhi's public stand for the Ali brothers was not successful as the government refused to release them on political grounds. However, Brown notes, "The Alis' case was the first all-India issue on which Gandhi showed his political skills and his potential as an all-India political protagonist."[13] It also introduced his strategy of working for Hindu–Muslim unity, which, at this stage, he argued was a precondition for the realization of Independence. In chapter 9, Roland E. Miller shows that this approach of Gandhi's won him significant backing from the

Muslim community but also became the basis for disaffection when Gandhi later seemed to change his priorities and put the noncooperation program and Independence ahead of improving Muslim–Hindu relations. As Miller indicates, the focus on Muslim–Hindu unity in the process of working for Independence was also fundamental to the support of Congress by the Muslims. M. A. Ansari, for example, was a key Muslim leader, twice president of the All-India Muslim League, a participant in Congress assemblies, and a supporter of Gandhi's satyagraha, which he called "a message of hope." During the early 1920s Gandhi and Congress retained Muslim support with the respected Muslim religious scholar Abdul Kalam Azad serving as Congress president in 1923. As Miller points out, although Azad became a lifelong supporter of Gandhi, he did not agree that nonviolent noncooperation was the correct response in all situations. However, he did agree with Gandhi in rejecting any idea that a separate country was needed to safeguard Muslim interests.

Gandhi's defense of the Ali brothers and his leadership in opposing the Rowlatt Act and responding to the Amritsar massacre enabled him to be seen as a linchpin by both Muslims and Hindus, and to become the leader of the Indian National Congress. At its meeting in September 1920 Gandhi moved a noncooperation resolution as the basis for India to obtain self-rule in one year. In his speech he outlined the various forms noncooperation needed to take including surrender of titles and honorary offices, refusal to attend government functions, withdrawal of students from government-controlled schools and colleges, boycott of British courts, refusal by the military to offer their services in the Khilafat disputes in Turkey, refusal to participate in elections to councils, and the boycott of all foreign goods.[14] Gandhi went on a speaking tour throughout the country and used his paper, *Young India*, to educate all sections of the public on how to participate in noncooperation. As Nanda states, "This program electrified the country, broke the spell of fear of foreign rule, and led to the arrests of thousands of *satyagrahis*, who defied laws and cheerfully lined up for prison."[15] In February 1922 the movement was sweeping the country when violence broke out in Chauri Chaura, a village in eastern India, causing Gandhi to call off mass noncooperation demonstrations. Muslim backers of the day were dismayed by Gandhi's lack of consultation in making this decision. Gandhi was arrested shortly after on charges of sedition and sentenced to six years in prison. Released two years later he found that much had changed. Tagore wrote the novel *Muktadara* indirectly criticizing Gandhi. The Congress Party had split in two and unity between the Hindu and Muslim communities, which had been a hallmark of the 1920–1922 satyagrahas, had disintegrated. Gandhi worked at drawing the two communities back together and in 1924 undertook a three-week fast to bring Hindus and Muslims back to a nonviolent approach.

In 1923 Besant started organizing a convention of moderates to develop the Commonwealth of India Bill, advocating self-rule, a village system of government, and a restricted franchise. The Hindu Nationalist movement in the form of the Hindu Mahasabha was revived and its intellectual leader, Savarkar published his key work *Hindutva* (see chapter 6). Also in 1923 Mohammed Ali delivered his presidential address to Congress stating his own belief that violence in self-defense is valid despite his agreement to abide by Gandhi's policy of nonviolence.

In the mid-1920s Gandhi took little interest in active politics. During this period Gandhi's friend the Christian minister C. F. Andrews was urging Gandhi to join forces with Dr Bhim Rao Ambedkar, the leader of the Untouchable community, to battle the evil of untouchability. Although he expressed deep feelings for the Untouchables, Gandhi could not let go of his focus on Independence and Muslim–Hindu unity. But he did attack untouchability in ways that were radical for a caste Hindu of his day. He had accepted an Untouchable family into his Ahmedabad ashram, and in 1924 he supported the use of satyagraha by the Untouchables against caste Hindus at the town of Vaikam. Gandhi went to Vaikam and debated with the Orthodox Brahmins against their interpretation of Hindu scripture that supported untouchability. Although winning a partial success for the Untouchables, Gandhi admitted that he was not able to change the minds of the Orthodox Hindus. During the debate Gandhi accepted the revealed status of Hindu scriptures and the laws of karma and rebirth. Through his newspaper *Young India*, he also supported Ambedkar when the latter led a satyagraha at Mahad to establish the right for Untouchables to drink water from the Chawdr tank located in a Brahmin locality. Gandhi commended the Untouchables for their self-restraint and Ambedkar for his leadership in refusing to do battle with a stick-wielding mob of caste Hindus. However as I show in chapter 2, a major difference between Gandhi and Ambedkar was that Gandhi wanted to solve the problem by reinterpreting Hindu scriptures and redefining Untouchables as shudras within the Hindu caste system, while Ambedkar said that the Hindu scriptures that justified untouchability should be burned and the caste system scrapped.

In 1925 Tagore wrote an article in the *Modern Review* criticizing Gandhi's emphasis on the home spinning of cotton. Gandhi responded to this criticism with an article in *Young India* entitled "The Poet and the Charkhā." Tagore, in 1927, also criticized Gandhi's defense of *varnasrama dharma* (the four caste structure of orthodox Hindu society) in an article

"The Shudra Habit" published in *Modern Review.* At the same time Besant published her book *India—Bond or Free?* in Britain to gain support for the Commonwealth of India Bill in parliament. In her book Besant explicitly criticized Gandhi's noncooperation movement. Gandhi appeared to be a spent force in Indian politics.

The new British parliament did not pass the Commonwealth of India Bill but formed the Simons Commission, with no Indian representative, to investigate constitutional reform in India. The *Nehru Report* (named for Motilal, father of Jawaharlal) responded to the Simons Commission by calling for dominion status and joint electorates without provision for minorities. Muslims opposed the report, as did young members of Congress led by Jawaharlal Nehru and Subhas Chandra Bose who would settle for nothing less than complete independence. At the Calcutta meeting of Congress, a split between the old guard and younger members was avoided by a compromise formula framed by Gandhi. As Nanda puts it, "The Congress passed a resolution accepting the *Nehru Report* on the condition that, if by December 31, 1929 [i.e., in one year] it was not accepted by the Government, the Congress would demand complete independence and fight for it, if necessary, by resorting to non-violent, non-cooperation."[16] Gandhi was back at the helm of the Congress Party. Responding to the *Nehru Report*, Jinnah unsuccessfully called for protection of the Muslim minority and Azad and Ansari founded the All-India Nationalist Muslim Conference to rally Indian Muslims.

About this time C. F. Andrews published his book *Mahatma Gandhi's Ideas*, which included a public critique of Gandhi's early support for recruiting Indians to fight in World War I, and of Gandhi's views on celibacy. As the "year of grace" for the British to grant India dominion status in response to the Calcutta Congress ran out, preparations were underway for the next Congress meeting in Lahore. Gandhi was urged to accept the presidency of Congress but declined and put up Jawalharlal Nehru for the position; and although (as Robert D. Baird points out in chapter 1) they continued to have major differences of viewpoint and style, there was a strong bond of loyalty and affection between the two men. Nehru was elected and a split between the old and young sections of Congress was avoided. Although Nehru was President of Congress, Gandhi was its effective leader. Gandhi decided the country was ready for a satyagraha to force some action from the British. So in March 1930 he launched a noncooperation campaign against the government tax on salt, which most affected the poorest part of the community. Perhaps the most successful of Gandhi's nonviolent campaigns against the British, the salt march resulted in the imprisonment of more than sixty thousand persons.

The British government responded by arresting Gandhi and by calling a Round Table Conference in London to discuss India's future constitution. At the 1930 conference, the Untouchables, led by Ambedkar, joined forces with Muslim and Sikh representatives to ensure that the proposed constitution would include separate electorates for minority communities. In India, after talks with Lord Irwin, Gandhi and other imprisoned Congress leaders reached a truce in which they called off their civil disobedience campaign and agreed that Gandhi, as sole representative of Congress, would attend the second Round Table Conference in London in 1931. This was a serious disappointment to the Indian Nationalists who saw it as a shift of focus from Independence to minority group issues. As I recount in chapter 2, it was at this meeting that Ambedkar and Gandhi clashed over who really represented the Untouchables, and the question of separate electorates for the Untouchables. Gandhi also claimed that as Congress represented not only Hindus but also all minority communities, and as he was the sole Congress representative at the conference, it was therefore he who ultimately spoke for the Muslims, Sikhs, Christians, and Untouchables—all of whom had leading representatives at the meeting. Gandhi attempted unsuccessfully to get the agreement of the British to separate electorates for minorities (achieved at the first conference) reversed in the case of the Untouchables. This further upset Ambedkar and other minority leaders who perceived Gandhi as having shifted his priorities and was now placing Independence in front of Muslim–Hindu–Sikh harmony. The Muslim leader Ansari wrote to Gandhi stressing the importance of Hindu–Muslim-Sikh harmony over independence, and Mohammed Ali reversed his pro-Gandhi stance and publicly criticized Gandhi for trying to make Indian Muslims subservient to the Hindu Mahasabha. Upon his return from London, Gandhi was arrested and the Congress Party outlawed. Gandhi considered his London efforts a failure.

In 1932 British Prime Minister Ramsay MacDonald announced the results of the London Round Table meetings as a Communal Award stating that separate electorates for all minority communities (including the Untouchables) were to be incorporated into India's new constitution. Although in prison, Gandhi launched an effective protest by announcing a "fast until death" unless the provisions of the Communal Award were changed so that the separate electorates for the Untouchables were revoked. Gandhi correctly saw that this provision could result in the loss of 50 million votes from a Hindu community of 250 million, a significant weakening of which Hindu nationalists would never accept. Ambedkar and other minority leaders visited Gandhi during his fast in the Yeravada prison and after days of negotiation produced the Poona

Pact granting more assembly seats to the Untouchables but eliminating separate electorates—an agreement which the British accepted. Gandhi saw this event as a "wakeup call" from God that he and all Hindus should make amends for their unjust treatment of Untouchables over the centuries.

Gandhi's fast and his moral soul-searching shook the country. Upon release from prison Gandhi launched a two-year all-India campaign to change the attitude of caste Hindus in their discrimination against Untouchables, but with the retention of *varna* (hereditary occupational groupings). He established a weekly paper dedicated to this cause, the *Harijan* (Gandhi's name for Untouchables). He also created the Harijan Sevak Sang and the Harijan Fund to assist in the "uplift" of the Untouchables. Despite invitations from Gandhi, Ambedkar rejected involvement in these organizations, which he saw as patronizing actions by caste Hindus. In spite of Gandhi's efforts, however, Hindu caste attitudes did not significantly change, and when an earthquake struck Bihir in 1934, Gandhi took it as a divine sign that he should end his untouchability campaign and put his efforts into aiding earthquake victims. In addition Gandhi resigned as both leader and a member of the Congress Party because he was not convinced that Congress's leading members were sufficiently committed to nonviolent noncooperation. Instead, Gandhi shifted his attention from politics to the education and uplift of grassroots rural India. Tagore, Nehru, and others were distressed by Gandhi's sudden shift of direction. In 1936 Ambedkar published *The Annihilation of Caste*, a devastating critique of the Hindu caste system, prompting Gandhi to reply in the *Harijan*. Ambedkar replied to Gandhi and in so doing announced that he was leaving the Hindu religion, prompting large numbers of Untouchables to join him in eventually becoming Buddhists.

With the outbreak of World War II, the struggle for Independence entered its final phase. Gandhi was very critical of both fascism and war. In the journal *Harijan*, Gandhi wrote an article criticizing Zionism, Judaism, and the Jews in Germany, who were then suffering from the evils of Nazism. Martin Buber replied criticizing Gandhi's essay but Gandhi did not respond.[17] Unlike Gandhi, the Indian National Congress was not committed to complete nonviolence and was ready to support the British war effort if Indian self-government was promised. The Government of India Act, based on the round table discussions, was passed approving the goal of Indian independence and guaranteeing Muslim representation. During the 1937–1939 period Nehru, Tagore, and Andrews all found themselves in disagreements with Gandhi. Congress swept the Indian elections with the Muslim League winning only 109 of 482 reserved seats, prompting Jinnah to begin mobilizing the Muslim grass roots. In so doing Jinnah accused Gandhi of compromising the principles of Congress and establishing a Hindu Raj. In 1940 Jinnah refused Azad's offer to reconcile the Muslims with Congress because, in Jinnah's view, Congress was a Hindu body. The Muslim League passed its Pakistan Resolution based on the concept that Indian Muslims were a distinct people in need of a homeland.

In 1940 Gandhi once more became politically active, launching a civil disobedience campaign demanding self-rule for India in exchange for support of Britain's war effort. In 1942 the British sent Sir Stafford Cripps to India to propose an interim government during World War II to be followed by full independence. However, British equivocation over the transfer of power and the encouragement given by British officials to conservative and communal forces causing Hindu–Muslim discord led Gandhi to demand a complete British withdrawal from India. The British responded to this "Quit India" movement by imprisoning Congress leaders and outlawing the Indian National Congress. This led to violent outbreaks that were sternly suppressed until the rupture between India and Britain became wider than ever. In 1944 Gandhi was released from jail. Jinnah met Gandhi at talks in Bombay and scorned Gandhi's refusal to accept Muslim self-rule. In Jinnah's view Gandhi had turned the Congress Party into a Hindu body. In 1945 Ambedkar published his most vigorous critique of Gandhi in his book *What Congress and Gandhi Have Done to the Untouchables*. Gandhi admitted that he had been unable to change the attitude of caste Hindus on untouchability and finally agreed with Ambedkar that Untouchables should become active in Indian politics. In the elections of 1945 the Muslim League swept the reserved Muslim seats in the elections for India's provincial and central assemblies.

The election of the Labour Party in Britain in 1945 signaled a new phase in Indo–British relations. During the next two years prolonged negotiations took place between the Congress leaders, the Muslim League led by Jinnah, and the British. During this period, as Baird shows in chapter 1, there were increasing tensions and differences of view between Nehru and Gandhi. Ambedkar organized massive satyagraha demonstrations of Untouchables before the state legislatures at Pune, Nagpur, Lucknow, and Kanpur but, despite this activity, the Congress Party took all of the scheduled caste seats in the election. Jinnah urged "direct action" to secure Muslim independence, resulting in general Hindu–Muslim unrest and many deaths in Calcutta. Gandhi directed his final efforts to the defusing of this Hindu–Muslim rioting. As a result of all of this activity the Mountbatten Plan of 1947, which included the partition of India into Pakistan and modern India, was accepted.

The British parliament approved the Indian Independence Act and India's first cabinet was formed with Nehru as prime minister and Ambedkar as law minister (on Gandhi's recommendation).

With the formation in mid-August 1947 of the two new dominions of India and Pakistan, there were massive movements of Muslims, Sikhs, and Hindus from one part of the country to the other, with much bloodshed. As Nanda points out, one of Gandhi's greatest disappointments was that Indian Independence was achieved without Indian unity, and with much violence. "When the partition of the subcontinent was accepted—against his [Gandhi's] advice—he threw himself heart and soul into the task of healing the scars of communal conflict, toured the riot-torn areas of Bengal and Bihar, admonished the bigots, consoled the victims and tried to rehabilitate the refugees."[18] Partisans in all communities blamed Gandhi for what they perceived as their losses. Gandhi's two final triumphs were the stopping of rioting in Calcutta in September 1947 through fasting, and the shaming of the city of Delhi into a communal truce in January 1948. A few days later, while on his way to evening prayers, Gandhi was assassinated by a young fanatic member of the Hindu Mahasabha. Shortly after his death, untouchability was made illegal in India.

In this brief outline of Gandhi's engagement in the Indian Independence movement, we see that his activities and ideas brought him into dialogue and conflict with many major figures in India. The following chapters recount many of these interactions in detail. In part I, Gandhi's relationships with Nehru, Ambedkar, Besant, Aurobindo, and Tagore are given detailed study through the analysis of Gandhi's *Collected Works* and the letters, speeches, and writings of these other leaders, who often found themselves critical of Gandhi's ideas or actions. In part II the critique of Gandhi is examined from the perspective of various Indian movements including the Hindu Right, the Christian Community, the Sikhs, and the Muslims. Finally, Gandhi's response to the issue of language—the Hindi-Urdu question—is critically analyzed.

NOTES

1. Mahatma Gandhi, *Swaraj in One Year* (Madras: Ganesh, 1921).
2. B. R. Nanda, *Gandhi and his Critics* (Delhi: Oxford University Press, 1985), vii.
3. Ibid., viii.

4. Ibid.

5. Eleanor Zelliot, *From Untouchable to Dalit: Essays on the Ambedkar Movement* (Delhi: Manohar, 1998), 151.

6. Raghavan Iyer, "Gandhi on Civilization and Religion" in *Gandhi's Significance for Today*, ed. John Hick and Lamont Hempel (London: Macmillan, 1989), 123.

7. Judith Brown, *Gandhi: Prisoner of Hope* (New Haven, Conn.: Yale University Press), 1989, 1.

8. Zelliot, *From Untouchable to Dalit*, 153.

9. For more general introductions to Gandhi see B. R. Nanda, *Mahatma Gandhi: A Biography* (London: Allen and Unwin, 1958); Judith M. Brown, *Gandhi: Prisoner of Hope* (New Haven, Conn.: Yale University Press, 1989); and J. F. T. Jordens, *Gandhi's Religion: A Homespun Shawl* (London: Macmillan, 1998). See also M. K. Gandhi, *The Story of My Experiments with Truth* (Washington, D.C.: Public Affairs Press, 1948) and Jawaharlal Nehru, *Mahatma Gandhi* (Bombay: Asia Publishing House, 1949). For earlier treatments of Gandhi and his critics see P. C. Roy Chaudhury, *Gandhi and His Contemporaries* (Delhi: Sterling Publishers, 1972) and Nanda, *Gandhi and his Critics*.

10. Brown, *Gandhi*, 97.

11. Ibid., 98.

12. Ibid.

13. Ibid., 124

14. Mahatma Gandhi, *Swaraj in One Year* (Madras: Ganesh, 1921), 11, 12.

15. B. R. Nanda, "Gandhi," *The New Encyclopaedia Britannica* (Chicago: Encyclopaedia Britannica, 1989), 652.

16. Nanda, *Mahatma Gandhi*, 277.

17. Haim Gordon, "A Rejection of Spiritual Imperialism: Reflections of Buber's Letter to Gandhi," *Journal of Ecumenical Studies* 36 (1999): 471–479.

18. Nanda, "Gandhi," 653.

Part I

Critiques of Gandhi by Individuals

1

The Convergence of Distinct Worlds: Nehru and Gandhi

ROBERT D. BAIRD

As Nehru saw it, Gandhi's world was religious, simple, and antitechnological. In many ways it was premodern. On the other hand, his world was secular, technological, and socialistic. Nehru held to a kind of scientific humanism.[1] His ultimate goal was creating for every person the possibility of development into a *"fully integrated human being."*[2] The values that he thought were unassailable were the values of being rational, scientific, modern, and Indian.[3] He accepted the distinction made in the Constitution of India between religion and the secular: distinct realms. Furthermore, each realm was insular to the other. Nehru held that politics, economics, and social theory are all governed by secular values and that religion has no place within their boundaries. A supporter of the Uniform Civil Code, he also believed in the secularization of law.[4] He recognized that "Hinduism" and "Islam" and many other traditions have sought to govern every aspect of human existence. In the modern world that must change. While Nehru fervently supported the freedom to "profess, practice and propagate religion," he also held that in the effort to maximize human freedom certain practices had to be curtailed if they limited the freedom of others. The propensity of Hindus and Muslims to extend the influence of their religion into areas of politics and social matters has to be restricted in the interest of the greater freedom of all citizens. Gandhi characterized his life as a search for truth. That search was a religious search and it extended to every dimension of life. Gandhi felt comfortable fasting for political ends or in other ways stressing the religious dimensions of the struggle for independence. In an earlier analysis, I summarized Nehru's thought: "Nehru's ultimate goal, then, is humanistic and scientific, it is rational, and, unlike antiquated 'religious' superstitions, it is modern. It includes a higher material standard of living while retaining an ethical and spiritual approach to reality. It is, in his terms, 'a fully integrated human being.'"[5]

Nehru was a politician who understood the art of compromise and the need to accommodate goals to particular circumstances. But he valued clarity of thought, precision in setting goals, and clearly worked out social, economic, and political programs. And he worked out these positions in the light of the ultimate principles to which he was committed: They would have to be rational, scientific, modern, and Indian. Nehru's outlook was decidedly this-worldly. He was more concerned with man than with God: "Essentially I am interested in this world, in this life, not in some other world or a future life. Whether there is such a thing as a soul, or whether there is a survival after death or not, I do not know; and important as these questions are, they do not trouble me in the least."[6]

In Nehru's writings, it is frequently mentioned that Gandhi was not easily understood, that he was imprecise, and that he was overly religious. As Nehru saw him, Gandhi seldom reflected on goals with logical precision, often interjected religious practice into the political arena, and operated on a level that, while advancing the cause for freedom and political independence, would be an inadequate basis for nation building.

Throughout the long association of Nehru and Gandhi in the Congress Party, Nehru was successively adoringly committed, angry, frustrated, and in a state of utter confusion. In the end, though it is difficult to imagine two worlds that differ more in philosophical orientation, the two never parted company, nor did their deep friendship erode or disappear.

THE ENDURING BOND

There were personal qualities in Gandhi that attracted Nehru. They were, in Nehru's description, qualities that also compelled the Indian masses to follow him. When Nehru first met Gandhi at the Lucknow Congress in December 1916, he had heard of his work in South Africa. That Gandhi was prepared to apply his methods to India was hopeful. Even Gandhi's voice differed from the usual run of politicians. His voice was quiet, soft, and gentle, yet Nehru sensed strength in it. Every word seemed to be spoken in deadly earnestness. The politics of condemnation was out of place, and ineffective resolutions of protestation were left unuttered. As Nehru saw it, this was a politics of action rather than talk.

In Nehru's estimation, Gandhi was not a politician who imposed himself from above, but rather someone who emerged from the Indian masses. Gandhi spoke the language of the masses and seemed to participate in their world. Nehru was continually amazed at Gandhi's ability to carry the masses with him and he often attributed it to Gandhi's personality along with his strategy of nonviolent resistance.

> How came we to associate ourselves with Gandhiji politically, and to become, in many instances, his devoted followers? The question is hard to answer, and to one who does not know Gandhiji, no answer is likely to satisfy. Personality is an indefinable thing, a strange force that has power over the souls of men, and he possesses this in ample measure, and to all who came to him he often appears in a different aspect. He attracted people, but it was ultimately intellectual conviction that brought them to him and kept them there. They did not agree with his philosophy of life, or even with many of his ideals. Often they did not understand him. But the actions that he proposed were something tangible that could be understood and appreciated intellectually.[7]

The pull of Gandhi's personality prevailed even in times when Nehru was angered by Gandhi's decisions. And when Gandhi's life was terminated, Nehru's comments summed up their relationship.

> Friends and comrades, the light has gone out of our lives and there is darkness everywhere. I do not know what to tell you or how to say it. Our beloved leader, Bapu as we called him, the father of the nation, is no more. Perhaps I am wrong to say that. Nevertheless we shall not see him again as we have seen him for these many years. We will not run to him for advice and seek solace from him and that is a terrible blow not to me only, but to millions and millions in this country, and it is a little difficult to soften the blow by any other advice that I or anyone else can give you.[8]

THE RANGE OF RELIGION

Nehru characterized Gandhi as "essentially a man of religion."[9] Furthermore, Gandhi was a Hindu at the very depths of his being. But Gandhi's conception of religion as well as his Hinduism "had nothing to do with any dogma or custom or ritual."[10] Rather, it revolved around his "firm belief in the moral law, which he calls the Law of Truth or Love. Truth and non-violence appear to him to be the same thing, or different aspects of one and the same thing, and he uses these words almost interchangeably."[11] Claiming to understand the "spirit" of "Hinduism," Gandhi was able to reject "every text or practice which does not fit in with his idealist interpretation of what it should be, calling it an interpolation or a subsequent accretion. 'I decline to be a slave,' he has said, 'to precedents or practice I cannot understand or defend on a moral basis.'"[12] Nehru had no disagreement with that. But there were elements in Gandhi's religion that were problematic. In Nehru's world, religion had no place in politics. Nor did Gandhi's stress on the religious and spiritual side of the freedom movement resonate with Nehru. The intrusion of religion into politics was inappropriate in the modern world.

> I used to be troubled sometimes at the growth of this religious element in our politics, on both the Hindu and the Moslem side. I did not like it at all. Much that Moulvies and Maulanas and Swamis and the like said in their public addresses seemed to me most unfortunate. Their history and sociology and economics appeared to me all wrong, and the religious twist that was given to everything prevented all clear thinking.[13]

Nehru's discomfort extended to Gandhi himself. "Even some of Gandhi's phrases sometimes jarred upon me—thus his frequent reference to *Rama Raj* as a golden age which was to return. But I was powerless to intervene, and I consoled myself with the thought that Gandhiji used the words because they were well known and understood by the masses. He had an amazing knack of reaching the heart of the people" (72).

Nehru continued by saying that he did not concern himself with such matters, but threw himself into his work. He confessed that Gandhi was "a very difficult person to understand; sometimes his language was almost incomprehensible to an average modern. But we felt we knew him quite well enough to realize that he was a great and unique man and a glorious leader, and, having put our faith in him, we gave him an almost blank check, for the time being at least" (72). Moreover, Nehru's inclination to dislike the way of exploitation by the so-called men of religion was toned down due to his association with Gandhi.

The intrusion of religion into politics in the form of a fast angered Nehru. It was inconceivable in Nehru's modern rational world. But in Gandhi's world it followed with ease. In September 1932, when Nehru and Gandhi were both in prison, Nehru was shaken by Gandhi's decision to undertake a "fast unto death." In disapproval of British Prime Minister Ramsay MacDonald's decision to give separate electorates to depressed classes, Gandhi announced such a fast.

Nehru experienced a wide range of emotions. He contemplated the fact that he might never see Gandhi again. That would be a deep personal loss. Nehru was particularly annoyed that Gandhi would choose such a "side issue" for his final sacrifice. How would this decision affect the freedom movement? For Nehru the goal was complete independence. In the light of that goal, the push for independence should be central. Nehru was concerned that that objective might be set aside. After so much sacrifice, was it prudent to give it all up for a side issue? "I felt angry with him at his religious and sentimental approach to a political question, and his frequent references to God in connection with it. He even seemed to suggest that God had indicated the very date of the fast. What a terrible example to set!" (237).

Then news came that the proposal for separate electorates had been set aside. Untouchability seemed doomed. Nehru marveled at what that "little man" could do while sitting in prison. Gandhi knew that his action would disturb Nehru and he wired him in prison. "During all these days of agony you have been before mind's eye. I am most anxious to know your opinion. You know how I value your opinion. Saw Indu [and] Swarup's children. Indu looked happy and in possession of more flesh. Doing very well. Wire reply. Love" (237). Nehru's reply was warm but forthright.

> Your telegram and brief news that some settlement reached filled me with joy. First news of your decision to fast caused mental agony and confusion, but ultimately optimism triumphed and I regained peace of mind. No sacrifice too great for suppressed downtrodden classes. Freedom must be judged by freedom of lowest but feel danger of other issues obscuring only goal. Am unable to judge from religious viewpoint. Danger your methods being exploited by others but how can I presume to advise a magician. Love. (238)

Gandhi's activities on behalf of the Harijans continued to frustrate Nehru. The movement to end untouchability had received a real impetus. One unhappy consequence was that civil disobedience in the interest of independence became minimal. "The country's attention had been diverted to other issues, and many Congress workers had turned to the Harijan cause. Probably most of these people wanted an excuse to revert to safer activities which did not involve the risk of jail-going or, worse still, lathee blows and confiscations of property" (238).

One shock seemed to follow another as Gandhi acted religiously and Nehru had to stand by and accept. In May 1933 Gandhi began a twenty-one-day fast. Again Nehru was shocked even though he tried to condition himself for such occurrences. Against some who urged Gandhi to give it up, Nehru felt that once it had been announced publicly, Gandhi's word was important. Nehru received a letter from Gandhi that required a reply. Nehru telegrammed, "Your letter. What can I say about matters I do not understand? I feel lost in a strange country where you are the only familiar landmark and I try to grope my way in the dark but I stumble. Whatever happens my love and thoughts will be with you" (239). Nehru continually vacillated between disapproval and disassociation and his deep desire not to hurt Gandhi. The very idea of a fast for some political end was abhorrent to Nehru. If he had been asked for advice beforehand he would have opposed it. But he wrote a second telegram to encourage Gandhi: "Now that you are launched on your great enterprise may I send you again love and greetings and assure you that I feel more clearly now that whatever happens it is well and whatever happens you win" (239).

Gandhi announced a new civil disobedience push among the Gujarat peasantry that resulted in his imprisonment. When he was denied the facilities in prison for carrying on harijan work as he had in the past, he initiated another fast. Nehru again looked on with bewilderment. When Gandhi was released just in time to spare his life, he met with Nehru and they had several discussions. Their worlds remained distant from each other, but Nehru expressed appreciation for the fact that Gandhi tried to come as close to him as he was able. "I was happy to see him again and to find that though weak, he was making good progress. We had long talks. It was obvious that we differed considerably on our outlooks on life and politics and economics; but I was grateful to him for the generous way in which he tried to come as far as he could to meet my viewpoint."[14]

SATYAGRAHA: RELIGION OR POLITICAL STRATEGY

For Gandhi Satyagraha was religion. Moreover, it was not only for the religiously elite but also a religion for the masses: "The religion of nonviolence is not meant merely for the Rishis and saints. It is meant for the common people as well. Nonviolence is the law of our species as violence is the law of the brute. The Spirit lies dormant in the brute, and he knows no law but that of physical might. The dignity of man requires obedience to a higher law—to the strength of the spirit."[15] For Gandhi, holding on to truth was a religious matter that manifested itself in the political arena. Since both the means and the end were about truth, there could be no compromise. Even in the face of invasion during World War II, Gandhi preferred nonviolence even though he struggled with the consequences. He could not gleefully accept a police force or a military in independent India.

But for Nehru and Congress, satyagraha was accepted as a political strategy to be affirmed in the subsequent light of its success. The massacre in Amritsar in the Jallianwala Bagh took place on April 13, 1919. Congress met in Amritsar in December 1919, and the next year it adopted Gandhi's program of nonviolent noncooperation. According to Nehru's report, the older and more experienced Congress leaders harbored some doubt. But the cries of *Mahatma Gandhi ki jai* (victory to Mahatma Gandhi) from the masses and the rank and file of Congress swept them along in spite of lingering doubts. That Muslims were also supportive added to the viability of this new approach.

While satyagraha was "a most civilized form of warfare" that avoided the growth of bitter racial and national hatreds, thus making an ultimate settlement easier, it was its effectiveness, its practical usefulness that finally captured the support of Nehru.[16] Nehru saw the futility of armed resistance against a power that had superior arms. The British had succeeded in striking fear in the hearts of the masses, not to speak of their leadership. But satyagraha filled the masses with confidence and strength. Rather than continued ineffectual resolutions or begging for crumbs, the masses lost their fear and became characterized by confidence and strength.

> But the dominant impulse under British rule was that of fear, pervasive, oppressing, strangling fear; fear of the army, the police, the widespread secret service, fear of the official class; fear of laws meant to suppress, and of prison; fear of the landlord's agent; fear of the moneylender; fear of unemployment and starvation, which were always on the threshold. It was against this all-pervading fear that Gandhi's quiet and determined voice was raised: Be not afraid.[17]

The erosion of fear was one consequence that appealed to Nehru. Peasants were enabled to join a movement that had thus far been dominated by the upper class. With such practical results, whatever disagreements Nehru might have had were secondary. Yet this nonviolent method was effectively disruptive and was a "refusal to help the government in its administration and exploitation of India."[18] Satyagraha was, for Nehru, a very practical and effective method given the particulars of India's situation.

In addition to the captivating personality that Gandhi exuded, then, Nehru was drawn to Gandhi's method of satyagraha as the only practical alternative on the horizon. Repeated resolutions of Congress had been ineffectual in gaining self-rule, and a military overthrow of the British seemed ill-advised. Noncooperation, however, had a chance of working and it seemed as though it had already been effectual in a number of ways. Satyagraha was, for Gandhi, essential to his search for truth.[19] For Nehru it was political expediency. For the secular politician compromise was always the link between principle and reality. Nehru espoused relativism with reference to truth. "What is truth? I do not know for certain, and perhaps our truths are relative and absolute truth is beyond us. Different persons may and do take different views of truth, and each individual is powerfully influenced by his own background, training and impulses. So also Gandhi. But truth is at least for an individual what he himself feels and knows to be true."[20]

Nehru continued by voicing a concern for the dominance of Gandhi's search for truth and its applicability to politics: "According to that definition I do not know of any person who holds to the truth as Gandhi does. That is a dangerous quality in a politician, for he speaks out his mind and even let's [sic] the public see its changing phases."[21] Gandhi's openness in this way may be appropriate in the area of personal growth, but in politics it is sometimes shockingly frank. It is not politically prudent to allow the public in on every change of mood or ideology. Nehru was a secular politician and that involved compromise and a careful concern for what was revealed to the public. The politician in him always tempered principle to the realities of the historical situation.

Even having heard Gandhi's arguments for the religious and uncompromising nature of satyagraha, Nehru could not think of satyagraha as unconditional.

> We were moved by these arguments, but for us and for the National Congress as a whole the nonviolent method was not, and could not be, a religion or an unchallengeable creed or dogma. It could only be a policy and a method promising certain results, and by those results it would have to be finally judged. Individuals might make of it a religion or incontrovertible creed. But no political organization, so long as it remained political, could do so.[22]

Nehru could not, then, give absolute allegiance to satyagraha. But he held in high regard its moral and ethical side and supported it because it seemed like "sound, practical politics" (72): "[T]he non-cooperation movement offered me what I wanted—the goal of national freedom and (as I thought) the ending of the exploitation of the underdog, and the means which satisfied my moral sense and gave me a sense of personal freedom" (73).

The difference in outlook between Nehru and Gandhi was highlighted in February 1922. Many of the leaders, including Nehru, were in prison, but Gandhi was still free. An incident took place near the village of Chauri Chaura, where a mob of villagers had retaliated against some policemen by setting fire to the police station and burning a half dozen officers in the process. Gandhi immediately suspended civil disobedience. It seemed to Nehru that the method had been going well, and now it was suspended because of this single incident on the part of some villagers. If satyagraha could only be used if every Indian were under complete control, then it could never be implemented. The suspension was resented by the Congress leadership as well as by Nehru. But there was nothing they could do about it. "We were angry when we learned of this stoppage of our struggle at a time when we seemed to be consolidating our position and advancing on all fronts. But our disappointment and anger in prison could do little good to anyone; civil resistance stopped, and non-cooperation wilted away" (79). Nehru had accepted the method because of its effectiveness and not as a religious principle.

Nor was Nehru drawn to the metaphysical aspects of the *Bhagavadgita*, even though he participated in the recitation of its verses every evening at Gandhi's ashrama prayers. He approved of its ethical dimensions which say what a person is to be like: "Calm of purpose, serene, and unmoved, doing his job and not caring overmuch for the result of his action" (73). Nehru thought this appealed to him even more because he was not very calm or detached himself.

The Rational And The Intuitive

Occasionally Nehru expressed frustration and disapproval of Gandhi's failure to articulate the clear basis for satyagraha, or something more than a vague meaning for swaraj. At base, this manifests Nehru's rational approach and Gandhi's propensity for deciding matters intuitively. It was this intuitive approach that often left goals imprecise and accounted for unexpected actions by Gandhi.

In Nehru's mind, Gandhi's goal was anything but clear and precise. It is possible that was its value, as I have earlier contended for the symbol "secular state."[23] Nevertheless, Gandhi's vagueness on swaraj and on economic issues for the independent state was unacceptable for Nehru.

It seems surprising now, how completely we ignored the theoretical aspects, the philosophy of our movement as well as the definite objective that we should have. Of course we all grew eloquent about *Swaraj*, but each one of us probably interpreted the word in his or her own way. To most of the younger men it meant political independence, or something like it, and a democratic form of government.[24]

Nehru and others also hoped that swaraj would address some of the burdens of the peasantry and lift their lives to places of dignity. But he was aware that for many the term *swaraj* meant something less than political independence. This vagueness carried them on, but it never ceased to trouble Nehru.

> But it was obvious to most of our leaders *Swaraj* meant something much less than independence. Gandhiji was delightfully vague on the subject, and he did not encourage clear thinking about it either. But he always spoke, vaguely but definitely, in terms of the underdog, and this brought great comfort to many of us, although, at the same time, he was full of assurances to the top dog also. Gandhiji's stress was never on the intellectual approach to a problem but on character and piety. He did succeed amazingly in giving backbone and character to the Indian people.[25]

Nehru admits that he went along as well. He put the need for reflective thought aside as he threw himself into the quest for independence.

> We ignored the necessity of thought behind the action; we forgot that without conscious ideology and objective the energy and enthusiasm of the masses must end largely in smoke. To some extent the revivalist element in our movement carried us on; a feeling that non-violence as conceived for political or economic movements or for righting wrongs was a new message which our people were destined to give to the world. We became victims to the curious illusion of all peoples and all nations that in some way they are a chosen race.[26]

And yet, his goal of an independent India was capable of rational articulation. It was expediency alone that set it aside. He was clear about what it was, even though Gandhi was not.

> Let us be clear about our national objective. We aim at a strong, free and democratic India where every citizen has an equal place and full opportunity of growth and service, where present-day inequalities in wealth and status have ceased to be, where our vital impulses are directed to creative and cooperative endeavor. In such an India communalism, separatism, isolation, untouchability, bigotry, and exploitation of man by man has no place, and while religion is free, it is not allowed to interfere with the political and economic aspects of a nation's life.[27]

The night of March 4, 1931, provided another shocker for Nehru. The goal of his involvement in nonviolent resistance was nothing short of independence. Gandhi had gone to the viceroy's house and returned at 2 A.M. and announced that "an agreement had been reached." The mention of "safeguards" in clause 2 of the agreement seemed to Nehru to compromise complete independence. Clause 2 read as follows:

> As regards constitutional questions, the scope of future discussion is stated, with the assent of His Majesty's Government, to be with the object of considering further the scheme for the constitutional Government of India discussed at the Round Table Conference. Of the scheme there outlined, Federation is an essential part; so also are Indian responsibility and reservations or safeguards in the interests of India, for such matters as, for instance, defense; external affairs; the position of minorities; the financial credit of India; and the discharge of obligations.[28]

Nehru strongly disagreed with the decision but, as often, felt helpless to do anything about it. He surely could not overthrow Gandhi nor break from him. Such sentiments were contemplated, but Nehru saw no future in that. For now the Civil Disobedience movement was ended. Gandhi had already agreed to a settlement. But Nehru was insistent that the goal of independence not be muted. Gandhi learned indirectly of Nehru's distress and asked Nehru to accompany him on his morning walk. Gandhi reassured Nehru, holding that the inclusion of the phrase "in the interests of India" guaranteed that the goal of independence was not compromised. Nehru was somewhat soothed, but was not convinced intellectually by what seemed to him a forced interpretation.

It was this intuitive way of making decisions that was troubling. Nehru expressed to Gandhi that his propensity for springing surprises on him was frightening and that no matter how close his association, he could not understand it. Gandhi admitted the presence of this "unknown element" in him, and that he himself could not answer for it or foretell to what it might lead.

Nehru continued to vacillate for a few days, wondering if he should disassociate himself from the clause. In the end he concluded it would not do anything beneficial for the larger cause. Gandhi went to Lord Irwin to clarify that Congress would only send representatives to the Round Table Conference to advance the claim for independence. Lord Irwin would not admit the claim to independence, but acknowledged the right of Congress to advance it. In the end the greater cause determined Nehru's decision: "So, I decided, not without great mental and physical distress, to accept the agreement and work for it wholeheartedly. There appeared to be no middle way."[29]

There were those who saw Gandhi's interpretation of the phrase "in the interests of India" as one that came as the result of an "ultimatum" issued by Nehru or a bargain Nehru struck with Gandhi. Such an interpretation of their relationship seemed preposterous to Nehru. His comment adds to our understanding of their working relationship: "So far as Mr. Gandhi is concerned, I have had the privilege of knowing him pretty intimately . . . and the idea of presenting ultimatums to him or bargaining with him seems to me monstrous. We may accommodate ourselves to each other; or we may, on a particular issue, part company; but the methods of the market place can never affect our mutual dealings" (197).

Modern And Premodern

Nehru repeatedly indicated that he was modern. Gandhi was traditional, connected to peasants, and in many ways premodern. At times, Gandhi's world seemed so inconceivable that Nehru contemplated the possibility that Gandhi did not mean the components literally himself, or that eventually he would be compelled by the circumstances of the modern world to come over to Nehru's position.

Nehru never espoused Gandhi's expressed ideas about machinery and modern civilization. He pondered the possibility that even Gandhi saw them "as utopian and largely inapplicable to modern Indian conditions" (75). Nehru admitted that he felt attracted to big machinery and to fast travel.

As Nehru saw it, Gandhi's conception of democracy illustrated his premodern position. Gandhi's conception had nothing to do with representation or numbers or majorities or voting as such. Gandhi considered himself a "born democrat" because he identified with the poorest of humanity and tried to live on their level. Nehru quotes Gandhi as saying, "I make that claim, if complete identification with the poorest of mankind, longing to live no better than they, and a corresponding conscious effort to approach that level to the best of one's ability can entitle one to make it" (189). Gandhi felt he was a democrat because he represented the spirit and aspirations of the masses. The number of people who could serve as delegates was irrelevant. Gandhi is quoted further by Nehru:

> Let us recognize the fact that the Congress enjoys the prestige of a democratic character and influence not by the number of delegates and visitors it has drawn to its annual function, but by an ever increasing amount of service it has rendered. Western democracy is on its trial, if it has not already proven

a failure. May it be reserved to India to evolve the true science of democracy by giving a visible demonstration of its success.

Corruption and hypocrisy ought not to be the inevitable table products of democracy, as they undoubtedly are today. Nor is bulk a true test of democracy. True democracy is not inconsistent with a few persons representing the spirit, the hope, and the aspirations of those whom they claim to represent. I hold that democracy cannot be evolved by forcible methods. The spirit of democracy cannot be imposed from without; it has to come from within. (189)

As Nehru pointed out, whether Gandhi was a democrat or not in the modern sense, he was more than a mere representation of the masses—he was "the idealized personification of those vast millions" (189). Gandhi had a peasant's outlook, accompanied by its limited vision. Nehru saw India as peasant India, an India Gandhi knew well. When the leadership of Congress failed to understand him, and he was a puzzle to the British, India seemed to understand. As Nehru saw it, even urban India had the imprint of the peasant upon her, and so it naturally related to Gandhi as well. Nehru described his own outlook differently.

Many of us had cut adrift from this peasant outlook, and the old ways of thought and custom and religion had become alien to us. We called ourselves moderns and thought in terms of "progress," and industrialization and a higher standard of living and collectivization. We considered the peasant's viewpoint reactionary; and some, a growing number, looked with favor toward socialism and communism. (190–191)

There are times when Nehru voiced the hope that Gandhi would eventually come over to his point of view. After all, he did have the knack of adjusting himself to historical circumstances. In the light of the demands of the modern world, how could Gandhi not eventually move in the direction of socialism. "It seemed to me almost inevitable then that he would accept the fundamental socialist position, as I saw no other way out from the violence and injustice and waste and misery of the existing order. He might disagree about the methods, but not about the ideal. So, I thought then, but I realize now that there are basic differences between Gandhi's ideals and the socialist objective."[30]

Nevertheless, he held out the hope that the compelling nature of the facts would eventually move Gandhi toward his position. It was because Gandhi was in the midst of a struggle for independence that he could not see it clearly. The time had not yet come.

For the present, I thought then, this question did not arise. We were in the middle of our national struggle, and civil disobedience was still the program, in theory, of the Congress, although it had been restricted to individuals. We had to carry on as we were and try to spread socialistic ideas among the people, and especially among the more politically conscious Congress workers, so that when the time came for another declaration of policy we might be ready for a notable advance. Meanwhile, Congress was an unlawful organization, and the British government was trying to crush it. We had to meet that attack.[31]

Nehru agreed with much of the criticism on the part of socialist members of Congress that was directed at Gandhi's application of his metaphysical positions to politics.[32] But Nehru could not countenance suspending civil disobedience. Gandhi might be reactionary, but "this reactionary knows India."

Yet, despite his support for Gandhi, Nehru's world remained different. He was a modern thinker who required modern and rational goals. India's social inequities would have to be addressed from a social perspective. Gandhi's objectives were never quite clear to Nehru. He even questioned if Gandhi was clear on them within himself. But Nehru continued on nevertheless.

One step is enough for me, he says; and he does not try to peep into the future or to have a clearly conceived end before him. Look after the means and the end will take care of itself, he is never tired of repeating. Be good in your personal individual lives, and all else will follow. That is not a political or scientific attitude, nor is it perhaps even an ethical attitude. It is narrowly moralist, and begs the question: What is goodness? Is it merely an individual affair or a social affair? Gandhiji lays all stress on character and attaches little importance to intellectual training and development. Intellect without character is likely to be dangerous, but what is character without intellect?[33]

On other occasions Nehru thinks he does understand Gandhi. He is premodern. Nehru returns to his recollection of Gandhi's 1909 writing in South Africa where he states that India's salvation consists in turning back the clock, in unlearning what she has learned in the past fifty years. As Nehru remembered it,

The railways, telegraphs, hospitals, lawyers, doctors and such like have all to go; and the so-called upper classes have to learn consciously, religiously and deliberately the simple peasant life, knowing it to be a life giving true happiness." And again: every time I get into a railway car or use a motor bus I know that I am doing violence to my sense of what is right; to attempt to reform the world by means of highly artificial and speedy locomotion is to attempt the impossible.[34]

In a letter dated October 5, 1945, Gandhi wrote Nehru about their growing differences. While he did not think they were fundamental, if they were, the differences should be public. Gandhi reflected on *Hind Swaraj*, which he wrote in 1908, and which he still affirmed. His letter reveals his village approach in the following words:

> If India is to attain true freedom and through India the world also, then sooner or later the fact must be recognized that people will have to live in villages, not in towns, in huts, not in palaces. Crowds of people will never be able to live at peace with each other in towns and palaces. They will then have no recourse but to resort to both violence and untruth. I hold that without truth and non-violence there can be nothing but destruction for humanity. We can realize truth and non-violence only in the simplicity of village life and this simplicity can best be found in the Charkhā and all that the Charkhā connotes.[35]

Gandhi continued that this village would be clean and free of disease and plague. Even some modern facilities in the form of railroads and telegraph offices would be possible. But the means of simplicity and nonviolence had to be followed first and then some of these things might be added.

Nehru's reply, in a letter dated October 9, 1945, was that it is not a difference between them of truth or untruth of violence or nonviolence. But he did not see why a village was the virtuous solution. "A village, normally speaking, is backward intellectually and culturally and no progress can be made from a backward environment. Narrow-minded people are much more likely to be untruthful and violent."[36] Nehru's perception is closer to the description presented in chapter 2 of this volume discussing Ambedkhar's experience of village life.

As for *Hindu Swaraj*, Nehru had this to say:

> It is many years ago since I read *Hind Swaraj* and I have only a vague picture in my mind. But even when I read it twenty or more years ago it seemed to me completely unreal. In your writings and speeches since then I have found much that seemed to me an advance on that old position and an appreciation of modern trends. I was therefore surprised when you told us that the old picture still remains intact in your mind. As you know, the Congress has never considered that picture, much less adopted it. You yourself have never asked it to adopt it except for certain relatively minor aspects of it.[37]

It seemed to Nehru that Gandhi was concerned with personal salvation and sin. Nehru's modern rational and scientific view, on the contrary, was concerned with social welfare. Nehru had little appreciation for the concept of sin.

I find it difficult to grasp the idea of sin, and perhaps it is because of this that I cannot appreciate Gandhiji's general outlook. He is not out to change society or the social structure; he devotes himself to the eradication of sin from individuals. "The follower of Swadeshi," he had written, "never takes upon himself the vain task of trying to reform the world, for he believes that the world is moved and always will be moved according to the rule set by God." And yet he is aggressive enough in his attempts to reform the world; but the reform he aims at is individual reform, the conquest over the senses and the desire to indulge them, which is sin."[38]

When word reached Nehru in the Alipore jail that Gandhi had withdrawn civil disobedience once again, he was disappointed. He reasoned that movements do not last forever. A few days later he received a copy of the weekly *Statesman* that included Gandhi's statement of his reasons for the withdrawal. As he read this, Nehru became angry and resentful. He recognized that Gandhi often acted intuitively and later constructed reasons to justify the act. The present reasons grew out of a discussion with his ashram inmates. Nehru held that Gandhi could treat his inmates as he liked since they had taken certain vows. Neither he nor Congress had taken such vows and the reasons given were completely irrational for a political movement. Gandhi revealed that an unnamed "friend" and long-standing companion was reluctant to perform his "whole prison task" and preferred to engage in his private studies. To Nehru, it was inconceivable that one would think of justifying the withdrawal of civil disobedience because a friend performed with such imperfections.

Then Gandhi proceeded to advise a course of action for congressmen that reminded Nehru once more of the huge gulf that separated him from Gandhi.

[T]hey must learn the art and beauty of self-denial and voluntary poverty. They must engage themselves in nation-building activities, the spread of khadi through personal hand-spinning and hand-weaving, the spread of communal community of hearts by irreproachable personal conduct toward one another in every walk of life, the banishing of untouchability in every shape or form in one's own person, the spread of total abstinence from intoxicating drinks and drugs by personal contact with individual addicts and generally by cultivating personal purity. These are services which provide maintenance on the poor man's scale. Those for whom the poor man's scale is not feasible should find a place in small unorganized industries of national importance which give a better wage.[39]

Such advice was out of place in Nehru's world. He did not value poverty and did not want to live on the level of peasants. Nehru would prefer to raise them to higher levels of education and economics. More than ever before, Nehru saw the chasm between their worlds and more than ever before was unwilling to attempt to bridge that chasm. Nehru wrote to Gandhi after his release indicating his disappointment.

> When I heard that you had called off the C.D. [Civil Disobedience] movement I felt unhappy. Only the brief announcement reached me at first. Much later I read your statement and this gave me one of the biggest shocks I have ever had. I was prepared to reconcile myself with the withdrawal of C.D. But the reasons you gave for doing so and the suggestions you made for future work astounded me. I had a sudden and intense feeling, that something broke inside me, a bond that I had valued very greatly had snapped. I felt terribly lonely in this wide world.[40]

From Nehru's point of view, Gandhi feared socialism and opted for a "muddled humanitarianism."[41] He avoided communism and socialism because of its association with violence. The phrase *class war* was repugnant to him. Moreover, Gandhi had no desire to raise the standard of living of the masses except beyond a certain level. Nehru's idea that socialism is capable of raising the standard of living greatly did not interest him.[42] As Nehru saw it, Gandhi "does not want people to make an ideal of ever increasing comfort and leisure, but to think of the moral life, to give up their bad habits, to indulge themselves less and less, and thus to develop themselves individually and spiritually."[43] For Gandhi, those who wish to serve the masses would do better going down to their level. Gandhi stressed the trusteeship of the rich in the name of the poor, but he was not interested in making the masses self-indulgent.

WARFARE AND DEFENSE

World War II presented a moral dilemma for both Gandhi and Congress. Gandhi was committed to nonviolence as a religious principle and under all circumstances. The threat of war and a possible invasion of India was something over which he anguished. He wanted Congress to follow a pacifist approach and commit itself to it even after Independence. But such an approach questioned the place of the military and of police in independent India. Congress was unwilling to commit to this view, nor was Nehru. But Nehru's approach to Gandhi was not so much a judgment or a critique as a sympathetic understanding of Gandhi's personal dilemma. Nehru was pragmatic, adjusting his view to circumstances. So was Congress, but nonetheless, its position bore the influence of Gandhi. Yet its conditions and limitations made its commitment to nonviolence less than complete.

> The All-India Congress Committee firmly believes in the policy and practice of non-violence not only in the struggle for *swaraj*, but also, in so far as this may be possible of application, in Free India. The Committee is convinced, and recent world events have demonstrated, that complete world disarmament is necessary and the establishment of a new and juster political and economic order, if the world is not to destroy itself and revert to barbarism. A free India will, therefore, throw all her weight in favor of world disarmament and should herself be prepared to give a lead in this to the world. Such lead will inevitably depend on external factors and internal conditions, but the state would do its utmost to give effect to this policy of disarmament.[44]

The statement fell short of what Gandhi might have hoped for with its qualifications and conditions. Although Gandhi preferred complete nonviolence, and although Nehru saw this as unrealistic, his tone remains more of sympathy than of judgment: "The approach of the war to India disturbed Gandhi greatly. It was not easy to fit in his policy and program of non-violence with this new development. Obviously civil disobedience was out of the question in the face of an invading army or between two opposing armies. Passivity or acceptance of invasion were equally out of the question. What then?"[45] Nehru pointed out that although Gandhi usually had the pulse of India, this time he did not. Although Gujarat was strongly influenced by the Jains and was influenced by nonviolence, other parts of India were less so. The Kshatriya class did not allow it to interfere with the hunting of wild animals. Other classes, including the Brahmans, were little influenced by it. Many Indian thinkers considered such an attachment to nonviolence as "farfetched." Nehru would surely be one of them. But Nehru's expressions were expressions of sympathy for Gandhi's dilemma. To his lengthy discussions with Gandhi, he attributed the latter's greater appreciation for international factors that would influence any such policy. In the end Gandhi compromised even though it was a bitter pill. Nehru put it this way:

> His love of freedom for India and all other exploited nations and peoples overcame even his strong adherence to non-violence. He had previously given a grudging and rather reluctant consent to the Congress not adhering to his policy in regard to defense and the state's functions in an emergency, but he had kept himself aloof from this. He realized that his half-hearted attitude in this matter might well come in the way of a settlement with Britain and the United Nations. So he went further and himself sponsored a Con-

gress resolution which declared that the primary function of the provisional government of free India would be to throw all her great resources in the struggle for freedom and against aggression and to cooperate fully with the United Nations in the defense of India with all the armed and other forces at her command. It was no easy matter for him to commit himself in this way, but he swallowed the bitter pill, so overpowering was his desire that some settlement should be arrived at to enable India to resist the aggressor as a free nation.[46]

CONCLUSION

At times, Gandhi exasperated Nehru. Nehru could not accept his basic philosophy, or many of his decisions. Nehru had no desire to join Gandhi in his antitechnological and irrational premodern world. While he was interested in character, Gandhi's stress on sin held no interest for him. Religion had its proper sphere, but politics and economics were to be governed by secular principles. Gandhi's world would be an inadequate base on which to build a modern nation.

But while satyagraha could never be an unquestioned dogma, it could be used in the interest of freedom. It was a program that enabled the weak and the poor to resist the strong. It was a political expedient. For this reason, Nehru accepted it and joined with Gandhi in the struggle for independence. If even the goals were not clearly identical, the method would still be effective in the march to independence. During that march Nehru and Gandhi were close comrades. A deep affection existed between them so that when they had to disagree, it was painful.

NOTES

1. Jawaharlal Nehru, *The Discovery of India* (Garden City, N.Y.: Doubleday, Anchor Edition, 1960), 407. See also the discussion in S. Abid Husain, *The Way of Gandhi and Nehru* (Bombay: Asia Publishing House, 1959), chap. 5.

2. R. K. Karanjia, *The Mind of Mr. Nehru: An Interview with R. K. Karanjia* (London: Allen and Unwin, 1960), 34 (emphasis in original).

3. Robert D. Baird, "Religion and the Legitimation of Nehru's Concept of the Secular State," in *Religion and the Legitimation of Power in South Asia*, ed. Bardwell L. Smith (Leiden: Brill, 1978).

4. Cf. Robert D. Baird, "Uniform Civil Code and the Secularization of Law," in *Essays in the History of Religions,* vol. 11 of *Toronto Studies in Religion* (New York: Peter Lang, 1991), chap. 9.

5. Baird, "Religion," 78.

6. Nehru, *The Discovery of India*, 12.

7. Jawaharlal Nehru, *Toward Freedom: The Autobiography of Jawaharlal Nehru* (Boston: Beacon Press, 1958), 191.

8. Address over All India Radio the night of Gandhi's assassination, quoted in Jawaharlal Nehru, *Nehru on Gandhi: A Selection, Arranged in the Order of Events, from the Writings and Speeches of Jawaharlal Nehru* (New York: John Day, 1948), 127ff.

9. Nehru, *The Discovery of India*, 279.

10. Ibid.

11. Ibid.

12. Ibid., 279–280.

13. Nehru, *Toward Freedom*, 71–72.

14. Nehru, *Nehru on Gandhi*, 85. For a discussion of a range of disagreements between Nehru and Gandhi, see B. R Nanda, *Gokhale, Gandhi, and the Nehrus: Studies in Indian Nationalism* (New York: St. Martin's, 1973), particularly chap. 6.

15. Nehru, *Toward Freedom*, 81.

16. Jawaharlal Nehru, *Glimpses of World History: Being Further Letters to His Daughter Written in Prison* (New York: John Day, 1942), 718.

17. Dorothy Norman, ed., *Nehru: The First Sixty Years* (New York: John Day, 1965), 1:42.

18. Nehru, *Glimpses of World History*, 716.

19. Cf. Boyd H. Wilson, "Ultimacy as Unifier in Gandhi," in *Religion in Modern India*, ed. Robert D. Baird (New Delhi: Manohar, 1981). See also the discussion in V. T. Patil, "Nehru and Gandhi: Their Impact on the Nationalist Movement," in *Studies on Nehru*, ed. V. T. Patil (New Delhi: Sterling, 1987), 202ff.

20. Nehru, *The Discovery of India*, 275.

21. Ibid.

22. Nehru, *Toward Freedom*, 82.

23. It is possible that the ambiguity of swaraj was its value, as I have argued for the symbol "secular state." An analysis of that term showed it to be a multivalent symbol that enabled persons who differed on basic issues to work together by filling the term with their own meaning. If swaraj had been as clear and unambiguous as Nehru wanted it to be, if it had filled his socialistic agenda for the new nation, support for it could have expected to lessen. Cf. Robert D. Baird, "'Secular State' and the Indian Constitution," in *Essays in the History of Religions* (New York: Peter Lang, 1991), 141–169.

24. Nehru, *Toward Freedom*, 74.

25. Ibid. For a discussion of these two approaches, the rational and the intuitive, see also R. C. Pillai, *Jawaharlal Nehru and His Critics, 1923–1947* (New Delhi: Gitanjali Publishing House, 1986), 45ff.

26. Ibid., 75.

27. Address at Allahabad University, December 13, 1947. Quoted in Nehru, *Nehru on Gandhi*, 125–126.

28. Norman, *Nehru*, 242.

29. Nehru, *Toward Freedom*, 194.

30. Nehru, *Nehru on Gandhi*, 66.

31. Ibid., 86.

32. Nehru, *Toward Freedom*, 257–258.

33. Ibid., 313–314.

34. Ibid., 314.

35. Jawaharlal Nehru, *A Bunch of Old Letters* (New York: Asia Publishing House, 1960), 507

36. Ibid., 509

37. Ibid., 510.

38. Nehru, *Toward Freedom*, 316.

39. Ibid., 311.

40. Nehru, *A Bunch of Old Letters*, 115ff.

41. Nehru, *Toward Freedom*, 318.

42. Ibid., 319.

43. Ibid., 319–320.

44. Nehru, *The Discovery of India*, 357–358.

45. Nehru, *Nehru on Gandhi*, 107.

46. Ibid., 114–115.

2

Gandhi, Ambedkar, and Untouchability

Harold Coward

Gandhi christened victims of untouchability as Harijans, Children of God. Ambedkar, however, wanted to see his people as full-fledged "Children of the Soil" with equal rights and privileges and not merely as "touchables" under the guise of another name.
—D. C. Ahir, *Gandhi and Ambedkar*

Untouchability was made illegal in India several months after Gandhi's death. When the measure was passed on November 29, 1948, Dr. Bhim Rao Ambedkar was present in the Constituent Assembly as its members shouted *"Mahatma Gandhi ki jai"* (victory to Mahatma Gandhi). In fact, Gandhi had opposed legal measures, believing that moral suasion of the caste Hindus was the best attack against untouchability. Ambedkar, himself an Untouchable, strongly disagreed with Gandhi's approach. Ambedkar believed that the Untouchables had to become educated and fight for their own freedom and equality—provisions that Ambedkar wrote into law as he drafted India's new constitution. How was it then that at the moment when untouchability was legally abolished in India, Gandhi rather than Ambedkar received the praise? In attempting to answer this question we will look at the efforts both men made to combat untouchability, and especially at Ambedkar's critique of Gandhi.

Untouchability Prior To 1920

Before examining the actions of Gandhi and Ambedkar toward the problem of untouchability, let us look at the situation of Untouchables prior to 1920 in India. What better place to begin than with Ambedkar's firsthand analysis.

In his book, *Untouchables or the Children of India's Ghetto*, Ambedkar describes the position of Untouchables under the Hindu social order as follows. Whereas Gandhi and Hindus generally tend to idealize the Indian village, to Ambedkar the village is the site of social evil. The Indian village as described by Ambedkar is a social unit consisting of castes divided into Touchables and Untouchables. The Touchables live inside the village and form a strong community, while the Untouchables are forced to live in separate quarters outside the village in a poor and dependent community. Socially, the Touchables are the rulers, and the Untouchables occupy the position of "hereditary bondsmen."[1]

In the village, says Ambedkar, there is a code established by the caste Hindus that the Untouchables have to follow. Breaking this code by acts of commission or omission by Untouchables is treated as an offense. The basic idea is that Untouchables are impure and must be separated from pure caste Hindus so as not to pollute them. A selection of the offenses listed by Ambedkar include living in the village; coming too close to or casting a shadow on a caste Hindu; acquiring wealth such as land or cattle; building a house with a tiled roof; wearing clean clothes, shoes, a watch, or silver or gold ornaments; sitting on a chair in the presence of a caste Hindu; riding on a horse through the village; speaking in a cultured language; and taking water from the village well or tank. Then there are the duties to be done by Untouchables for the caste Hindus of the village without remuneration such as carry messages of death or marriage to relatives living in other villages; work at a caste Hindu house when a marriage is taking place; perform menial service when a village is preparing for a special celebration such as Halos; at certain festivals Untouchable women must submit themselves to members of the village community to be made the subject of indecent fun. Punishment for offenses, even when committed by an individual, is always upon the whole Untouchable community (23).

Ambedkar also describes how the Untouchables are allowed to earn their living. They are not usually allowed to purchase land, so they are unable to practice agriculture except as landless laborers at wages the Hindu farmers choose to pay. The Untouchables may be paid in cash or privy corn (*gobaraha*)—corn that bullocks, while treading corn on the threshing floor, have eaten but not digested (because of excessive consumption) and is then sieved out of their dung. This corn is given to the Untouchable workers as their wages. When the agricultural season is over, Untouchables cut grass and firewood from the jungle (by bribing the forest guard) and sell it in a nearby town. Some find work as sweepers and cleaners of latrines. They also remove dead animals and skin and tan their hides (23–25). But the main means of livelihood for sixty million Untouchables in India, says Ambedkar, is begging for food from caste Hindus. "If anyone were to move in a village after the usual dinner time, he will meet with a swarm of untouchables moving about the village begging for food" (24–25). Untouchable families are attached to different touchable families as servants and this serves to organize the begging process. Should an Untouchable be employed in a government job, the value of the food obtained by begging is taken into account in establishing the wage to be paid.

In this traditional village structure, says Ambedkar, the law is made by the Touchables, and the Untouchables have no choice but to accept it and obey. Untouchables have no rights or equality, they can only ask for mercy and be content with what is offered. In the village society one's position is established on a hereditary basis (once a Brahmin, always a Brahmin; once a sweeper, always a sweeper) and justified by the law of karma. According to karma, the position one is born into in this life is a direct result of the freely chosen actions of one's previous life. Thus the favorable or unfavorable status one has in this life is a just result of one's self-made karma from previous lives. Ambedkar observes that this karma approach has no relationship to the merits of persons living under it. "An Untouchable, however superior he may be mentally and morally, is below a Touchable in rank, no matter how inferior he may be mentally or morally" (25). Consequently, inside Indian village life there is no room for democracy, equality or fraternity. It is the rule, says Ambedkar, "of the Touchables, by the Touchables and for the Touchables. . . . It is a kind of colonialism of the Hindus designed to exploit the Untouchables."[2] From his experience of growing up under such conditions, Ambedkar was more inclined to trust the British than the caste Hindus who dominated the Congress Party and Independence politics. Thus, his opposition to Gandhi's strategy of putting aside the Untouchable problem until after he had dealt with Hindu–Muslim tensions and achieved Independence. Then, said Gandhi, he would deal with the untouchables. Ambedkar was not willing to trust a caste Hindu–dominated independent India to give justice to the Untouchables. Rather, he wanted equality for himself and his community from the British and the Congress prior to or as part of the conditions for independence.

Untouchability is not just the creation of the rural village, as Ambedkar suggested. Nor, as he also believed, would modernization itself make untouchability a thing of the past. As Susan Bayly shows, urban modernization in India has, in some ways, made the Touchable–Untouchable social division even more rigid and deeply ingrained than it was in its earlier rural village setting.[3] Perhaps Gandhi sensed something of this in his opposing of modernization and his idealizing of the village. In any case, having achieved a clearer understanding of the practice of untouchability in India prior to 1920, let us now take a close look at how Gandhi and Ambedkar attempted to deal with this problem.

DEVELOPMENTS FROM 1920 TO 1932 AND THE POONA PACT

As we have seen, untouchability was a key issue in India in the decades before Gandhi and Ambedkar brought it to the fore. For many people it was intimately tied to the question How could India advance to independent nationhood if it remained as a caste society? The issue of caste and its correlate "untouchability" was a matter of concern for many of India's politicians and social commentators in the decades leading up to independence. Vivekananda and Gandhi condemned "untouchability as impurity" while attempting to maintain but redefine caste so as to somehow uplift Untouchables to equality. Ambedkar strenuously opposed this view, believing that caste division itself was the root problem. Yet during the 1920–1932 period, culminating in the Poona Pact, Gandhi and Ambedkar, while they frequently clashed, were often appreciative of each other and able to cooperate in practical advances for Untouchables.

In 1920 Gandhi criticized the practice of untouchability not in its own right but rather on the grounds that its continued existence obstructed national unity and thus harmed the fight for independence. Writing in *Young India* he said, "Non-cooperation against the government means cooperation among the governed, and if Hindus do not remove the sin of untouchability there will be no *Swaraj* whether in one year or in one hundred years."[4] However, Gandhi qualifies this statement in a 1921 letter to C. F. Andrews: "[Untouchability] is a bigger problem than that of gaining Indian independence but I can tackle it better if I gain the latter on the way. It is not impossible that India may free herself from English domination before India has become free of the curse of untouchability."[5] Andrews urged Gandhi not to try to achieve two goals but rather to join forces with Ambedkar and make his single focus the removal of untouchability.

Although he had deep feelings for the untouchables, Gandhi could not let go of his objectives of independence and Muslim–Hindu unity.[6] But he did attack untouchability in both his words and his actions in ways that were radical for a caste Hindu. On several occasions in 1920–1921 he suggested during speeches that sufferings the Indians were experiencing from the British rule were punishments for the Hindu treatment of the Untouchables: "We make them crawl on their bellies; we have made them rub their noses on the ground; with eyes red with rage, we push them out of railway compartments—what more than this has British rule done?" (*CW* 19:572). In his actions Gandhi set an example for other caste Hindus by accepting Untouchable students into Gujrat Vidyapith, the university he started, and by integrating an Untouchable family into his Ahmedabad ashram—over the objections of his wife and his brother. At this time Gandhi, like Ambedkar, was urging Untouchables not to trust caste Hindus to reform, but to change their own behavior and so improve themselves. Untouchables, by their own purity and cleanliness, are to make Hindus feel ashamed, said Gandhi. Untouchables should no longer "accept leavings from plates, however clean they may be represented to be. Receive only good sound grain, not rotten grain—and that too only if it is courteously offered. . . . May God give you strength to work out your salvation" (*CW* 19:569–575).

During this period Gandhi also supported the use of satyagraha by the Untouchables against the caste Hindus. In 1924 at the town of Vaikam, Gandhi backed an Untouchable satyagraha against a denial of the use of public roads adjacent to a temple and Brahmin residences.[7] Gandhi personally went to Vaikam—the only time he took part in a satyagraha against untouchability. Gandhi debated with the orthodox Brahmins against their interpretation of scripture and managed to get the road past the temple opened to all, although Untouchables were not allowed to enter the temple until 1936. In a 1925 speech to a Depressed Classes Conference at Bombay, Ambedkar recounted the Vaikam satyagraha events and expressed appreciation for Gandhi's involvement—the first politician in India to support the Untouchables' cause.[8] But Ambedkar also expressed his disappointment that Gandhi was still placing Hindu–Muslim unity and the fight for independence ahead of the Untouchables' cause.

The Vaikam action and its partial success may have encouraged the 1927 satyagraha at Mahad, led by Ambedkar, over the right of untouchables to drink water from the Chawdar tank located in the midst of a Brahmin locality—a right the Mahad municipality had approved (*CW* 33:268). A "Correspondent's Report" printed in Gandhi's *Collected Works* records the following. Dr. Ambedkar led the Untouchables to the tank where they drank water with cries of "*Hara Hara Mahadev.*" Touchable caste Hindus came to see what was happening and were filled with rage. The Untouchables went back to their meeting hall for lunch, but within an hour a mob of Touchables with sticks gathered in the temple having been falsely told that the Untouchables were planning to enter the temple. Finding no Untouchables attempting to enter the temple the Touchable crowd went into the streets, beating any Untouchable they came across. At the meeting hall under Ambedkar's leadership, the Untouchables, who outnumbered the stick-wielding Hindu mob, refused to come out, thus avoiding a major calamity (*CW* 33:267). Following the report, which he printed in *Young India*, Gandhi commends the Untouchables for their admirable self-restraint under very provoking circumstances. He condemns the action of the Touchables and commends Ambedkar for his leadership in putting the resolutions of the Bombay Legislative Council and the Mahad municipality to the test in a satyagraha fashion. The evil of untouchability must be eradicated, Gandhi said (*CW* 33:268). Later in 1927 about fifteen thousand Untouchables again assembled at Mahad under Ambedkar's leadership to further demonstrate the Untouchables right to use public water. When it looked as if the action would turn violent, Ambedkar abandoned the satyagraha style action in favor of a ten-year court case which he won. However, at this conference a copy of the *Manusmriti* was publicly burned. This radical action resulted in the loss of many of Ambedkar's caste Hindu supporters, and highlighted a major difference between Ambedkar and Gandhi. Ambedkar noted that as the Orthodox Brahmins at Vaikam had used Hindu scripture to justify their position to Gandhi, such scriptures should be burnt: "Either we should burn all these scriptures or verify and examine the validity of their rules regarding untouchability. . . . Truly these scriptures are an insult to people. The government should have confiscated them long ago."[9]

Gandhi also opposed Hindu scripture's provisions for untouchability but used the approach of one wanting to work from within the tradition by suggesting that such passages were interpolations or not part of the true Hindu canon.[10] Gandhi found himself forced into this position when the Vaikam pundits, in their three-hour debate with Gandhi on March 10, 1925, led Gandhi to state that he believed in the divinity of the Hindu *shastras* (scriptures), the law of karma, and reincarnation. These beliefs, the Brahmin pundits argued, required them to treat Untouchables as born into an unapproachable caste due to their bad karma in a previous life. Recognizing that he was trapped, Gandhi then appealed to reason over scripture—a move that the pundits of course rejected, unless it was advised by an *avatar* (incarnation of a Hindu diety) rather than an ordinary person such as Gandhi. There the debate rested. In a speech following this debate Gandhi acknowledged that the orthodox pundits had listened to him patiently, "I appealed to their reason. I appealed to their humanity. And I appealed to the Hinduism in them. I am sorry to confess to you that I was not able to produce the impression that I had expected that I would be able to."[11] This experience led Gandhi to change his approach to untouchability. To win the confidence of the Orthodox Hindu community he had to be seen by them more as a fighter to preserve Hinduism and less as a reformer. Thus he began to present himself as a committed sanatanist Hindu, saturated with the spirit of Hinduism as he interpreted it, who could speak for all Hindus.[12] Emphasizing allegiance to his religion Gandhi began to underplay his reformist goals (including the eradication of untouchability) but he did not give them up. We see this approach manifested at the Round Table Conferences and in his "fast unto death" at Poona where he and Ambedkar had their first open clash.

THE ROUND TABLE CONFERENCE AND THE POONA PACT

In 1930 a Round Table Conference was called in London by the British government to discuss India's future constitution. Ambedkar and Dewan Bahadur R. Srinivasan were chosen by the government to attend as Untouchables. This helped in no small measure to consolidate Ambedkar's leadership position among the Untouchables. Ambedkar presented himself as an Indian nationalist but equally as a fighter for the Untouchable cause. While agreeing with Congress politicians that "no country is good enough to rule over another," he added, "it is equally true that no class is good enough to rule over another class."[13]

For Ambedkar, engagement in nationalist politics and the structuring of the future constitution gave Untouchables a chance of getting political power into their own hands with which they could change their situation. This remained Ambedkar's goal, although the methods he adopted to achieve it varied depending on the circumstances in which he found himself. At the first Round Table Conference Ambedkar came out strongly for separate electorates for the Untouchables, and continued to hold this position through the three Round Table Conferences. Even though he knew that separate electorates could result in increased disunity (Gandhi's position), Ambedkar chose to join with the Muslim and Sikh appeal for separate electorates to safeguard their minority status, which the British seemed willing to grant.

Gandhi was not present at the first meeting; however, he was selected to represent the Congress Party at the Second Round Table Conference in 1931. Before leaving for London, Gandhi, who had not yet met Ambedkar, invited him to a meeting in Bombay to exchange views. This was their first meeting. (D. C. Ahir quotes their discussion in full.[14]) Gandhi opened by recounting his many efforts to have the Congress Party include dealing with the Untouchable problem as a plank in its platform and expressing surprise that Ambedkar should offer opposition to him and Congress. Acknowledging that it was due to Gandhi's leadership that Congress had given recognition to the Untouchable problem, Ambedkar challenged Congress saying,

> Had [Congress] been sincere it would have surely made the removal of untouchability a condition, like the wearing of Khaddar for becoming a member of Congress. No person who did not employ untouchable women or men in his house . . . or take food with an untouchable student at least once a week should have been allowed to be a member of Congress. . . . I also say Hindus have not shown a change of heart in regard to our problem and so long as they remain adamant we would believe neither the Congress nor the Hindus."[15]

Ambedkar then asked Gandhi what his position was on the separate electorates recommended for both Muslims and the Depressed Classes or Untouchables at the first Round Table Conference. Gandhi responded, "I am against the political separation of the Untouchables from the Hindus. That would be absolutely suicidal."[16] Ambedkar rose and left saying they now knew where they stood.

At the Second Round Table Conference held in London in September 1931, Gandhi and Ambedkar publicly clashed for the first time over two issues: separate electorates and the question of who represented the Untouchables. In his first speech Gandhi strongly opposed the demands Ambedkar put forth on behalf of the Untouchables. Gandhi's stand was to some degree governed by the Congress mandate to him. Congress, he argued, represented the masses of India including the Untouchables. However Gandhi's way of presenting this varied throughout the conference. At one point he allows that he and Congress "will share the honour with Dr. Ambedkar of representing the interests of the untouchables" (*CW* 48:34). Later, however, *The Hindustan Times* reports Gandhi as saying to British governments, "It is only with Congress that your Government will have to reckon . . . though I do not represent Dr. Ambedkar, I do represent the Depressed Classes" (*CW* 48:290). Gandhi made a similar claim regarding the representation of Muslims, Sikhs, and Christians—namely, that Congress, not their faith participants, represented them. The *Proceedings of the Round Table Structure and Minorities Committee* dated October 8, 1931, detail Ambedkar's response to Gandhi's claim: "The Mahatma has always been claiming that the Congress stands for the Depressed Classes, and that the Congress represents the Depressed Classes more than I or my colleague can do. To that claim I can only say that it is one of the many false claims which irresponsible people keep on making."[17] Ambedkar then presented a telegram from the president of the Depressed Classes Union in the United Provinces expressing no confidence in Congress and that "if all the Depressed Classes of India were given the chance of electing their representatives to this Conference, I would find a place here. [Therefore] whether I am a nominee [of the Government] or not, I fully represent the claims of my community" (*Writings* 2:661). Gandhi immediately responded that while he had the greatest regard for Dr. Ambedkar and his efforts to uplift the Untouchables, "I claim . . . to represent the vast mass of the Untouchables. Here I speak not merely on behalf of Congress, but I speak on my own behalf, and I claim that I would get, if there was a referendum of Untouchables, their vote, and that I would top the poll" (*Writings* 2:663).

This battle played out on the conference floor as to who truly represented the Untouchables must have been disconcerting for the British hosts and the other Indian minority leaders. Gandhi and Ambedkar were the intellectual heavyweights at the conference and most minority leaders lined up behind Ambedkar with parallel concerns, opposing Gandhi and Congress. This cut Gandhi to the quick (remember that he was twenty-two years older and far more experienced than Ambedkar). But in their one-upmanship battle as to who could speak for Depressed Classes with authority, Ambedkar held the trump card for he himself was an Untouchable. Gandhi admitted that he had at first taken Ambedkar to be a Brahmin obsessed with helping the Untouchables. It was not until their clash in London that Gandhi realized that Ambedkar was an Untouchable—which says much about Gandhi's stereotype of Untouchables as the "dumb millions" that he and Congress maintained they represented (*Writings* 2:660).

However, over and above the representation question, there was a fundamental disagreement between Gandhi and Ambedkar as to how the Untouchable problem was to be resolved in a free India. At the First Round Table Conference, which Gandhi did not attend, Ambedkar had been successful in obtaining a recommendation of separate electorates for Untouchables—just as were proposed from Muslims and Sikhs. At the second conference in 1931 the idea of separate electorates for the Untouchables was strongly opposed by Gandhi and the Congress Party. While accepting separate electorates for Muslims and Sikhs (for historical reasons) as a necessary evil, Gandhi maintained it would be a positive danger for Untouchables: It would simply perpetuate their current stigma and render permanent the discord between the Untouchables and the Orthodox Hindus in villages. Rather than separate electorates, said Gandhi, the problem must be solved by the Orthodox Hindus doing penance through "active social reform and by making the lot of the untouchables more bearable by acts of service" (*CW* 48:223). At the final sitting before the Second Round Table Conference broke up in failure, Ambedkar reiterated his demand for separate electorates, and Gandhi restated his opposition as follows:

> I am opposed to [the Untouchables'] special representation. . . . What these people need more than election to the legislature is protection from social and religious persecution. Custom, which is often more powerful than law[,] has brought them to a degradation of which every thinking Hindu has need to feel ashamed and to do penance. . . . Thank God, the conscience of Hindus has been stirred, and untouchability will soon be a relic of our sinful past. . . .
>
> Let this Committee and the whole world know that today there is a body of Hindu reformers who are pledged to remove this blot of untouchability. We do not want on our register and on our census Untouchables classified as a separate class. Sikhs may remain as such in perpetuity, so may Muhammadans. . . . Will Untouchables remain untouchables in perpetuity? . . . it is not a proper claim which is registered by Dr. Ambedkar when he seeks to speak for the whole of the Untouchables of India. It will create a division in Hinduism. (*Writings* 2:663)

In Gandhi's mind this division would be perpetuated by separate electorates between the Touchable and Untouchable Hindus in the villages and result only in increasing violence and discrimination by the Touchables on the Untouchables. Should Untouchables want to convert to Islam or Christianity, said Gandhi, that is tolerable. What would be intolerable, he said, is the setting up of separate rights and electorates for the Untouchables: "If I was the only person to resist this thing I would resist it with my life" (*Writings* 2:663). And that indeed was what happened in round three.

Following the Second Round Table Conference, Gandhi returned to India feeling that he had lost to Ambedkar and the leaders of the other minority groups. He tried to stall the granting of political rights to the Untouchables by writing a series of letters to the secretary of state for India warning the British government of disastrous consequences if the Untouchables were granted separate electorates. One week after his return to India, Gandhi was arrested and put in jail as the government outlawed the Congress and jailed eighty thousand people. On August 20, 1932, British Prime Minister Ramsay MacDonald announced the Communal Award voting pattern to be incorporated into India's new constitution. According to the award separate electorates were granted to Muslims, Sikhs, Indian Christians, Anglo-Indians, Europeans, and Untouchables.[18] Ambedkar had won. A month later, while still in the Yeravda prison, Gandhi launched his fast-unto-death in protest. In response, the government said that the award would be revised only if caste Hindus and the Untouchables agreed on an alternative. Gandhi maintained that his fast was against the caste Hindus, not the Untouchables or the government. My aim, he said, is "to sting the Hindus conscience into right religious action" (*CW* 51:62). Gandhi, himself, also seems to have been stung by his defeat and used the fast to signal a radical change of direction: "The Cabinet's decision came like a violent alarm waking me from my slumber and telling me this is the time . . . to give my life for the untouchables" (*CW* 51:vi). No longer could the plight of the Untouchables wait until Independence was achieved and Muslim–Hindu tension overcome; it had to be dealt with immediately by the Orthodox Hindu community throughout India. If the Hindu majority showed remorse, Ambedkar and the Untouchables might relent on their demands for separate electorates. But if the Hindus were not prepared to wipe out untouchability now Gandhi said that he would gladly give his life as a poor penance for the atrocious wrongs Hindus have heaped upon helpless men and women of their own faith. Ambedkar, by his successes at the Round Table Conferences, had set off an alarm bell that Gandhi saw as "a God-given opportunity for a final act of satyagraha in the cause of the downtrodden" (*CW* 51:55).

Gandhi warned Orthodox Hindus that this fast was just the beginning of ending the persecution of the Untouchables, and that this case which would be carried forward by an army of reformers far surpassed the gaining of Independence. The fast began inside Yeravda prison on September 20, 1932, and on September 21 Gandhi gave an interview outlining his immediate reform expectations to caste Hindus and his negotiating position to Ambedkar (namely, that he would accept reserved seats but not separate electorates).

> If I had my way I would insist on temple-entry and the like being included in any pact that may be concluded and I would invite all reformers and the untouchables to do so. . . . I would accept any pact that has not a tinge of separate electorate about it. I would, with utmost reluctance, tolerate reservation of seats under a joint electorate scheme. But I should insist on what is to me the vital part of the pact, the social and religious reform. (*CW* 51:126)

The response of the country to Gandhi was summed up by Tagore: "Our sorrowing hearts will follow your sublime penance with reverence and love" (*CW* 51:109). Hindu caste leaders in Bombay resolved that "one of the earliest Acts of the Swaraj Parliament" would be to guarantee Untouchables equal access to "public wells, public schools, public roads and all other public institutions" (*CW* 53:130). All over India temples were opened to Untouchables, and Brahmins and Untouchables ate together. Gandhi described it as a modern miracle and that it was a new birth for himself and for Hinduism. This may have been the happiest and most spiritual moment of Gandhi's life:. "God was never nearer to me than during the fast" (*CW* 51:186). And although he experienced considerable physical suffering he commented, "There is a deep unconscious joy felt during such purifying agony" (*CW* 51:157).

In the midst of this countrywide response, Ambedkar with other Untouchable leaders came to Gandhi's bedside in prison and after several days of negotiations, in which Ambedkar fought very hard, agreement was finally reached. By that historic pact (referred to as the "Yeravda Poona Pact") Untouchables "would be assured of 147 seats on provincial councils, rather than the 71 awarded to them by the prime minister's scheme; they would also hold 18 percent of the Central Assembly seats, as long as they ran for election by the general electorate rather than under any separate rubric."[19] Ambedkar in fact had gained more guaranteed representation for Untouchables, while Gandhi had won his requirement of "no separate electorate for untouchables." Untouchables would be merged with caste Hindus in a reformed Hinduism. The British cabinet accepted the Poona Pact as an amendment to the Communal Award. Gandhi ended his fast just seven days after it started, and the following week was celebrated throughout India as "Untouchability Abolition Week."[20] However, it took another two decades for untouchability to be abolished by law. Gandhi conveyed his "Hindu gratitude" to Ambedkar and the Untouchables who he said had acted out of forgiveness when they could have chosen the path of revenge. Ambedkar gave a large part of the credit to Gandhi. For the moment, they reached a meeting of the minds.[21] Gandhi believed that the Poona Pact mechanism of reserved seats rather than separate electorates, together with the use of persuasion and example to change the moral outlook of caste Hindus, would avert a crisis. In the view of one commentator, "The agreement between the Mahatma and Ambedkar saved a society from turning upon itself and committing collective suicide."[22] Still in prison, Gandhi followed up the agreement by committing himself to an all-out attack on untouchability and the reform of Hinduism required to merge Untouchables and caste Hindus into a single stream.

THE CHANGING POSITIONS OF GANDHI AND AMBEDKAR: 1933–1947

The Poona Pact spirit of agreement and mutual appreciation between Gandhi and Ambedkar was not destined to last. Despite Ambedkar's urging Gandhi could only devote himself to the Untouchables cause for a short period before returning to Hindu–Muslim unity and independence as his major concern. For Ambedkar, however, "social democracy was more vital than independence from foreign rule" (*Writings* 7:i).

After the Yeravda fast and for the period 1932–1934, Gandhi devoted all his energy to the anti-untouchability campaign for the welfare of Harijans or "Children of God," as he called them. Ahir summarizes Gandhi's activities during this period as follows:

> In February 1933 he founded the Weekly Paper "Harijan" in English and Hindi in place of the "Young India" founded by him in 1919. He also founded the Harijan Sevak Sangh to look after the interests of the Depressed Classes. To give impetus to the anti-untouchability campaign, Gandhi set out on a country-wide tour on November 7, 1933. He also started a Harijan Fund and collected about Rs. 8 lakhs for it. . . . Between December 1932 and July 1934 he undertook three fasts against the practice of untouchability. These were: the two day fast in December 1932 (against untouchability); 21 day fast in May 1933 (for self-purification against untouchability); and 7 day fast in July 1934 (against opponents of untouchability).[23]

Gandhi's anti-untouchability campaign came to a sudden stop in August 1934 when he gave up his focus on the Untouchable problem in order to help the victims of an earthquake that had devastated Bihar. Concluding his effort Gandhi claimed again, as he had previously at the London Round Table Conference, that untouchability was on its last legs and would soon be a relic of the Hindu sinful past (*Writings* 2:661)—a claim that, as Ambedkar continued to make clear, was simply not true.

At the start of his anti-untouchability campaign Gandhi attempted to co-opt Ambedkar to his cause. Gandhi asked Ambedkar to send a message for the first issue of *Harijan*. Ambedkar sent this statement: "The outcaste is a by-product of the caste system. There will be outcastes so long as there are castes. Nothing can emancipate the outcastes except the destruction of the caste system" (*CW* 53:260). Even though Ambedkar had completely contradicted Gandhi's own view, Gandhi published Ambedkar's statement with the following counterstatement: "Untouchability is the product, not of the caste system, but of the distinction of high and low. . . . The attack on untouchability is thus an attack on this 'high-and-low' ness. The moment untouchability goes, the caste system itself will be purified (*CW* 53:261). Gandhi also attempted to win over Ambedkar by naming him to the first board of the All-India Anti-Untouchability League, later renamed the Harijan Sevak Sang (Servants of Untouchables Society) founded in 1932 as a means of sensitizing the Nationalist movement to the cause of the Untouchables. Ambedkar, however, resigned when he found that the organization would not launch a civil rights movement for Untouchables, and that the caste Hindu majority on the board saw the organization's goal as not to change the views of the Orthodox Hindus but rather to collect money from caste Hindus to "uplift" or "civilize" the unclean and immoral Untouchables. Ambedkar found this patronizing and little different from what the Ramanandi gurus and other devotional Hindu leaders had said decades earlier, namely, "adopt our pious brand of ascetic purity, offer yourself in humble submission to our preceptorship, and you will be admitted on sufferance to our mystical communion."[24]

Another problem with the Harijan Sevak Sangh was the "ideal untouchable" Gandhi designed for its use. Along with Harijan, Gandhi used the term *Bhangi* (the Gujarate caste name for hereditary household waste removers) for Untouchables in general. The Sevak Sangh used the image of the uplifted and idealized Bhangi—the godly and dutiful Untouchable "bringing the benefits of cleansing humble service to his home community, and through it to the whole nation."[25] In Gandhi's mind, this ideal image would eventually be embraced by all Hindus of whatever caste until India became an all-Bhangi utopia, and it was the Harijan Sevak Sangh's job to make this happen. Setting the example, Gandhi himself cleaned the latrines at a Congress conference and called on others to do likewise. The Sevak Sangh, attempting to follow Gandhi's example, gave scholarships to Untouchable children, set up hostels, ran industrial schools, and sank wells in as many villages as its very limited funds would reach. While inspiring to some caste Hindus, the Sevak Sangh approach said to Ambedkar and the Untouchables that they should be patient and let the caste Hindus save them. As Bayly puts it, the Untouchables were to be grateful to the caste Hindu Gandhians of the Sevak Sangh on two counts: first, for having been made into clean, vegetarian, teetotaler sweepers; and second, for being allowed to act as instruments of repentance and spiritual cleansing for the high-caste benefactors who had uplifted them.[26] Ambedkar quickly distanced himself from this kind of Gandhian thinking, which he clearly saw was going nowhere. An Untouchability Abolition Bill introduced into the Legislative Assembly in March 1933 was not passed because of opposition from caste Hindus and lack of Congress support.[27] It took Gandhi eight more years to reach Ambedkar's conclusion—namely, that all caste conceptions had to go.

GANDHI'S CHANGING POSITIONS ON CASTE

All through the anti-untouchability campaign Gandhi argued for a reformed view of caste, purged of notions of untouchability. He opened his campaign with dual thrusts directed at the actions and thoughts of caste Hindus. In terms of actions, Gandhi pushed hard for the opening of temples to Harijans through the education of public opinion (*CW* 52:148). Opening the temples, he believed, was an indispensable test of the removal of untouchability and would open the hearts of both caste Hindus and Harijans to receive new light (*CW* 53:vii). Temple entry was to be achieved not by coercion (e.g., through threats of a fast) but rather through a change of spiritual convictions. To foster the new light and new spiritual convictions Gandhi engaged in a reinterpretation of Hindu scriptures. The Hinduism of the *Gita*, the *Upanisads*, and the *Bhagavata*, he said, teach us "that all life is one, and that in the eye of God there is no superior and no inferior" (*CW* 53:171). Thus Hinduism must be purified of all notions of untouchability, and temple entry would help. He also urged close contact with Untouchables. Setting the example, Gandhi stayed in Untouchable colonies, adopted an Untouchable girl, and shared his meals with them.[28] These measures were also followed in Gandhi's ashram which he saw as "the measuring rod by which people can judge me" (*CW* 53:291). To the proposal that Untouchables should undergo a purification ceremony before being admitted to temples, Gandhi responded that it was for the caste Hindus "to undergo purification for having done a violent wrong to the untouchables" (*CW* 52:126). Against the Orthodox Hindu contention that the Hindu scriptures (*shastras*) enjoined untouchability as a part of the caste laws (*varnashrama dharma*), Gandhi could not find one scriptural authority supporting untouchability (*CW* 52:351).

Gandhi's interpretation was supported by numerous scholars and pundits who issued a public statement "that untouchability as practiced in modern times had no warrant in the Shastras and that . . . any community hitherto considered untouchable could acquire all the privileges of caste Hindus 'by clean living and initiation into the Shaiva or Vaishnava worship'" (*CW* 52:vii). Gandhi attacked all fundamentalism, all blind faith in the inerrancy and literal authority of the shastras and instead emphasized that Hinduism (and its shastras) was a dynamic and progressive realization of the unity of all life. The shastras, he argued, contained ample evidence of continuous progress and adaptability to new circumstances (*CW* 52:viii). Rather than attacking the caste system as such (which would have united pro-Orthodox Hindus in opposition), Gandhi's strategy during this period was to attack an evil no one could defend, namely, untouchability. Even so Orthodox Hindus felt threatened and protested against him as he campaigned across India against untouchability. Protestors waved black flags and shouted slogans against him. In Poona a car thought to be carrying him was bombed. In Banaras his portrait was burned. In Karachi, a Hindu carrying an ax was arrested before he could use it against Gandhi. Orthodox Hindu supporters began withholding money from his cause because he had forsaken the dharma or scriptural teaching.[29]

What was Gandhi's interpretation of caste during the anti-untouchability campaign? He attempted to argue that you could have an ideal caste system (based on the teaching of the shastras) that did not incorporate distinctions of "high and low." It was the notions of high and low, he argued, that created untouchability. When they were removed, untouchability would disappear and the caste system would be purified (*CW* 53:261). As there is no fifth caste in the Shastras, Untouchables should be regarded as *shudras* (servants)—a view acceptable to some Orthodox Hindu leaders of the day. While the role of shudras was to serve the other castes, it was to possess equality of status if not opportunity. As Gandhi put it, "One born a scavenger must earn his livelihood by being a scavenger, and then do whatever else he likes. For a scavenger is as worthy of his hire as a lawyer or your President."[30] Thus, although Gandhi criticized current caste practice with its divisions of superior and inferior, he held to a traditional view (varnashrama dharma) of the divinely ordained division of society into four caste groups defined according to duty as the way to allow for both a harmonious society and the spiritual growth of the individual soul. In this Gandhi was largely following earlier reformers such as Vivekananda who also interpreted the Hindu shastras as calling for equal and harmoniously integrated castes.[31] And it was this idealized view of the purified caste system as a solution to the problem of untouchability that Ambedkar strongly rejected.

Ambedkar's goal was to integrate Untouchables into Indian society in modern, not traditional, ways. In contrast to Gandhi's ideal shudra or Bhangi who would continue to do sanitation work even though theoretically his or her status would be equal to that of a Brahmin, Ambedkar's ideal was to raise the educational standards of the Untouchables so that they could aspire to rise to the level of the highest Hindu and be in a position to use political power as a means to that end.[32] For Ambedkar equality did not mean equal status of the castes but rather equal social, political, and economic opportunities for Untouchables. Ambedkar did not find Gandhi's condemnation of untouchability radical enough because it did not attack the root of the problem: the caste system.

In 1935 Ambedkar was invited to give a presidential address to the Annual Conference of the Jat Pat Todak Mandal of Lahore—an organization of caste Hindu reformers who wanted to do away with the caste system. The talk, prepared by Ambedkar and titled "The Annihilation of Caste," aroused problems with the Mandal's organizing committee because in it Ambedkar announced that he intended to give up Hinduism for another religion. The Mandal first postponed and then canceled the conference. Ambedkar, at his own expense, then published his talk which evoked a comment from Gandhi in the form of two articles in the *Harijan* dated July 11 and 19, 1936. Ambedkar responded with "A Reply to the Mahatma," which be published as an appendix in the second edition of his *Annihilation of Castes* in 1937.[33] This is the key exchange between the two on their different views regarding Hinduism, caste, and untouchability and thus deserves careful examination.

In his talk Ambedkar set out to destroy the religious notions within Hinduism upon which caste practice was founded. The prescription Ambedkar proposed to the caste Hindus of the Mandal was that they continue with intercaste meals and intercaste marriages (practices they had already approved) but that to get to the root of the problem the Hindu belief in the sanctity of their scriptures must be destroyed—for it is through these shastras that caste and untouchability are rooted in the common mind of the people. Citing Buddha and Nanak for support, Ambedkar says that what is wrong with Hindus is their religion and its scriptures that have produced in Hindus the notion of sacredness of caste (73–75). Ambedkar summarizes the key points of his talk as follows:

1. That caste has ruined the Hindus;

2. That the reorganization of Hindu society on the basis of purified *varna* (as proposed by Gandhi and others) is harmful because it degrades the masses by denying them the opportunity to acquire knowledge or organize themselves with political power;

3. That Hindu society must be reorganized so as to recognize the principles of Liberty, Equality and Fraternity;

4. To achieve this objective the sense of religious sanctity behind Caste and *Varna* must be destroyed only by discarding the divine authority of the *shastras*, as did Buddha and Nanak. (114)

Ambedkar believed such a reorganization of Hindu society to be impossible because Brahmins and the higher castes would not be willing to give up the rights and privileges caste status afforded them, and because reason cannot trump revelation in the interpretation of the shastra rules for caste and *varna* (hereditary occupational groupings) as set out by Manu and others. Thus Hinduism had become a religion of rules that must be destroyed and could not be reformed. Consequently, said Ambedkar, "I have decided to leave Hinduism and change my religion" (96).

Gandhi's response, which was published in the *Harijan* in July 1936, focused on Ambedkar's final point, namely, the divine sanction of Hindu scripture for untouchability and caste. Gandhi organizes his reply around the questions What are the scriptures? Are any parts to be rejected as unauthorized interpolations? Once unacceptable interpolations have been removed, what is the view of Hindu scripture on questions such as untouchability, caste, and equality of status? (101). Gandhi's answer to the first question is that the "Vedas, Upanisads, Smritis and Puranas including the Ramayana and Mahabharata are the Hindu Scriptures" (102). In answer to the second question, Gandhi argues that as every generation has added to the scriptures, not everything can be accepted. The Smritis, which Ambedkar quotes from at length in making his case, contain much that cannot be accepted as God's word. Acceptable scriptures, says Gandhi, must present eternal truths, appeal to any conscience and pass the test of reason. And even a text cleared of unacceptable interpolations will still need interpretation. This is a task, not for the learned, but for the saints who embody God's word in their lives (102). It is by using this theory of interpretation that Gandhi then presents the understanding of untouchability, caste, and varna that he finds in the Hindu scriptures.

> Caste has nothing to do with religion. . . . *Varna* and *Ashrama* are institutions which have nothing to do with castes. The law of *Varna* teaches us that we have . . . to earn our bread by following the ancestral calling . . . there is no calling too low and none to high. All are good, lawful and absolutely equal in status. The callings of a Brahmin—a spiritual teacher—and a scavenger are equal and their due performance carries equal merit before God, and at one time seems to have carried identical reward before man . . . there is nothing in the law of *Varna* to warrant a belief in untouchability. (103)

Gandhi suggests that he finds traces of such an approach, even in these degenerate times, in some villages. He contends that is wrong to judge (as he thinks Ambedkar does) the law of Varna by those who make it a caricature in their lives. One should judge a religion by its best expression, not its worst. Can a religion that was professed by Chaitanya, Ramakrishna, Raja Ram Mohan Roy, Debendranath Tagore, and Vivekananda be as devoid of merit as Ambedkar has suggested?

Reading Gandhi's response to Ambedkar in the *Harijan* caused the Jat Pat Todak Mandal of Lahore (where Ambedkar's talk was to be given) to write a letter to Gandhi, which he published in an August 1936 issue of the paper. In their letter this reform caste Hindu group supports Ambedkar's critique and takes Gandhi to task for his interpretation:

> Your philosophical difference between caste and *varna* is too subtle to be grasped by people in general, because for all practical purposes in Hindu society caste and varna are one and the same thing. . . . Your theory of *varnavyavastha* is impracticable in this age and there is no hope of its revival in the near future. But Hindus are slaves of caste and do not want to destroy it. So when you advocate your ideal or imaginary *varnavyavastha* they find justification for clinging to caste. Thus you are doing a great disservice to social reform. . . . To try to remove untouchability without striking at the root of *varnavyavastha* is simply to treat the outward symptoms of a disease. (106)

This comment from reform-minded caste Hindus not only agrees with Ambedkar's critique of Gandhi but also puts its finger on the conceptual weakness inherent in Gandhi's anti-untouchability campaign.

Ambedkar's own reply to Gandhi picks up the points made by the Mahatma one by one. To Gandhi's charge that Ambedkar focused on interpolated and inauthentic texts, Ambedkar admits that he is not an expert on Hindu scripture but that the texts he cited were "all taken from the writings of the late Mr. Tilak who was a recognized authority on the Sanskrit Language and the Hindu *Shastras*" (115). Ambedkar goes on to ask what does it matter if the texts he cited are interpolations or have been differently interpreted by the saints? The Hindu masses, he says, do not make distinctions between genuine and interpolated texts. They believe what they have been told, namely, that the shastras require as a religious duty the observance of caste and untouchability. With regard to the saints, says Ambedkar, their teachings have been ineffective on these issues because they were believers in untouchability, and the masses have been taught that even though a saint (due to his special purity) might break caste, the common person may not. Therefore, while the saint may be honored as a pious person, he or she never becomes an example to follow. Thus saints have had no effect on the masses who continue as believers in caste and untouchability.

Ambedkar concludes his reply by attacking Gandhi's contention that one should follow the varna of one's ancestral calling. First, he points out that in his own life Gandhi does not practice what he preaches. Although born a Bania, he has never been a trader but instead chose to follow law and a calling which is closer to that of a Brahmin. In fact Gandhi's position, that one should follow one's ancestral calling, is a step backward from the teaching of Dayananda Saraswati who understood Vedic varna in terms of a calling suited to one's natural aptitudes rather than the calling of one's ancestral birth. Ambedkar pushes the argument a step further. Must a person follow an ancestral calling if it does not suit one's capacities or if due to changing conditions one can no longer make a living by it? Or what if one finds one's ancestral pattern to be immoral as when one is born into a family of pimps or prostitutes? Is Gandhi willing to accept the logical conclusions of his doctrine? Ambedkar concludes that Gandhi's "ideal of following one's ancestral calling is not only an impossible and impractical ideal, but it is also morally an indefensible ideal" (121). Gandhi did not reply.

Ambedkar's announcement that he was leaving the Hindu religion influenced other Untouchables. In 1936 a conference of Mahars held in Bombay decided to leave Hinduism by converting to some other religion. Christian, Muslim, and Sikh leaders announced that they were ready to receive Untouchable converts, however, Ambedkar wanted another religion that was Indian in origin.[34] It was Buddhism that attracted him, but at that time there were no effective Buddhist organizations in India. In any case Ambedkar immediately became so caught up in political activity that the question was postponed. During the period 1937–1947 Ambedkar formed the Independent Labour Party (which had some electoral success); established the Scheduled Castes Federation in the hope of uniting all Untouchables into a political power; and was elected to the position of minister of labour on the Viceroy's Executive Council. Even though improved educational opportunities and the reservation of government jobs gave some advance to Untouchables, the situation for the vast majority remained unchanged. By the mid-1940s Ambedkar's frustration at the slow pace of change showed in his most vigorous attack on Gandhi: *What Congress and Gandhi Have Done to the Untouchables.*[35] In it Ambedkar restates his contention (with numerous illustrations) that to attain political rights Untouchables require separate electorates. He also offers a strong criticism of Gandhi's teachings and actions. The Harijan Sevak Sangh, which Gandhi said was for the uplift of Untouchables, is held to be political charity intended to bring Untouchables into the Congress camp (145). Ambedkar's assessment of Gandhi's anti-untouchability campaign was that "after a short spurt of activity in the direction of removing untouchability by throwing open temples and wells the Hindu mind returned to its original state" (114). Detailed study is made of several temple-entry movements to show that these activities were often concerned more for Congress political success than for the well-being of Untouchables (115–125).

Gandhi's repeated statement that if his fellow caste Hindus, who have taken pledges for the removal of untouchability, fail to make good on their pledges, then he would "have no interest left in life" is judged by Ambedkar to be an empty vow which Gandhi gives up to preserve political power (124–125). Ambedkar repeats from the Annihilation of Caste lecture his critique of Gandhi's theory of caste and describes Gandhi's attempt to make the Bhangi soil remover an ideal for all Hindus and the nation as "a cruel joke on the helpless classes which none but Mr. Gandhi can perpetuate with equanimity and impunity" (304). Untouchables, concludes Ambedkar, must continue to beware of Gandhi (and the Congress) for their attitude is "let Swaraj perish if the cost of it is the political freedom of the Untouchables" (283–284). Eleanor Zelliot concludes that Ambedkar's words exerted little influence on the British in their political planning for India's Independence in which they provided no special political rights for Untouchables. In response Ambedkar organized "huge satyagraha demonstrations before the state legislatures at Pune, Nagpur, Lucknow, and in the industrial city of Kanpur from July to October 1946. This effort failed to move the planners of India's future."[36]

When Ambedkar indicated that he and the Untouchables should find another religion and leave the Hindu fold, Gandhi was shocked to see Christians, Muslims, and Sikhs vying with each other to convert Untouchables. In a conversation with the Christian leader John Mott, Gandhi said that such activities hurt him and were an ugly travesty of religion (*CW* 64:35). Aside from it being an unseemly competition, said Mott, should Christians not preach the gospel to Untouchables who were thinking of leaving Hinduism? Gandhi's response did not endear him to the Untouchables: "Would you preach the gospel to a cow? Well, some of the untouchables are worse than cows in understanding . . . they can no more distinguish between the relative merits of Islam and Hinduism and Christianity than a cow" (*CW* 64:37). Christians should not preach with words but only with examples of service, then they would not get in the way of Gandhi's anti-untouchability campaigns.

From 1935 on Gandhi become more open in his criticism of the caste system itself. Nehru reported that Gandhi "did not believe in the caste system

except in some idealized form of occupation. . . . I am undermining it completely, he said, by my tackling untouchability. . . . If untouchability goes . . .
the caste system goes. So I am concentrating on that."[37] In the 1940s
Gandhi's emphasis seemed to change, perhaps as a result of his continually
having to contend with Ambedkar's critique. Rather than continuing to exalt
a purified caste order purged of untouchability, be began to call for the full repudiation of caste.[38] It was becoming clear to him that the attitudes of caste
Hindus were not changing. In a 1945 conversation Gandhi debates the possibility of going on another fast but doubts it would change Hindus—a
marked reversal of his earlier thinking at the time of his Poona fasts (*CW*
81:119). Even the Harijan Sevak Sangh, he says, needs to rethink its goal
from the uplift and education of Untouchables to the reeducation of caste
Hindus. Gandhi suggests that it is easier to educate Untouchables than caste
Hindus: "You can educate Harijans by giving them scholarships, hostels, etc.,
but no such way is possible among the caste Hindus" (*CW* 81:119). While
his attempt to prick the conscience of the caste Hindus through the anti-untouchability campaign did change the lives of some Hindus and may have
sensitized the nation to the evil of untouchability, the vast majority did not
significantly alter their behavior. Gandhi, in 1945, seems to adopt Ambedkar's approach when he asks educated Harijans to participate in politics and
be more than a match for their political competitors. While Harijans can take
assistance from caste Hindus (the previously stated goal of the Harijan Sevak
Sangh), the more Harijans lean on such assistance, the less likely are they to
uplift themselves and the rest of society (*CW* 81:120). This is far from
Gandhi's counsel of the 1920s and 1930s when he urged Untouchables to remain passive but become clean in personal habit, while he convinced the caste
Hindus to change their sinful ways. In the end Gandhi seems to adopt the
strategy (with regard to untouchability) that Ambedkar had advocated all
along. Perhaps that is why, as independence approached, Gandhi advised
Nehru and Patel to include Ambedkar in India's first cabinet.[39]

CONCLUSION

Untouchability was a central issue for both Ambedkar and Gandhi. Ambedkar had no choice. Born an Untouchable and scared in childhood by injustices visited upon him, he devoted his life to the cause of equality and
opportunity for his people. Gandhi, in 1946 said, "I have become a Harijan
by choice."[40] That choice, too, may go back to childhood when at age twelve

Gandhi told his mother it was wrong to consider contact with Uka, the Untouchable cleaner of the family's latrines, as sinful.[41] Throughout his life, removing the evil of untouchability from Hinduism and India remained a major concern—although he and Ambedkar more often than not sharply disagreed on how that goal was to be achieved. While Gandhi's political approach was not successful, his wisdom and humility led him not only to propose Ambedkar for the new cabinet but to change the minds of Nehru and other Congress leaders who, at first, were not in favor of Ambedkar's appointment. On his side Ambedkar showed a statesman-like attitude in his willingness to join the caste Hindu–dominated Congress cabinet. As law minister, chairman of the Drafting Committee, and the guiding hand behind the passage of the constitution, Ambedkar was able to put into the Constitution of India many of the equality and justice rights for Untouchables that he had fought for (usually against Congress) throughout his life. Without Gandhi's intervention, it is unlikely that Ambedkar would have been given that opportunity. Gandhi, while finally deferring to Ambedkar's political approach, maintained his moral fight against untouchability up to the end. During his last two years, Gandhi set a moral example by living in Untouchable settlements in Delhi. Although an impossibly romantic ideal, Gandhi said that rather than Nehru for President, India should choose "a chaste and brave Bhangi girl" to complement the seventeen-year-old British queen (*CW* 89:223). Throughout his life Gandhi touched the Untouchables and his example led many of them to follow him and to vote Congress, resulting in a sweep of the Scheduled Caste seats in the 1945–1946 election.

Looking back on the contributions of both men it seems clear that they needed and benefited from each other. But for Ambedkar's stand at the Round Table Conferences there would have been no need for Gandhi's Poona fast. But for the fast Gandhi may never have launched the anti-untouchability campaign. Ahir points out that "prior to the fast Gandhi was even opposed to the entry of Untouchables into the Hindu Temples. After the fast he . . . advocated the opening of the temples, wells, roads and other public places."[42] Ambedkar's refusal to go along with the Harijan Sevak Sangh's patronizing policy of serving Untouchables rather than politically empowering them may have eventually helped Gandhi see that his narrow religious view of untouchability within the varnashrama context not only reinforced Harijan passivity but betrayed his own political insight "that no system of oppression could be ended without the active involvement and consequent political education and organization of its victims."[43] Gandhi's blindness on this point not only rendered the Sevak Sangh ineffective but also the

Congress Party. Sharing Gandhi's philosophy of serving the untouchables rather than challenging caste practice, Congress did little to get them into positions of political power. Ambedkar's withering critique of this approach in his *Annihilation of Castes*, and his subsequent debate with Gandhi, seems to have caused Gandhi to start to doubt the wisdom of his thought and action.

Both Ambedkar and Gandhi had a vision of equality for Untouchables. Gandhi's traditional outlook, his concern for rural masses, and his political drive for independence had little appeal for Ambedkar and his Mahar colleagues who wanted to integrate themselves into a modern Indian society, at the highest level. Equality, for Ambedkar, did not mean equal status of the varnas but rather equality of economic, social, and political opportunity—the rights for Untouchables and all others that he built into the Indian constitution. Ambedkar's statements to his fellow Untouchables on the need to live clean, moral lives parallel some of Gandhi's teachings. But Ambedkar, from the beginning, went much further than Gandhi in awakening Untouchables to their oppressed state and showing them how to obtain equality through education and the modern use of political and legal rights. Aware of the powerful inertia in the caste system, Ambedkar led his community into choosing to change their religion from Hinduism, with its scripturally based caste system, to Buddhism and its view of equality. Ambedkar was more radical than Gandhi or any other Untouchable leader of his day. Yet it was Gandhi's action in getting Ambedkar into India's first cabinet that made it possible for Ambedkar to achieve, at least partially, his equality vision. In 1948, shortly after Gandhi's death, when the Constituent Assembly finally voted to abolish untouchability and cries of "victory to Mahatma Gandhi" rang out, Ambedkar may have felt that in spite of and together with Gandhi he had achieved something of his goal.

NOTES

1. B. R. Ambedkar, "Untouchables or the Children of India's Ghetto" in *Dr. Babasaheb Ambedkar Writings and Speeches*, comp. by Vasant Moon (Bombay: Government of Maharastra, 1989), 5:18–26.

2. Ibid., 26. Ambedkar's description of the position of untouchables prior to 1920 is given confirmation by Susan Bayly, *Caste, Society, and Politics in India from the Eighteenth Century to the Modern Age*, vol. 4.3 of *The New Cambridge History of India* (Cambridge: Cambridge University Press, 1999). For a general discussion of purity and impurity, see John B. Carman and

Frederique Marglin, eds., *Purity and Auspiciousness in Indian Society* (Leiden: E. J. Brill, 1985).

3. Bayly, *Caste, Society, and Politics*, 230

4. M. K. Gandhi, *Young India*, 29 December 1920.

5. *The Collected Works of Mahatma Gandhi* (Delhi: Government of India, 1971), 19:289–290. Hereafter cited parenthetically in the text as *CW* followed by volume and page(s).

6. Rajmohan Gandhi, *Revenge and Reconciliation* (Delhi: Penguin Books, 1999), 244.

7. Gandhi, *Revenge and Reconciliation*, 246.

8. For these events, see the recounting of Eleanor Zelliot, *From Untouchable to Dalit* (Delhi: Manohar, 1998), 160–163.

9. As quoted by Zelliot, *From Untouchable to Dalit*, 163.

10. Bhikhu Parekh, *Colonialism, Tradition, and Reform* (New Delhi: Sage, 1989), 217ff.

11. Quoted in ibid., 223.

12. Ibid., 224. Gandhi defines himself sanatanist as follows: "I call myself a sanatanist Hindu because I believe in the *Vedas*, *Upanisads*, the *Puranas*, and the writings left by the holy reformers. This belief does not require me to accept as authentic everything that passes as *Shastras*. I am not required to accept the *ipse dinit* or the interpretation of Pundits" (quoted in ibid., 224). In the *Harijan* of December 23, 1939, Gandhi commented further: "A sanatanist is one who follows the Sanatana *Dharma*. According to the *Mahābhārata*, it means observance of *Ahimsā*, *Satya*, non-stealing, cleanliness and self-restraint. As I have been endenvouring to follow these to the best of my ability, I have not hesitated to describe myself as a sanatanist."

13. Quoted in Zelliot, *From Untouchable to Dalit*, 102.

14. D. C. Ahir, *Gandhi and Ambedkar: A Comparative Study* (New Delhi: Blumoon Books, 1995), 38–41.

15. Ibid., 39.

16. Ibid.

17. Vasant Moon, ed., *Dr. Babasaheb Ambedkar: Writings and Speeches* (Bombay: Government of Maharashtra, 1982), 2:661. Hereafter cited parenthetically in text as *Writings* followed by volume and page.

18. Stanley Wolpert, *A New History of India* (New York: Oxford University Press, 2000), 319.

19. Ibid., 320.

20. Ibid.

21. Gandhi, *Revenge and Reconciliation*, 251.

22. Ravinder Kumar, *The Making of a Nation: Essays in Indian History and Politics* (Delhi: Manohar, 1989), 157.

23. Ahir, *Gandhi and Ambedkar*, 43.

24. Bayly, *Caste, Society, and Politics*, 250.
25. Ibid., 251.
26. Ibid.
27. Parekh, *Colonialism, Tradition, and Reform*, 239.
28. Ibid., 241.
29. Gandhi, *Revenge and Reconciliation*, 253.
30. From *Harijan*, 6 March 1937. Quoted in Zelliot, *From Untouchable to Dalit*, 154.
31. See Vivekananda's "The Rationale of Caste . . ." in *Sources of Indian Tradition*, ed. Stephen Hay (New York: Columbia University Press, 1988), 2:74. Says Vivekananda, "Caste is a natural order."
32. Zelliot, *From Untouchable to Dalit*, 158.
33. B. R. Ambedkar, *Annihilation of Caste with a Reply to Mahatma Gandhi* (Julhindur, Punjab: Bheem Patrika Publications, 1968).
34. Zelliot, *From Untouchable to Dalit*, 170–171.
35. B. R. Ambedkar, *What Congress and Gandhi Have Done to the Untouchables* (Bombay: Thacker and Co., 1945).
36. Zelliot, *From Untoucable To Dalit*, 172.
37. Quoted in Gandhi, *Revenge and Reconciliation*, 253.
38. Bayly, *Caste, Society, and Politics*, 251. Bayly observes, "In the 1940s Gandhi called for full repudiation of caste rather than his earlier goal of a purified caste order purged of untouchability" (note 40).
39. Gandhi, *Revenge and Reconiliation*, 256.
40. *Harijan*, 9 June 1946 as quoted in Zelliot, *From Untouchable to Dalit*, 160.
41. As revealed in a *Young India* article quoted in ibid., 154–155.
42. Ahir, *Gandhi and Ambedkar*, 44.
43. Parekh, *Colonialism, Tradition, and Reform*, 243.

3

Of Many Mahatmas: Besant, Gandhi, and Indian Nationalism

Joy Dixon

In 1917, Annie Besant was one of the most (in)famous women in the British Empire. Externed from the Bombay Presidency in 1916 as a threat to public order, she was interned by the Madras government a year later for her pro-Nationalist activities. When the Indian National Congress met in Calcutta in 1917 she served as its president. This was not Besant's first moment in the political limelight: She was a notorious public figure long before she arrived in India in 1893. While in England she had gone from being the unhappy wife of an Anglican clergyman to a scandalous public life as a secularist, a socialist, and an advocate of birth control. In 1889 her conversion to Theosophy opened up a new career for her as a religious leader and Indian Nationalist. She lived in India for much of the 1890s, and in 1907 she was elected president of the Theosophical Society and established her base at the theosophical headquarters at Adyar, near Madras (now Chennai), in south India.

Once in India, Besant became part of the movement for the revival of Hinduism, which included both Conservative Hindus, who called for an end to western influence in India, and Hindu reformers, who were working to "purify" Hinduism through a return to a more noble past in which modern abuses (such as child marriage or a rigid caste system) did not exist. As Nancy Anderson notes, during her first years in India Besant attempted to steer a cautious course between these two poles, and she was reluctant to criticize Hindu custom. Instead, she worked to assimilate herself to Indian culture—adopting the sari, furnishing her home in Indian style, and bathing in the Ganges—and avoided discussion of present political conditions by emphasizing the achievements of the ancient Aryan civilization. By the turn of the century, Besant had begun to advocate for reform, and in 1913 she "dropped almost all attempts to compromise with orthodox Hinduism."[1]

In the same year, Besant joined the Indian National Congress, and immediately began working to expand its activities. At the Congress meeting in 1914 she proposed that delegates prepare "a definite scheme for self-government to be presented to Great Britain at the end of the war." That campaign failed, but in 1915 Congress adopted the idea.[2] Her All-India Home Rule League, developed over the next few years, was to become one of the most important Nationalist organizations in India.

When she met the viceroy, Lord Chelmsford, and the secretary of state for India, Edwin Montagu, in 1917, Besant claimed that her entry into Nationalist politics had grown out of her educational concerns, as she realized that educational work was useless without political reform.[3] Among her fellow Theosophists, however, she told a different story. In that version, she claimed that in 1913 she was summoned by the members of the Great White Lodge to their headquarters in Shamballa. Shamballa, the center of activities for this occult hierarchy, did not appear on any worldly map, but was located somewhere in the Gobi Desert, invisible to profane eyes. There Besant met with the Rishi Agastya, the "Regent of India in the Inner Government," who commanded her to take up the cause of India's political freedom.[4] Many years later, in 1929, Besant revealed to the public the instructions she had been given on that momentous day. The chief point was to "Claim India's place among the Nations." In pursuit of that goal Besant was warned to "be firm but not provocative," and she was assured that "the end will be a great triumph, take care it is not stained by excess." Besant concluded that "Liberty for India, but within the British Federation, was the goal for which I was to work . . . Dominion Status . . . gives exactly what is wished—Independence within India, with an equal and friendly link with Britain through the Crown."[5]

When Besant was elected president of the Congress in 1917 she seemed to be well on her way to fulfilling the Rishi Agastya's command. However, 1917 was the height of her popularity. Even at the Congress itself, opposition was already emerging. By the 1920s, Gandhi's vision of swaraj had displaced Besant's Home Rule movement. For Besant, Home Rule was not intended to mean independence, but "Self-Government within the Empire on Colonial Lines." Home Rule, Besant argued in 1917, "does not mean that England and India ought to be torn apart. It means only that India shall be mistress in her own household."[6] According to Besant, the Gandhian Non-cooperation movement destroyed all hope of achieving self-government for India within an imperial federation; it was disorderly, revolutionary, and (most serious, in her view) it directly contradicted the process of spiritual evolution, which had brought England and India together for the good of all humanity.

INDIAN NATIONALISM AND THE THEOSOPHICAL SOCIETY

Besant's entry into the Indian Nationalist movement was eased by the fact that members of her Theosophical Society (TS) had been actively involved, for almost thirty years, in the Indian Nationalist movement. The TS was founded in New York in 1875 by the Russian émigré Helena Petrovna Blavatsky and the American lawyer Henry Steel Olcott. In 1879 the two founders moved to India, and in 1882 they moved their headquarters to Adyar. By the late 1870s Blavatsky had begun to make India the source of her inspiration, and to identify "esoteric" versions of both Buddhism and brahminical Hinduism as the basis of her theosophy or "divine wisdom."[7] At the same time, the "true founders" of the TS—the mysterious Masters who gave Blavatsky her instructions—began to be identified with a specifically Hindu spiritual tradition, as "Mahatmas" or great souls. According to Blavatsky, the Mahatmas were not supernatural beings, but men who "by special training and education, [have] evolved those higher faculties and [have] attained that spiritual knowledge which ordinary humanity will acquire after passing through numberless series of reincarnations during the process of cosmic evolution."[8] Two of these Mahatmas—Morya, originally from the Punjab, and the Kashmiri Koot Hoomi Lal Singh—had taken a special interest in the Theosophical Society.

The Theosophical Society was, officially at least, apolitical, but the Theosophists had made contact with the Indian Nationalist movement even before they arrived in India. In 1878 the TS had entered into a short-lived alliance with the Arya Samaj whose leader, Dayananda Saraswati, advocated a reformed Hinduism that appeared to be broadly compatible with theosophical teaching. There were very real differences between the two organizations, which led to an acrimonious break in 1882. While it lasted, however, the alliance helped to establish the Theosophical Society's reputation in India, and by 1884 the TS had founded more than one hundred branches across the subcontinent.[9]

At the theosophical conference in Madras that year Ragunath Rao, the former *diwan* of Indore state, called on Indian Theosophists to involve themselves in work for reform. When Blavatsky insisted that the society must preserve its political neutrality in India, Rao and other members formed a separate organization, the Madras Mahajana Sabha, to work toward an all-India political association. Most important of all was the Indian National Congress, which first convened in Bombay in December 1885. A. O. Hume, widely regarded as the "father" of the Congress, was a liberal and a former member of the Indian Civil Service; he was also a former Theosophist and he exploited the connections provided by the TS in his political activities.[10] All of these activities were endorsed by Theosophy's Mahatmas: According to Blavatsky, the "*main* object of K. H. and M." was to encourage the TS in doing "real practical good . . . for the Natives."[11] These pro-Nationalist Mahatmas provided very real inspiration for Nationalist activity. According to Blavatsky, when Hume (who had rapidly become disillusioned with the TS) denounced Blavatsky and rejected her Mahatmas as fictions, Ragunath Rao and other "leaders of Hindus" in the society reacted with "disgust," arguing that "they all believed in the Mahatmas . . . [and] would have no more their names desecrated."[12] For some years Hume himself had relied on these Mahatmas for political insight; letters "precipitated" to him by occult means warned of political unrest throughout India, and urged him to promote reform and to encourage Nationalist activity. Even after he left the TS, Hume continued to work with a group of "advanced initiates" who, he claimed, directed his reform activities.[13]

GANDHI AND THE THEOSOPHICAL SOCIETY

It was precisely this concern with the occult—the belief in a powerful and secret Great White Lodge and that ordinary men and women could develop their psychic powers in order to become Mahatmas themselves—that Gandhi rejected in Theosophy. Writing to Dr. Pranjivan Mehta in 1911, Gandhi recorded that he had conclusively rejected Theosophy in 1899: "They pressed me hard that year to join the Society but I refused in no uncertain terms, saying that, though the Society's rule respecting brotherhood appealed to me, I had no sympathy for its search for occult powers. . . . One who runs after occult powers cannot but become so intoxicated."[14] The problem, as he put it in 1926, was the society's "secret side—its occultism. It has never appealed to me. I long to belong to the masses. Any secrecy hinders the real spirit of democracy."[15]

During his student years in London, however, the Theosophical Society provided Gandhi with important contacts and introduced him to new ways of thinking. He began his first real reading of the *Bhagavad Gita* with two theosophical friends, who also introduced him to the Blavatsky Lodge of the TS and to Madame Blavatsky and her new convert, Annie Besant. It was, he later recalled, Blavatsky's *The Key to Theosophy* that "stimulated in me the desire to read books on Hinduism, and disabused me of the notion fostered by the missionaries that Hinduism was rife with superstition."[16] Gandhi applied for an associate membership in the lodge on March 26, 1891, but he was never an active participant in the society.[17]

Gandhi remained sympathetic to the Theosophists' belief in "Universal Brotherhood," and he shared their concern for religious tolerance. This was the point he emphasized in a series of lectures on Hinduism that he gave to the Theosophical Society in Johannesburg in 1905: that "there was, among the objects of the Theosophical Society, this one, viz., to compare the various religions, find out the truth underlying these and show the people how those religions were only so many roads leading to the realisation of God, and how one ought to hesitate to dub any of them false."[18] Like Besant, he was firmly committed to a belief in the religious (though nonsectarian) basis of political life and reform. In a speech given on Besant's birthday in 1928, Gandhi acknowledged her contribution to the Nationalist cause in precisely these terms: "'It was Dr. Besant,' declared Mahatmaji, 'who bridged the gulf between religion and politics. Bereft of religion politics would be like a body without soul. Without religion swaraj would be of no avail. It was Dr. Besant,' concluded Gandhiji, 'who had awakened India from her deep slumber.'"[19]

The Home Rule Movement

In recent years, a number of excellent studies of Besant's political thought have appeared. Mark Bevir has traced the political implications of Besant's Orientalist reconstruction of a Hindu golden age which, he argues, allowed her to challenge the "legitimating discourse of empire." Besant's neo-Hinduism not only provided an alternative to the Christian justification of British rule in India, but it also asserted the superiority of indigenous religious and political institutions over their western counterparts.[20] In another important study, Gauri Viswanathan has traced the ways in which Besant's embrace of theosophical theories of "race" and "racial evolution" led her to a theory of empire as a "family of nations," a vision that (at least according to Besant) was more "organic" and more benevolent than the existing imperial arrangements.[21] In both of these studies, however, the explicitly occult basis of Besant's activities receives relatively little attention. For Viswanathan the controlling context is the scientific elaboration of evolutionary racial "science," and for Bevir, it is academic Orientalism and Christian theology. On one level, this effort to downplay the most bizarre elements of Besant's work is an understandable reaction to earlier accounts, which tended to use them for comic effect. But the result is that we lose sight of the context in which Besant herself understood and explained her own activities. Recent scholarship on Gandhi makes similar links: Joseph Alter's *Gandhi's Body*, for example, revisits Gandhi's obsessions with hygiene, nutrition, and sexual desire, arguing that these supposedly marginal details are, in fact, central to Gandhi's political philosophy.[22]

In Besant's own accounts of her work for Indian Nationalism the occult dimensions of her reform activities are clearly emphasized, even in works written for a non-theosophical audience. Although she remained, for many years, quite reticent about the supposed commission she had received from the Rishi Agastya in 1913, her political interventions had always been justified in terms of her duty to her guru or master the Mahatma Morya. As she put it in the final lines of her autobiography, first published in 1893 just before her departure for India, "in life, through death, to life, I am but the servant of the great Brotherhood, and those on whose heads but for a moment the touch of the Master has rested in blessing can never again look upon the world save through eyes made luminous with the radiance of the Eternal Peace."[23]

In response to her Master's command, Besant began her work for Indian Nationalism by bringing together a group of her closest associates in India in a new organization, the "Brothers of Service." These Indian Theosophists pledged themselves to work for social reform by disregarding caste restrictions, discouraging child marriage, promoting education among women and the people, and working to support the Indian National Congress. The Brothers of Service were committed to the belief that "the best interests of India lie in her rising into ordered freedom under the British Crown, in the casting away of every custom which prevents union among all who dwell within her borders, and in the restoration to Hinduism of social flexibility and brotherly feeling." In October of the same year, Besant delivered a series of lectures in Madras, laying out her social and political program. The titles of the lectures—"Foreign Travel," "Child-Marriage and Its Results," and "The Passing of the Caste System," among others—indicated her new interests, and the success of the lectures established Besant as a new force in Nationalist politics.[24]

In January 1914, Besant launched a new weekly, *The Commonwealth*, with the motto "For God, Crown and Country." The official history of the

Theosophical Society later summarized the goals of the paper: "It stood for Religious and Political Reform, the latter to deal with the building-up of a complete Self-Government from village councils upwards to a National Parliament. Also, to draw Great Britain and India nearer to each other through better understanding."[25] Besant went to England in the spring of 1914 to try to form an Indian party in Parliament. When that initiative failed, it strengthened her belief in the importance of Home Rule. At a meeting in the Queen's Hall, London, she called publicly for Home Rule in India, and "in answer to an absurd suggestion that India's loyalty to British Rule must be 'unconditional,' declared that 'the price of India's loyalty is India's Freedom.'"[26] In July 1914 Besant bought the *Madras Standard* and relaunched it as *New India*. By the end of the year, circulation had risen from just more than one thousand to more than ten thousand.[27] In Bombay, a group of dedicated young Theosophists, under the leadership of Jamnadas Dwarkadas, founded *Young India* to publicize Besant's program.[28] In 1915, Besant announced plans for an all-India Home Rule League. The league, which relied heavily on Besant's theosophical contacts, was set up in September 1916. Within a year Besant's league boasted twenty-seven thousand members and more than two hundred local branches, mostly in Madras Presidency.[29]

Besant and *New India* soon fell afoul of the anti-sedition clauses in the Press Act of 1910, and in 1917 she and her colleagues, George S. Arundale and B. P. Wadia, were interned. For Besant, the internment forced her to abandon the work the Rishi Agastya had laid upon her; according to Arundale, the psychic shock of that forced inactivity could have killed her.[30] Gandhi, on the other hand, used Besant's imprisonment as an opportunity for action, and called for satyagraha, the militant nonviolence of "truth-force," to be deployed on her behalf. Since armed action and petitioning were, he argued, clearly useless, the only alternative was to court arrest by participating in Besant's activities.[31] At one point, he proposed to lead one hundred volunteers on a walking pilgrimage from Bombay to Coimbatore to draw attention to Besant's plight and force her release. While that plan was abandoned as unrealistic, the concept of satyagraha was now widely discussed, even in *New India* itself.[32]

Besant rejected the notion that Gandhi's call for satyagraha had played any part in her release. Besant's criticisms of satyagraha, and of Gandhi's policies more broadly, can all be traced back to her belief in the priorities outlined in the Rishi Agastya's injunction to "Claim India's place among the Nations." Gandhi, she believed, was deliberately attempting to be "provocative," and independence achieved through his methods would be "stained by excess."

The broader imperial federation into which she hoped India would be incorporated could never emerge under Gandhi's leadership.

BESANT AND THE OPPOSITION TO NONCOOPERATION

Besant's distrust of Gandhi and his tactics became clear soon after his return to India, when he was a relative newcomer to Indian politics, and Besant had already built a national reputation as a reformer and Nationalist. On February 6, 1916, Besant and Gandhi clashed on the platform at the opening ceremonies for the Benares Hindu University (which had subsumed and ultimately replaced Besant's theosophical Central Hindu College).[33] Gandhi's speech belittled the "great empire" Besant hoped to preserve, rejected the vision of social hierarchy that underpinned her understanding of Indian history and the Aryan polity, and seemed to advocate precisely the violence and disorder that she had pledged to avoid. He ridiculed the idea that the new university would produce "finished citizens of a great empire." Rather than welcoming educational reform as a means of social uplift, he condemned English education for its tendency to split an educated elite off from the mass of the people. Educated Indians, he argued, had become "foreigners in their own land"; isolated by language not only from the poor but also from their own families, they had been cut off from the "heart of the nation." The "richly bedecked noblemen" of India (some of whom were sitting with Besant on the platform at the time) were criticized for their failure to do more for the "millions of the poor." The speech ended with what was (in retrospect) clearly intended as a criticism of violence and anarchy within the Nationalist movement. Besant, however, understood Gandhi to be advocating violence, and demanded that he be silenced.[34]

From 1916 onward, Besant continually pointed out the supposed contrasts between her own peaceful, reformist, law-abiding, and constitutional activities and the violence, disorder, and revolutionary activities of Gandhi and his followers. Recounting the events that led to her release from internment, she underlined the constitutional character of the agitation and the lawful nature of the protests, which she attributed to her own moral authority and calming influence:

> Crowds of people and many popular leaders joined the Home Rule League. . . . They preserved perfect order; never a window was broken; never a riot occurred; never a policeman was assaulted; never man, woman

or child went to gaol. For three months the vehement agitation continued unbrokenly, without ever breaking a law, and the students who wanted to strike were kept in their schools and colleges.[35]

Gandhi made the opposite argument, and also claimed credit for the avoidance of violence. "The internments [of Besant and her colleagues] are a big blunder," he wrote in a letter to the viceroy's private secretary. Public protest over the internments had exponentially increased her popularity. If she were not released "there will be no rest in the country and the cult of violence will surely spread," a tendency he was actively attempting to combat with "soul force or truth force or love force which for want of a better term I have described as passive resistance" (satyagraha).[36] In fact, *pace* Besant's claim that none of her activities had ever been unconstitutional, the government's decision to treat her Home Rule movement as political and constitutional rather than as revolutionary was primarily a tactical decision, not a validation of her own valuation of her activities.[37] As Besant's former colleague Bhagavan Das put it in 1920, "'Constitutional' or 'unconstitutional' are terms whose use only betrays the jugglery of British officers."[38]

In the months immediately following her internment, Besant was at the high point of her political popularity. While still interned, she had been elected president of the next Indian National Congress; breaking with historical precedent she claimed the right to exercise her presidential prerogatives throughout the entire year of her office, and not simply for the few days when the Congress was in session. Thanks to her, Gandhi argued in a speech at Ahmedabad in 1918, "'Home Rule' has become a household word all over India."[39] Almost immediately, however, her popularity began to erode. Her election to the presidency had aroused considerable opposition in Nationalist circles; her speeches at the Congress were widely perceived as authoritarian and irrelevant.[40]

The real turning point, however, came with her opposition to Gandhi's doctrine of satyagraha and to its political deployment in the noncooperation campaigns. In early 1919 the Rowlatt Acts, which extended wartime restrictions on civil liberties into the postwar period, were passed into law. Gandhi and his followers responded with an all-India mass protest, the Rowlatt satyagraha. Besant mistrusted Gandhi's campaign from the beginning. She recognized that the Rowlatt legislation constituted a slur on Indian loyalty, but she believed that the educated classes could overlook that slur, because they recognized the real advantages of the "British connection." The "ignorant masses," on the other hand, could not be trusted to understand their real

interests. She distrusted noncooperation precisely because it was a movement
"of Mass Direct Action, directly revolutionary."[41] She worried that noncooperation threatened "the very existence of India, her spiritual life, and her
spiritual mission to humanity," and she called on Theosophists to oppose
Gandhi's appeal to the masses in the name of order and freedom.[42] Gandhi
drew special attention to the antidemocratic elements in Besant's thought in
a backhanded compliment delivered at the Annie Besant Felicitation Meeting
in Bombay in October 1919, when he "pointed out to the audience how
Mrs. Besant stood by her own convictions, which made her believe that satyagraha had its shortcomings and the common people were not able to grasp
the full significance of satyagraha."[43]

Early in Gandhi's noncooperation campaign Besant predicted, in conversation with him in Bombay, that civil disobedience would lead to "burning
of post offices, cutting of telegraph wires, loss of respect for law and order, rioting and every kind of violent upheaval."[44] When rioting broke out in Delhi
after Gandhi called a *hartal* (a day of prayer and fasting) in protest against the
Rowlatt Acts, Besant thundered in *New India* that "a Government's first duty
is to stop violence." In words that came back to haunt her for the rest of her
political career she went on to argue that "before a riot becomes unmanage-
able brickbats must inevitably be answered by bullets in every civilized country." Shortly afterward Besant compounded her error with a hasty defense of
the soldiers involved in the massacre at Amritsar, issued before the full story
of the atrocities had become known, and confirmed her reputation as a
defender of (British) law and order rather than (Indian) freedom.[45]

BESANT AND THE MAHATMAS

At least part of Besant's opposition to Gandhi's campaign came from her belief that loyalty to her, and to her Mahatmas, had to be undivided. According
to Gandhi, Besant had formally declared "that she is not a satyagrahi" when
some of her close colleagues, such as Sir S. Subramania Iyer, vice president of
the TS from 1907 to 1911, joined Gandhi's movement. She accused Gandhi
of "'leading young men of good impulses to break their most solemn
pledges.'"[46] The "solemn pledges" Besant referred to included, presumably,
those taken by members of the Theosophical Society's Esoteric Section. In
1911 Besant had reorganized this occult school within the TS, and demanded
that members pledge themselves "to support before the world the Theosophical Society, and in particular to obey, without cavil or delay, the orders

of the Head of the Esoteric Section [Besant] in all that concerns my relation with the Theosophical movement."[47] Loyalty, Besant argued, had to be un-conditional, in the political as well as in the spiritual realm. B. G. Tilak, whose Maharashtra Home Rule League paralleled Besant(s, criticized her stand (and perhaps, by implication, Gandhi's as well): "Though I admire her eloquence, learning, and unfailing energy for work, I cannot bear for a moment the su-premacy which she claims for her opinions in matters political under the guise that she is inspired by the Great Souls [the Mahatmas] and that such orders from them as she professes to receive must be unquestionably obeyed." He went on to argue that "Autocracy may be, and sometimes is, tolerated in the-ological and Theosophical Society matters, but in democratic politics we must go by the decisions of the majority. . . . Congress recognizes no Mahatma to rule over it except the Mahatma of majority."[48] Besant was, however, unwill-ing to recognize the authority of that "Mahatma of majority."

Besant was no democrat, and her understanding of authority and hierar-chy was shaped by her belief in the occult hierarchy of which the Rishi Agastya was a high-ranking member. According to theosophical theories of cosmic evolution, spiritual, physical, and political hierarchies emerged together. In the ancient kingdoms of Lemuria and Atlantis super-evolved "King-Initiates" ruled as autocrats, occupying the finest, most refined, and most noble physical bodies.[49] A truly ideal state would recognize natural distinctions, and on that basis Besant called for a restored and purified caste system:

> When we are able to re-form a caste of teachers, a cast[e] of legislators and ad-ministrators of justice, a caste of those who organise industry and accumulate wealth, a class of manual labourers. . . all equally honourable and equally nec-essary, and all equally essential to the nation's welfare, and when the old idea of duty returns and each knows his duty and does it, then shall we again make the golden age, and a happier day shall break upon our earth.[50]

These types of claims reflected Besant's support for political brahminism which "yoked together caste pride and patriotic sentiment [and] lent the politics of nationalism as it obtained in the Madras presidency a distinctive cultural weight and resonance."[51] Besant did recognize the very real prob-lems that faced the mass of the Indian people—during debate at the All-Parties Conference held in Delhi in 1925, for example, she burst out that "Swaraj is the only solution to the problem of poverty and starvation. 'Shall India live or die?' is the question, not trifling quarrels. To me that is the vital thing. I think of it day and night."[52] But her political solution was always a restoration of power to those most able to make use of it, and throughout

Besant's voluminous writings, that invariably meant an appeal to an "India" which was Aryan, Hindu, Brahmin, middle class, and educated.

THE COMMONWEALTH OF INDIA BILL

In February 1919 Besant's Home Rule League split apart over the question of Gandhi's campaign of passive resistance against the Rowlatt Acts. According to Kanji Dwarkadas who, with M. A. Jinnah, was a leading figure in Besant's original Home Rule League, Gandhi and his supporters effectively took over Besant's league, changing its name from the Home Rule League to Swaraj Sabha, and substituting "non-violent agitation of any type" for constitutional agitation.[53] Having lost control of her original Home Rule League, Besant formed a new organization, the National Home Rule League, with Kanji Dwarkadas as general secretary. The new league committed itself to "the strengthening of the British connection" and announced that it was "open to all who have Home Rule as their goal, who work only in law-abiding ways, who stand by the British connection, and by the Free Nationhood of India under the Crown of George V and his successors." As a first step the National Home Rule League worked to promote a modified version of the Montagu–Chelmsford Reform Bill.[54] As time went on, the league poured its resources into the support of the Commonwealth of India Bill, Besant's last real contribution to Nationalist political debate.

In 1922 she had begun to agitate for a convention that could frame a new constitution for the country. The result was a series of meetings held in Delhi between 1923 and 1925 which drew together a group of moderate politicians who (like Besant) opposed Gandhi's Non-cooperation movement.[55] The convention duly produced a draft bill according to which "India will be placed on an equal footing with the Self-Governing Dominions, sharing their responsibilities and their privileges." The system of government was to be organized on a series of levels, beginning with local or village government, and ascending through the districts and provinces to the whole of India. The most controversial element of the plan was its adoption of a restricted franchise: "The franchises for the various Legislative bodies have been graded, commencing with universal adult suffrage in the Village, and restricted by higher educative, or administrative, or property or other monetary qualifications in the case of each higher body."[56]

In *India—Bond or Free?*, which Besant published in 1926 to publicize the bill and raise support for it in Britain, Besant identified the village *pañchāyaṭ* (the village council of elders) as the traditional and natural government of India. Drawing freely from the work of well-known Orientalist scholars and historians of India as well as from clairvoyant investigations that located the origin of the original Indo–Aryans in the lost continent of Atlantis, she identified these ancient Aryans (as distinct from Kolarian and Dravidian peoples) with the history of freedom as it was embodied in the village republic.[57] The village republic represented a hierarchical and ordered "freedom," which reflected Besant's suspicion of mass democratic action. The view of democracy contained here was similar to that which she had outlined in her pamphlet *The Future Socialism*, first written in 1908. British democracy, she argued, was "full of menace for the future": "A democratic Socialism, controlled by majority votes, guided by numbers, can never succeed; a truly aristocratic Socialism, controlled by duty, guided by wisdom, is the next step upwards in civilisation."[58]

The Commonwealth of India Bill received little support, either in Britain or in India. It contained no effective mechanism for imposing sanctions on the British government if the bill were to be rejected; it exacerbated tensions between Brahmin and non-Brahmin; it provided no resolution for communal tensions between the Hindu and Muslim communities. The new Conservative government in Britain was unwilling to sponsor the bill, and the Labour Party Conference refused to support it because of its restricted franchise. The bill was finally introduced by Besant's old ally George Lansbury as a Private Member's Bill, but it failed to get a second reading.[59]

HINDUSTAN OR ENGLISTAN?

Gandhi and Besant represented two incompatible approaches to reform in India. They differed not only over tactics (i.e., satyagraha) but also over goals. Besant's syncretic vision—England and India in federation—was radically opposed to Gandhi's emphasis on independence. Gandhi had always denied that India's admission to Dominion status would represent true swaraj. In *Hind Swaraj*, for example, he had rejected the model of self-government as it existed in Canada or South Africa because "[i]n effect it means this: that we want English rule without the Englishman. You want the tiger's nature, but not the tiger; that is to say, you would make India English. And when it becomes English, it will be called not Hindustan but *Englistan*. This is not the *swaraj* that I want." English education had brought enslavement, not liberation; English improvements (such as railways, doctors, and lawyers) had only impoverished the country.[60] This, Besant argued, was a "new primitivism." If Gandhi had his way it would leave India "with no railways, no machines, no electricity but only spinning wheels, donkeys and candles."[61] While Besant had some sympathy with the antimodernist argument (she encouraged hand-spinning in support of Gandhi's swadeshi campaign at Adyar, for example) she could not countenance the complete rejection of England and Englishness that Gandhi called for.

The final pages of *India—Bond or Free?* betrayed the fears behind Besant's position. Surveying the world situation, she contrasted the growing populations of China and the rest of Asia with the vast open spaces of the United States and the white settler colonies. She foresaw a movement of "economic compulsion, an inevitable irresistible movement of the hungry towards the empty fertile lands where Nature will reward labor with food. If resisted by legislation, it will burst into war, war implacable and sustained. Once the struggle blazes into war, numbers must tell. . . . And such a war will not end before the present civilization has received its death blow." To avoid that future, India needed to be brought in as "an equal partner in the firm instead of a servant"; an Indo–British Commonwealth of Colored and White Nations would bridge the racial divide and avoid the conflagration of a war based on the "clash of color." The union between England and India was, therefore, part of a cosmic plan to avoid that conflagration; "personally," Besant wrote, "I regarded the union between India and Great Britain as the one great defence against a war of the white and colored races."[62]

Besant and the Theosophical Society had, in effect, come to India because, as Besant put it in her pamphlet *England and India*, "when two nations come together, each has something to teach and something to learn." In terms of religion, India had more to teach than she had to learn; in education, on the contrary, "England has more to teach there than to learn."[63] As she put it in *India—Bond or Free?*, "The Future of India will, I hope, be united with that of Britain for the sake of both Nations and for the sake of Humanity at large, for they supply each other's defects, and united can do for the world a service that neither can do alone."[64] In pamphlet after pamphlet, lecture after lecture, Besant drove home the same point: "The greatest mutual advantage of all, however, would be that by the union of India and England as equal partners in a mighty Commonwealth, the strong concrete mind of Britain would be permeated and illuminated by the sublime spirituality of India." How, she asked, "can the relationship be symbolised by a wedding ring rather than by handcuffs?"[65]

The wedding ring was an odd symbol for Besant to choose, given that her own marriage, which had broken down almost fifty years earlier, was not a happy one. The relationship between England and India was clearly to be based on love and cooperation, rather than on tyranny and force. This metaphor (much more common in Besant's writing than the "equal partners" model) disavowed male privilege within marriage in order to emphasize the naturalness of the tie between husband and wife. A similar impulse underpinned Besant's use of the term *Home Rule* itself, which she preferred to self-government or swaraj because "Home Rule connoted control over a 'National Household.'"[66] Here, the image of the household or home, a space that was governed by love rather than by law, disavowed the privileges of caste or class within the nation. Besant similarly disavowed her own colonial privilege as a white, British woman in India. Even before her first visit to India she privileged her "Irishness" over her "Englishness," identifying with the colony rather than with the colonizer: "It has always been somewhat of a grievance to me that I was born in London, 'within the sound of Bow Bells' [the definitive mark of the true Londoner], when three-quarters of my blood and all my heart are Irish." In a racialized reading of the dichotomy between secular and spiritual, she associated Ireland, like India, with the mystical and religious.[67]

Besant idealized India and attempted to embody Indian aspirations. But to most devout Hindus (as Sri Prakasam, the son of Bhagavan Das, put it) "she was no different from any ordinary untouchable in the caste sense."[68] Her critics were even less charitable. G. K. Khaparde, one of B. G. Tilak's followers, described Besant as an "aunt Putna," an incarnation of the female demon who, according to the editor of Gandhi's letters, "attempted to kill the infant Lord Krishna by suckling him, but was herself sucked to death by the child."[69] While Gandhi noted that Besant "love[d] India with the devotion of a daughter" he also suggested, by implication at least, that Theosophy's religious syncretism was a violation of *swadeshi*, of self-sufficiency. In February 1916, shortly after his conflict with Besant on the platform at the Benares Hindu University, Gandhi argued that "Swadeshi is that spirit in us which restricts us to the use and service of our immediate surroundings to the exclusion of the more remote": "Thus, as for religion, in order to satisfy the requirements of the definition, I must restrict myself to my ancestral religion. That is the use of my immediate religious surroundings. If I find it defective, I should serve it by purging it of its defects."[70] The point is brought out explicitly in I. M. Muthanna's *Mother Besant and Mahatma Gandhi*, a vehemently anti-Gandhian book which suggests that Besant was a better Indian, and a better Hindu, than Gandhi ever was. "One can rightly conclude," Muthanna argues, "that Mrs. Besant had to with-[d]raw because of her old age and also due to her being a Britisher, when Indians needed a 'god' of their own and not the one of foreign-make. That was a time when there was a great compaign [sic] going on for SWADESHI goods."[71]

Besant often spoke as an "Indian" only temporarily occupying an English body. As she put it in a lecture first delivered in Negapatam, "I went to the West to take up this white body, because it is more useful to India, because it gives me strength to plead, and because it gives more weight to what I say—even with you, alas, the words from a white mouth have a little more influence." That claim simultaneously reinforced her racial authority as a white woman and redefined her as an "Indian" insider.[72] The authority vested in her by the occult hierarchy, and by the Rishi Agastya, "Regent of India in the Inner Government," also enabled Besant to speak "for" India. She founded not only her own authority but the legitimacy of the Theosophical Society itself on the will of her Masters, the Mahatmas, the "ever-living Rishis":

> My own life in India, since I came to it in 1893 to make it my home, has been devoted to one purpose, to give back to India her ancient Freedom. I had joined the Theosophical Society in 1889, and knew that one of the purposes for which it was intended by the ever-living Rishis . . .was the rescue of India from the materialism which was strangling her true life by the revival of ancient philosophical and scientific religions.[73]

Ironically enough Besant and *New India* were among those who helped to popularize the use of the term *Mahatma* to refer to Gandhi. In 1924, Jamnadas Dwarkadas was shouted down at a meeting because of his failure to use the honorific Mahatma. "I adore him," Dwarkadas said, "because, though a human being like all of us, he is the best among us—and not because he is a Mahatma."[74] Gandhi defended him, noting that "I knew that I was not a 'Mahatma,' I did know that I was an *alpatma* [small soul]." "Much dirty work," he pointed out elsewhere, thinking perhaps of Besant as well as of his own followers, "has been done in the shadow of "Mahatma.'"[75]

NOTES

1. Nancy Fix Anderson, "Bridging Cross-Cultural Feminisms: Annie Besant and Women's Rights in England and India, 1874–1933," *Women's History Review* 3, no. 4 (1994): 567, 571–573.

2. Joanne Stafford Mortimer, "Annie Besant and India 1913–1917," *Journal of Contemporary History*, 18 (1983): 66.

3. Anne Taylor, *Annie Besant: A Biography* (New York: Oxford University Press, 1992), 294–295.

4. Arthur H. Nethercot, *The Last Four Lives of Annie Besant* (London: Rupert Hart-Davis, 1963), 217.

5. Annie Besant, *The Theosophist* (January 1929), 341, cited in Josephine Ransom, *A Short History of the Theosophical Society, 1875–1937* (Adyar: Theosophical Publishing House, 1938), 407–408.

6. Annie Besant, *Home Rule and the Empire. New India Political Pamphlets* No. 13 (Adyar: Commonweal Office, 1917), 10.

7. Mark Bevir, "The West Turns Eastward: Madame Blavatsky and the Transformation of the Occult Tradition," *Journal of the American Academy of Religion* 62, no. 3 (1994): 747–767.

8. H. P. Blavatsky, "Mahatmas and Chelas," *The Theosophist* (July 1884), cited in Sylvia Cranston, *HPB: The Extraordinary Life and Influence of Helena Blavatsky, Founder of the Modern Theosophical Movement* (New York: G. P. Putnam's Sons, 1993), 207.

9. W. Travis Hanes III, "On the Origins of the Indian National Congress: A Case Study of Cross-Cultural Synthesis," *Journal of World History* 4, no. 1 (1993): 84–86.

10. Hanes, "On the Origins of the Indian National Congress," 88–92.

11. H. P. Blavatsky to A. P. Sinnett, 20 June [1882], in A. T. Barker, ed., *The Letters of H. P. Blavatsky to A. P. Sinnett* (New York: Frederick A. Stokes, [1923]), 19.

12. Appendix, H. P. Blavatsky to A. P. Sinnett, 17 March [n.d.], in Christmas Humphreys and Elsie Benjamin, eds., *The Mahatma Letters to A. P. Sinnett*, 3rd rev. ed. (Adyar: Theosophical Publishing House, 1979), 461–462. On Hume's troubled relationship with Theosophy's Mahatmas, see Joy Dixon, *Divine Feminine: Theosophy and Feminism in England* (Baltimore: Johns Hopkins University Press, 2001), 26–29.

13. Mark Bevir, "Theosophy as a Political Movement" in *Gurus and Their Followers: New Religious Reform Movements in Colonial India*, ed. Antony Copley (New Delhi: Oxford University Press, 2000), 159–179; K. Paul Johnson, *The Masters Revealed: Madame Blavatsky and the Myth of the Great White Lodge* (Albany: State University of New York Press, 1994), 234–241.

14. M. K. Gandhi, Letter to Dr. Pranjivan Mehta, 8 May 1911, *The Collected Works of Mahatma Gandhi* (hereafter *CW*) (Delhi: Government of India, 1971), 11:64–65.

15. Gandhi, "Notes: A Tissue of Misrepresentations," *Young India*, 9 September 1926; *CW*, 31:377.

16. M. K. Gandhi, *An Autobiography or the Story of My Experiments with Truth*, 2nd ed., trans. Mahadev Desai (Ahmedabad: Navajivan Publishing House, 1940), 60. On Gandhi's early contact with Theosophy, see

Stephen Hay, "The Making of a Late-Victorian Hindu: M. K. Gandhi in London, 1888–1891," *Victorian Studies* (Autumn 1989): 83–87; and James D. Hunt, *Gandhi in London* (New Delhi: Promilla and Co., 1978).

17. *Minute Books of the Blavatsky Lodge of the Theosophical Society* (London: Archives of the Theosophical Society in England, 1887–1899), 1:84. More enduring than his membership in the TS was his association with the Esoteric Christian Union, which was similar in many ways to the TS, though more Christian in its emphasis. Gandhi acted as the agent for the union while in Durban.

18. Gandhi, "Lectures on Religion," *Indian Opinion*, 15 April 1905, *CW*, 4:405.

19. Gandhi, (Speech on Annie Besant's Birthday, Ahmedabad," 1 October 1928, *The Hindu*, 2 October 1928, *CW*, 37:321.

20. Mark Bevir, "In Opposition to the Raj: Annie Besant and the Dialectic of Empire," *History of Political Thought*, 19 no. 1 (1998): 61–77.

21. Gauri Viswanathan, *Outside the Fold: Conversion, Modernity, and Belief* (Princeton, N.J.: Princeton University Press, 1998), esp. 177–207.

22. Joseph S. Alter, *Gandhi's Body: Sex, Diet, and the Politics of Nationalism* (Philadelphia: University of Pennsylvania Press, 2000).

23. Annie Besant, *An Autobiography*, 3rd ed. (1893; Adyar: Theosophical Publishing House, 1939), 332.

24. Appendix to Annie Besant, *India—Bond or Free? A World Problem* (London: G. P. Putnam's Sons, 1926), 203–206.

25. Ransom, *Short History*, 407.

26. Besant, *India—Bond or Free?*, 164.

27. Ransom, *Short History*, 409.

28. Bevir, "Theosophy as a Political Movement."

29. Sumit Sarkar, *Modern India, 1885–1947*, 2nd. ed. (London: Macmillan, 1989), 151.

30. Nethercot, *Last Four Lives of Annie Besant*, 261.

31. Gandhi, "Satyagraha—Not Passive Resistance," [c. 2 September, 1917], *CW*, 13:525.

32. Nethercot, *Last Four Lives of Annie Besant*, 262–263.

33. On the problems at the Central Hindu College, and its relationship to the new university, see Taylor, *Annie Besant*, 295–296.

34. Gandhi, "Speech at Benares Hindu University," 6 February 1916, *CW*, 13:210–216.

35. Besant, *India—Bond or Free?*, 175.

36. Gandhi, Letter to Private Secretary to Viceroy, 7 July 1917, *CW*, 13:464–465.

37. Ransom, *Short History*, 424; Peter Robb, "The Government of India and Annie Besant," *Modern Asian Studies* 10, no. 1 (1976): 123.

38. Bhagavan Das, quoted in Mahadev Desai, *Day-to-Day with Gandhi: Secretary's Diary* (Rajghat, Varanasi: Sarva Seva Sangh Prakashan, 1969), 2:268.

39. Gandhi, "Speech at Ahmedabad Meeting," 13 March 1918, *CW*, 14:251.

40. Taylor, *Annie Besant*, 311–312.

41. Besant, *India—Bond or Free?*, 191; Annie Besant, *Apart or Together?* (Madras: National Home Rule League, n.d.), 2.

42. Annie Besant, Diary; cited in Ransom, *Short History*, 435–436.

43. Gandhi, "Speech at Annie Besant Felicitation Meeting," *The Bombay Chronicle*, 2 October 1919, *CW*, 16:200.

44. Kanji Dwarkadas, *Gandhiji through My Diary Leaves, 1915–1948* (Bombay: Kanji Dwarkadas, 1950), 20–21.

45. Annie Besant, *New India* (31 March 1919), quoted in Taylor, *Annie Besant*, 317.

46. Gandhi, "Letter to B. G. Tilak," 25 August 1918, *CW*, 15:31–32; "Letter to Annie Besant," 10 May 1919, *CW*, 15:300–301.

47. On the Esoteric Section and the pledge, see Dixon, *Divine Feminine*, 76. The pledge also bound members to Jiddu Krishnamurti, the young Telugu brahmin whom Besant believed to be the "World-Teacher."

48. Adyar Archives, Indian National Congress Papers, 585; cited in Taylor, *Annie Besant*, 315.

49. Annie Besant, *Some Problems of Life* (London: Theosophical Publishing Society, 1900), 40–42.

50. Annie Besant, *The Ancient Indian Ideal of Duty* (Adyar: Theosophical Publishing House, 1917), 12.

51. V. Geetha and S. V. Rajadurai, "One Hundred Years of Brahminitude: Arrival of Annie Besant," *Economic and Political Weekly* (15 July 1995): 1769.

52. Desai, *Day-to-Day with Gandhi*, 5:242.

53. Dwarkadas, *Gandhiji through My Diary Leaves*, 29–30. Gandhi also took over as editor of *Young India*.

54. Annie Besant, *National Home Rule League: Why Founded and How* (Adyar: Published for the N.H.R.L. by the Commonweal Office, 1919), 5–6.

55. Taylor, *Annie Besant*, 320.

56. Appendix to Besant, *India—Bond or Free?*, 211–216.

57. Besant, *India—Bond or Free?*, 16–17, 35.

58. Annie Besant, *The Future Socialism* (1908; 1912; Adyar: Theosophical Publishing House, 1916), 22.

59. Taylor, *Annie Besant*, 321.

60. M. K. Gandhi, *Hind Swaraj* (1909; rev. ed., 1939), in Raghavan Iyer, ed., *The Moral and Political Writings of Mahatma Gandhi*, vol. 1,

Civilization, Politics, and Religion (Oxford: Clarendon Press, 1986), 208, 219, 253.

61. Annie Besant, *New India*, cited in I. M. Muthanna, *Mother Besant and Mahatma Gandhi* (Vellore: Thenpulam, 1986), 282.

62. Besant, *India—Bond or Free?*, 191, 196–197.

63. Annie Besant, *England and India* (1906; Adyar: Theosophical Publishing House, 1921), 2–3.

64. Besant, *India—Bond or Free?*, 198.

65. Besant, *Apart or Together?*, 5, 7.

66. Ransom, *Short History*, 414.

67. Besant, *Autobiography*, 3, 13.

68. Ransom, *Short History*, 435; Sri Prakasam, cited in Muthanna, *Mother Besant*, 89.

69. Quoted in Gandhi, "Letter to Sarladevi Chowdhrani," 2 May 1920, *CW*, 17:376.

70. Desai, *Day-to-Day with Gandhi*, 4:110; Gandhi, "Speech on Swadeshi at Missionary Conference, Madras," 14 February 1916, *CW*, 13:219.

71. Muthanna, *Mother Besant*, 211.

72. Besant, *Home Rule and the Empire*, 15–16.

73. Besant, *India—Bond or Free?*, 26–27.

74. Desai, *Day-to-Day with Gandhi*, 4:150–151.

75. Gandhi, "Never to be Forgotten," *Young India*, 4 September 1924, *CW*, 25:72; Gandhi, "Speech at Excelsior Theatre, Bombay," 31 August 1924, *CW*, 25:56.

4

Sri Aurobindo's Dismissal of
Gandhi and His Nonviolence

Robert N. Minor

He was a widely known Indian Nationalist leader, a major figure in the more extremist wing of the Indian National movement until 1910. Even after his "temporary" retirement in 1910 to Pondicherry in south India to develop an activist
"Integral Yoga," he was repeatedly asked to return to lead the Indian National
Congress. He would become a cultural hero for the Indian nation and a widely
lauded Indian "freedom-fighter." Unlike most of the figures in this volume Sri
Aurobindo Ghose (1872–1950) never met Gandhi, nor corresponded with
him. Gandhi knew Aurobindo by reputation as a guru in an ashram, and pic-
tured Aurobindo in idealistic Gandhian terms.[1] But they did not meet and Aurobindo was never, then, subject to the personal charm that blunted many of
Gandhi's other critics. On his part, Aurobindo never accepted the centrality of
Gandhi's message of "nonviolence" nor Gandhi's emphasis on voluntary suffering and self-abasement. Sri Aurobindo was not a "Gandhian."

What we know of Aurobindo's criticism, we learn from private letters to
his disciples. Gandhi would never hear his criticisms nor would most of India.
Aurobindo preferred to avoid public debate over Gandhi's ideas and methods. But Aurobindo was clear in these letters that he could not identify with
Gandhi's approach. In them he told those who encouraged him to become
involved in Congress politics again that he would not return. To the dismay
of many, he never did. In 1962, Prime Minister Jawaharlal Nehru reminisced
about the disappointment this engendered in Congress leaders: "[W]hen
Gandhiji started his non-co-operation movements and convulsed India, we
expected Sri Aurobindo to emerge from his retirement and join the great
struggle. We were disappointed at his not doing so."[2]

The fact was, though Aurobindo supported its goal of Indian independence, he could not identify with the overall methods of any of the parties

in Congress leadership. As he wrote B. S. Moonje, the chairman of the Reception Committee of the Indian National Congress in response to Moonje's letter requesting that Aurobindo preside over the 1920 Congress session: "I am entirely in sympathy with all that is being done so far as its object is to secure liberty for India, but I should be unable to identify myself with the programme of any of the parties."[3]

As an exclusive ideology and strategy, Aurobindo fully rejected Gandhi's program of satyagraha. In correspondence with a disciple, he quickly dismissed Gandhi's ideas as the typically limited ideas of normal human minds. They were not even worth the effort it would take to criticize them.

> Gandhi's theories are like other mental theories built on a basis of one-sided reasoning and claiming for a limited truth (that of non-violence and passive resistance) a universality which it cannot have. Such theories will always exist so long as the mind is the main instrument of human truth-seeking. To spend energy trying to destroy such theories is of little use; if destroyed they are replaced by others equally limited and partial.[4]

He dismissed other elements of Gandhi's thought again when he told another correspondent that Gandhi's emphasis on the greater nobility of low status and service in the spirit of "suffering love," "is Christian rather than Hindu—for the Christian, self-abasement, humility, the acceptance of a low status to serve humanity or the Divine are things which are highly spiritual and the noblest privilege of the soul."[5] There is no nobility in low status and no honor in suffering, and the "Hindu tradition," Aurobindo would say, does not teach its nobility. Aurobindo responded to Gandhi's claims of the nobility of lower caste status, that the scavenger on the street may be equal to the upper caste Brahmin before God, but is in no sense superior to the Brahmin.

Two factors in Sri Aurobindo's life and thought help us understand his quick minimization and dismissal of Gandhi's ideas. This chapter intends to trace both factors to describe the theoretical and experiential context in which Sri Aurobindo—the Indian Nationalist, cultural hero, and internationally renowned Yogi—dismisses Gandhi in such a fashion.

THE REALM OF EXTREMIST POLITICS

Though he showed interest much earlier, Aurobindo's open activity in Indian national politics began in 1902 when he attended the Ahmedabad session of the Indian National Congress. There he met and spoke at length with Maharashtra political leader, Bal Gangadhar Tilak who conversed with him privately for about an hour. Tilak expressed his contempt for the moderate Congress reform movement and explained his own philosophy and methods of action in Maharashtra.[6] Aurobindo aligned himself immediately with the party known to other leaders of the Congress as the Extremists, or to themselves as Nationalists. The Nationalist approach to British control of India was to favor immediate revolution to achieve independence. Its advocates were committed to swaraj, which to them meant full Indian independence from Britain by any means possible including violent overthrow of their "oppressors." From 1905 until his retirement to Pondicherry in 1910, Aurobindo was primarily a political journalist in the revolutionary wing of nationalism in which he had found a home. He wrote for and soon became editor of the voice of extremism, a journal called *Bande Mataram*, and his writings became some of the chief statements of Extremist policy.

This was not the beginning of his identification with radical, revolutionary politics. Aurobindo was always a revolutionary, and from the earliest records we have of Aurobindo's activities and thought, he identified with an approach to Indian independence and other causes that believed in the utility of violence. As a student from Bengal sent to England by his father to prepare him for employment in the Indian Civil Service, he made revolutionary speeches at the meetings of the Indian Majlis. Near the end of his stay he also joined the London-based Lotus and Dagger society, a student organization sworn to revolutionary overthrow of the British. While at Cambridge his father had been sending him passages from the *Bengalee* with cases of British mismanagement highlighted. Whether intended or not, the immediate result was that Aurobindo lost all desire to serve in the Indian Civil Service. He sealed his fate by refusing three times to appear for the equestrian portion of the examination. In early December 1892 he learned of his rejection. Reports say he was "delighted."[7]

Within only four months of arriving back in India in 1893, twenty-two-year-old Aurobindo wrote an article for the *Indu Prakash* of Bombay that would result in a series entitled "New Lamps for Old." This anonymous series appeared between August 1893 and March 1894.

These first public political writings set the tone in India for Aurobindo's immoderate political stance as he criticized the leaders of the Indian National Congress and their "moderate" policies. He disparaged these moderates, whom Aurobindo at times labeled "Loyalists," for their loyalty to their British oppressors. He called them "the blind leading the blind," upper-class elitists who were out of touch with the Indian people, and misguided leaders who

led the Congress only to failure. He accused them of "bare-faced hypocrisy"
and "timidity."

> I say of the Congress, then, this—that its aims are mistaken, that the spirit in
> which it proceeds towards their accomplishment is not a spirit of sincerity
> and whole-heartedness, and that the methods it has chosen are not the right
> methods, and the leaders in whom it trusts, not the right sort of men to be
> leaders;—in brief, that we are at present the blind led, if not by the blind, at
> any rate by the one-eyed.[8]

While the leaders of the Congress were calling Queen Victoria "Our
Mother," "Victoria the Good," and "Our Sovereign," Aurobindo wrote of
her as "an old lady so called by way of courtesy, but about whom few Indians
can really know or care anything." While Congress leaders spoke of liberal
British Prime Minister William Gladstone as the friend of India, Aurobindo
described him as "a statesman who is not only quite unprincipled and in no
way to be relied upon, but whose intervention in an Indian debate has always
been of the worst omen to our cause." In spite of this, these Congress leaders went out of their way, Aurobindo says, to flatter Gladstone.

Many people in Bombay knew that Aurobindo was the author of the series. He therein threw down his gauntlet against anything that to him seemed
conciliatory. The British rulers in India, however "rude and arrogant," however "ordinary" they are (they are "not only ordinary men, but ordinary Englishmen"), or however badly they govern, are merely "commonplace men
put into a quite unique position." They are not our real enemy, he wrote, and
are hardly worth the anger one might waste upon them. Instead, in these articles it is the weakness of Congress leadership that he wanted to expose for
all to see. "Our actual enemy is not any force exterior to ourselves, but our
own crying weaknesses, our cowardice, our selfishness, our hypocrisy, our
purblind sentimentalism."[9]

The series threatened Congress leaders and they responded. M. G.
Ranade, the Maratha judge and influential Congress moderate from Bombay,
personally warned the owner of the *Indu Prakash* that he could be prosecuted
for sedition if he continued to publish the articles. As a result, the editor, who
was Aurobindo's old friend, persuaded Aurobindo to tone them down, but
Aurobindo soon lost interest in "these muzzled productions" and ended the
series completely.

With the end of this early series, Aurobindo published nothing political
for about a decade. He turned his literary interests toward the study of Sanskrit literature, particularly the thought of the ancient *Upanisads*. However,

he continued to work behind the scenes, apparently attempting to encourage an uprising against the government from within the Indian army.[10] In 1902, besides attending the Ahmedabad session of the Congress, in which the presidential address delivered by Surendranath Banerjea, pleaded for "the permanence of British rule in India," he also joined a secret society of those convinced that the way to freedom was armed revolution.

Such covert activity would be his arena of action until he joined the Congress Extremists in the hope that their approach would dominate Congress policy. Behind the scenes Aurobindo helped build a group of revolutionaries in Bengal. Though he personally preferred a full-scale revolution, he apparently authorized the group's individual acts of bombings and even the assassination of British officials.[11] In later life he took pains to correct any misperception from those who wanted to believe he was in agreement with Gandhi that he ever rejected such violence.

> In some quarters there is the idea that Sri Aurobindo's political standpoint was entirely pacifist, that he was opposed in principle and in practice to all violence and that he denounced terrorism, insurrection, etc., as entirely forbidden by the spirit and letter of the Hindu tradition. It is even suggested that he was a forerunner of the gospel of Ahiṁsā. This is quite incorrect. Sri Aurobindo is neither an impotent moralist nor a weak pacifist. . . . Sri Aurobindo has never concealed his opinion that a nation is entitled to attain its freedom by violence, if it can do so or if there is no other way. . . . Sri Aurobindo's position and practice in this matter was the same as Tilak's and that of other Nationalist leaders who were by no means Pacifists or worshipers of Ahiṁsā.[12]

In 1904, Aurobindo's brother, Barindrakumar, with whom Aurobindo had allied himself in the revolutionary struggle, proposed the establishment of an order of sannyasis who would prepare the Indian nation for revolution. He also persuaded Aurobindo to start a Bengali newspaper entitled *Yugantar* (*Jugantar*) which would advocate "open revolt and the absolute denial of the British rule and include such items as a series of articles containing instructions for guerrilla warfare."[13] The paper was begun as an alternative to the moderate papers in Bengal, and Aurobindo wrote some of the articles in its early numbers. It advocated open revolt against the British and survives today only in the form of very poor English translations made by government servants. When word of the viceroy's proposal to divide Bengal in two became public, Aurobindo wrote a pamphlet with the not surprising title "No Compromise" which was distributed in Calcutta but also does not survive.

Another pamphlet Aurobindo produced during this time, also as a result of his brother's persuasion, was intended to be a statement of the ideals of the new order of Nationalist sannyasis. Entitled "Bhawani Mandir," it was meant, as Aurobindo later recalled, "for revolutionary preparation of the country." Here Aurobindo first identified India as "the Mother," the goddess in all her power and strength. It is this strength, Aurobindo wrote, that India needs today if she is to "purge barbarism (Mlechchhahood) out of humanity and to Aryanise the world." Calling upon symbols of devotion to *sakti*, the "energy" that is the Mother Goddess, the pamphlet never explicitly calls for government overthrow, but it does challenge Indians to actively shake off their stupor and create a nation "out of strength." India is to be "reborn." "It rests with us what we shall create; for we are not, unless we choose, puppets dominated by Fate and Maya; we are facets and manifestations of Almighty Power."[14]

There was little question that, though veiled, these were the words of one who sought revolution, and the British so understood it. The pamphlet was cited by the writer of a secret police report for containing "the germ of the Hindu revolutionary movement in Bengal."[15]

It was on August 6, 1906, that the first issue of the English counterpart of *Yugantar* appeared. It was to become the "voice of Extremism" and was called *Bande Mataram*, (Hail Mother) despite the fact that shouting this phrase was declared an offense by Bengal authorities. Aurobindo was a major contributor to *Bande Mataram*. Though it continued to advocate the Nationalist position, its tone was less violent than its Bengali counterpart.

In fact one of the series of articles Aurobindo authored, which appeared daily from April 11 to April 23, 1907, came to be known under the general title the "Doctrine of Passive Resistance." Though the notion of nonviolence was hardly new in India, as Peter Heehs points out, this series was one of the first extensive public statements of that approach. It set forth the purpose and methods, but also the limitations, of "passive resistance."[16]

The politics of the Indian National Congress were ready for a change, Aurobindo declared in the series. This meant that they must move from the tentative and partial changes for which the so-called Moderates had been petitioning the British government to the complete and total withdrawal of the British. In the *Bande Mataram* series, he called the Extremist cause the "new politics," politics for the new century.

> This is the object which the new politics, the politics of the twentieth century, places before the people of India in their resistance to the present system of Government—not tinkerings and palliatives but the substitution for the autocratic bureaucracy, which at present misgoverns us, of a free constitutional and democratic system of Government and the entire removal of foreign control in order to make way for perfect national liberty.[17]

Aurobindo still could book no place for the earlier Moderates who dominated the Congress. These previous Indian leaders, he said, "could not realise" the elementary truths of modern politics because they were taught their politics by "English liberal 'sympathisers' and 'friends of India'" who inculcated in them the ideas of English superiority and Indian inferiority. These Moderates were "unaccustomed to independent political thinking" and lacked the perspective provided by a knowledge of world politics. But times have changed. There is no longer a place for the "self-development" that these Moderates believed India needed before the call for full swaraj. There is only a place for persuading the British by force.

This sense of a "new politics," which made previous Indian national leadership out of date and useless in the fight to achieve nothing less than complete British withdrawal, set the tone for Aurobindo's political methods and evaluation of the place of passive resistance. He said that there are three possible and legitimate courses that resistance might take passive resistance; an organized and aggressive campaign of assassination and a confused welter of riots, strikes, and agrarian risings all over the country; and armed revolt. All three can be effective and all three have their place. Thus, even though he could concede that passive resistance might be the most effective means in the present, he was quick to maintain the morality and justifiability of aggressive and violent methods.

> The choice by a subject nation of the means it will use for vindicating its liberty, is best determined by the circumstances of its servitude. The present circumstances in India seem to point to passive resistance as our most natural and suitable weapon. We would not for a moment be understood to base this conclusion upon any condemnation of other methods as in all circumstances criminal and unjustifiable.[18]

In these articles, Aurobindo joined those modern revolutionaries who used the revered, second century B.C.E text, the *Bhagavad Gita*, to justify bloodshed. By so doing he could show that armed warfare was in reality "traditional" for Hindus. He thereby took the text's battle scene on the field of Kurukshetra as a literal battle, and the god Krishna's call to battle given to the reluctant warrior Arjuna as a real call to take up arms. "Under certain circumstances a civil struggle becomes in reality a battle and the morality of war is different from the morality of peace. To shrink form bloodshed and violence under such circumstances is a weakness deserving as severe a rebuke as Sri Krishna addressed to Arjuna when he shrank from the colossal civil slaughter on the field of Kurukshetra."[19] The *Bhagavad Gita* provided a solid precedent for armed resistance especially among the Extremists. By the beginning of the twentieth century its presence on the persons of a number of assassins and revolutionaries whom the British detained resulted in government identification as a terrorist of anyone in possession of more than one copy of the text.[20]

Gandhi would also revere the *Bhagavad Gita* as his "prayer book," but he would maintain his belief in the exclusivity of nonviolence through an allegorical and symbolic interpretation of the call to battle. His understanding of the battle as the war between good and evil in the human heart would be influential for many. But not Aurobindo who believed that the setting of the text at the beginning of a great war actually anticipated India's struggle with the British. Like his Nationalist protégé, Tilak, symbolic, psychological, and allegorical interpretations must not negate the *Bhagavad Gita*'s political purpose and its call to use violence as the solution. Even after retiring from active nationalism, Aurobindo would never give up the sense that the *Bhagavad Gita* was speaking of violence. Violence, he would say in his nonpolitical, yogic period, was an important element in the evolution of the eternal spirit to higher levels of consciousness. "Destruction in itself is neither good nor evil. It is a fact of Nature, a necessity in the play of forces, as things are in this world."[21]

Passive resistance, therefore, has its place, he argued in the *Bande Mataram* series, but only when appropriate: "It is the nature of the pressure which determines the nature of the resistance."

> Where, as in Russia, the denial of liberty is enforced by legalised murder and outrage, or, as in Ireland formerly, by brutal coercion, the answer of violence to violence is justified and inevitable. Where the need for immediate liberty is urgent and it is a present question of national life or death on the instant, revolt is the only course. But where the oppression is legal and subtle in its methods and respects life, liberty and property and there is still breathing time, the circumstances demand that we should make the experiment of a method of resolute but peaceful resistance which, while less bold and aggressive than other methods, calls for perhaps as much heroism of a kind and certainly more universal endurance and suffering.[22]

India is actually, Aurobindo asserted, more on the verge of national life or death. This would at first seem to call for the appropriateness and exclusivity of open revolt—after all, he said, at such times revolt is the only course. However, in this series Aurobindo was willing to approve of passive resistance because, he believed, there is still time to experiment with it. To be successful, however, it must unite the Indian people and they must be ready to sustain it to the end. Its value is its possibility of success, not its exclusive morality. Yet to use it in the wrong circumstances is actually "to sin against the divinity within ourselves and the divinity in our motherland" (1:114).

Aurobindo's relationship as a revolutionary to the Indian National Congress came to a head with the Surat session of the Congress in December 1907. Nationalists, including Aurobindo, hoped this would be the chance for their approach and leadership to prevail. The Nationalists were, however, out-maneuvered and the Congress ended in an infamous, general melee. Aurobindo apparently gave the order to "break" the Congress and to refuse to join what he later called "the new-fangled Moderate Convention" (26:49). As for Gopal Krishna Gokhale, the leader of the Moderates, Aurobindo said that it was impossible to maintain any great respect for him as a politician (26:49).

From the earliest record we have of Aurobindo in the realm of politics, then, he embraced, supported, and believed in the efficacy and sometime necessity of violence. Nonviolence was at best only one of the methods available to humanity in its struggles, but no more valuable, moral, effective, or traditionally Hindu than violence. Though others might prefer to picture Aurobindo as a devotee of nonviolence and might want to turn him into a Gandhian, he would have to correct their misunderstanding throughout his life. For example:

> There seems to be put forth here and in several places the idea that Sri Aurobindo's political standpoint was entirely pacifist, that he was opposed in principle and in practice to all violence and that he denounced terrorism, insurrection etc. as entirely forbidden by the spirit and letter of the Hindu religion. It is even suggested that he was a forerunner of Mahatma Gandhi and gospel of Ahiṁsā. This is quite incorrect and, if left, would give a wrong idea about Sri Aurobindo. He has given his ideas on the subject, generally, in the *Essays on the Gita*, First Series (Chapter VI) where he supports the Gita's idea of Dharma Yuddha and criticizes, though not expressly, the Gandhian idea of soul-force. If he had held the pacifist ideal, he would never have supported the Allies (or anybody else) in this War, still less sanctioned some of his disciples joining the Army as airmen, soldiers, doctors, electricians, etc. . . . Sri Aurobindo has never concealed his opinion that a nation is entitled to attain its freedom by violence, if it can do so or if there is no other way; whether it should do so or not, depends on what is the best policy, not on ethical considerations of the Gandhian kind. (26:40–41)

The realm of politics for Aurobindo was a violent place and nonviolence was a possible method only if and when it would work.

GANDHI AND THE REALM OF INTEGRAL YOGA

It would be a mistake to distinguish the political from the religious in Aurobindo's life and thought. Aurobindo never did. Though his later followers,
and even the Indian Supreme Court, distinguished the secular from the religious and asserted that Aurobindo did too, for Aurobindo politics and all else
were also religious. His aspirations for India were to be understood as including every aspect of life and in the context of his devotion to the Mother Goddess, to the god Krishna, to his yogic practices, and to his study and
affirmation of the teachings of religious texts such as the ancient *Upanisads*
and the *Bhagavad Gita*. He did not hesitate to use the term *religion* to refer
to his teachings.[23]

However, it was not merely the fact that Aurobindo was a political activist who from the start affirmed the role of violence that stood behind his
rejection and minimization of Gandhi's ideas and practice. In his mind, particularly later during his period as a yogin and writer in Pondicherry, his understanding of his own yogic experiences and the view of Reality behind what
he called his "Integral Yoga," left Gandhi behind as an inferior thinker.

Crucial to the view of Reality Aurobindo more fully developed in the final
stage of his life at Pondicherry was the sense that it must be an integral view,
which Gandhi's, he believed, was not. Integral Yoga must include the multiple
ways of seeing reality, even those that seemed contradictory. This was so important an emphasis for him that it dominated the work of his retirement period.
One of the early goals of his experiments with Yoga was to integrate what
seemed to be two contradictory convictions. The first was that Reality is an undifferentiated, never-changing unity, Pure Being, which would apparently make
the diversity that is the world about one less than ultimately real. This viewpoint
had been represented in traditional Indian thought by the idea of Brahman,
particularly as conceived by the eighth-century Advaita Vedanta thinker
Shankara. However, there was an important and apparently contradictory idea
about Reality that was just as true. Aurobindo was also convinced that the
world about us in all its diversity and change was as real as its Unity. He came to
see this phenomenal world as the eternal Becoming of Reality. Both unchanging Being and ever-changing Becoming, he concluded, were irrefutable realities, though to the human mind they were logically contradictory.

The great Shankara failed to see both of these truths because he could
not reconcile them rationally. Therefore, Aurobindo says that Shankara promoted, like the Buddhists before him, the way of "illusionism," and a "philosophy of world negation." For Aurobindo, in contrast, the world had to be

a place of ultimate meaning. It could not be negated or relegated to Being, but fully and absolutely integrated.

Full affirmation of the reality of this evolving world was crucial to the multiple senses of the integral nature of Aurobindo's Integral Yoga. He not only sought to bring together the seemingly contradictory doctrines of Unity and Diversity and the full reality of the immutability of Being and the eternal change of Becoming, he also sought to promote a Yoga that would not negate the physical but would transform the whole human being, integrating the spirit, the psyche, and the body.[24] He further sought to affirm a multiplicity of spiritual paths known as *bhakti yoga, jnana yoga,* and *karma yoga,* integrated as "the triple Path of devotion, knowledge and works" (22:32).

This reconciliation of body and spirit, unity and diversity, and the multiple layers of consciousness which constitute the evolving universe was a major effort. Its importance to him is clear in his 1946 recollection that this was the major problem he had to solve through the Yoga of his retirement:

> The only real difficulty which took decades of spiritual effort to work out towards completeness was to apply the spiritual knowledge utterly to the world and to the surface psychological and outer life and to effect its transformation both on the higher levels of Nature and on the ordinary mental, vital and physical levels down to the subconscience and the basic Inconscience and up to the supreme Truth-Consciousness or Supermind in which alone the dynamic transformation could be entirely integral and absolute. (26:86)

Given the centrality of the process of integration in Aurobindo's thought, one would expect that he would integrate the theories and strategies of violence and nonviolence as well. Thus he declared Gandhi's exclusive emphasis on nonviolence as an affirmation of only one side of the duality of violence and nonviolence that he found in the Indian tradition. It is not surprising that he labeled Gandhi's view "one-sided" and "limited." In a system like Aurobindo's which seeks to integrate ideas and reject none, there must be a place for violence and it must be as crucial as nonviolence.

Yet, for Aurobindo, it was not merely a conceptual disagreement founded in philosophy and ideas that elevated his integral view above Gandhi's one-sided stand. Aurobindo regularly denied that he was developing a logically argued position. Such rational systems, he believed, were too mental, that is, too limited to logic. Arguing on the basis of philosophy was a misunderstanding of reality as he experienced it. That is why he replied to a disciple: "There is very little argument in my philosophy—the elaborate metaphysical reasoning full of abstract words with which the metaphysician tries to establish his conclusions is not there" (26:374). More authoritative than logic, for Aurobindo, is experience, especially the experiences he identified with his personal yogic practices. These, in turn, he identified with the experiences of the seers who wrote the classical *Upanisads*, but not necessarily those of later Indian Vedantins such as Shankara.

Gandhi, too, spoke of the authority of his experiences. They were, as his biography is entitled, "Experiments with Truth." But those were very different from the experiences Aurobindo held authoritative. So, in isolation from the political action of India, though not unaware of it, Aurobindo sought other types of experiences.

Especially after his retirement to Pondicherry to develop and experiment with Yoga, Aurobindo became more fully convinced that his own yogic experiences were authoritative. Though the importance of spiritual experiences was not a new idea for him, the primary goal of his retirement from active political involvement was to develop and further the experiential realization of what he believed were higher levels of consciousness that sprung from his yogic practices. And this more developed definition of Reality, which he believed was based on these experiences, further convinced him of the authoritative nature of his experiences.[26] As such, the importance of the integration of both Being and Becoming was tied to the realizations of higher, more evolved levels of consciousness which he believed he was discovering through his yogic practices.

Aurobindo's conviction that the higher levels of consciousness he was progressively experiencing through his yogic practices were true insights into Reality was what gave him permission to judge the experiences and thought of others. Those whose ideas are not the ideas of Integral Yoga, he could assume, must not be seeing Reality adequately. They must not, he would conclude, have the higher experiences that reveal the more integral nature of Reality. However, Aurobindo did not believe his criticism of others began with their inadequate ideas. He believed experience was the prior issue. These others must not be experiencing these higher levels of consciousness and, thus, they have inadequate theories. As such, Aurobindo believed his own religious experiences, not the fact that the ideas of others are faulty, were the measure of the experience and theories of others. His yogic experiences revealed the integral nature of reality. They revealed the importance of the integral itself. They also revealed the theoretical inadequacies of others as well as the reason for those inadequacies.[27]

The key to his yogic experiences was that they revealed what Aurobindo taught were levels of consciousness which are "higher" and more evolved than the level on which the vast majority of humans find themselves at present, including Gandhi. His experiences revealed that these levels are stages in the evolution that is the eternal Becoming of Reality as Consciousness–Force. This evolution moves upward toward the highest level of consciousness, which Aurobindo called "the Supreme Saccidananda Unmanifest."

The Absolute, which he sometimes calls Spirit, as Consciousness–Force had previously involuted from this highest consciousness to its least conscious state, that of the physical or Matter. From that most inconscient level it has begun its evolution through the organic consciousness of plant forms (the "Vital") and the level of animal consciousness ("Psyche" or "Soul"), to the level of consciousness currently most common among human beings, the level he called "Mind."

The level of consciousness that is Mind with all its logic and argumentation, however, is not the end of the Spirit's evolution, no matter how humans may tout it as such. Mind is neither the final nor the best way of knowing reality, for above the level of Mind Aurobindo saw seven more-evolved levels of consciousness.[28] By definition, then, Mind is actually an inferior level of knowing Reality compared with those above it, just as the levels of consciousness below Mind are inferior to Mind.

Aurobindo therefore describes the level of Mind as a limited and only indirectly illuminated consciousness that is characterized by ignorance because it views reality from its own limited standpoint through an exclusive self-identification of the soul with the temporal. It is not an integrating consciousness but a dividing one. Mind consciousness sees the multiplicity but stops without seeing the unity that is also there. It then takes the divided as the truth that is to be known and the consciousness of division as the true means of knowing: "it has lapsed from the dividing into the divided mentality."[29] On this level, the individual knows something of Reality, for Mind is the level of consciousness that enables self-conscious participation in the evolution of the universe. It likewise enables one to know the multiplicity in a self-conscious manner. There are, however, three difficulties that result from the acceptance of Mind as a means of knowing. First, mental knowing prevents the individual from being aware of its total being. It is only capable of knowing one's "surface" mentality, life, and physical being, and not even all of that. The vast majority of Reality is unknown to Mind including the deeper Self that unites the human being with all else and that is actually the Spirit striving for higher consciousness. Second, Mind separates the human being from the Universal and therefore from one's "fellow creatures." It does not relate to the all with a conscious identity but only indirectly and imperfectly through inferences, theories, observations, and some sympathy. Third, Mind divides force from conscious-ness in the evolutionary existence, separating and even warring with Matter and Life. In summary, Mind does not know reality in its unity. Though it is a stage in the evolution of Spirit, Mind in itself is only that, a stage that must be integrated with higher levels of knowing.

The yogic experiences that raise one's consciousness to higher levels provide the yogin with the opportunity to bring these insights from higher levels of consciousness down to lower levels, including the level of Mind. Mind can be transformed and "raised" to higher knowing if its insights are in-tegrated with those of the higher levels of consciousness. Integral Yoga, Au-robindo taught, is the personal acceleration of the evolutionary process that is the Becoming of the All. It is "a means of compressing one's evolution into a single life or a few years or even a few months of bodily existence" (20:2). The goal of the practitioner of Integral Yoga is to transform not only oneself (spirit, psyche, and body) but the entire "Earth Consciousness." In sum, the yogin is one who promotes the evolution of the universe.

What hinders the evolution of the Becoming Aurobindo calls "egoism." And this arises on the level of Mind. It is not that "ego" in itself is evil. The de-velopment of the ego is a valuable stage in the evolutionary process. The ego is necessary for the discovery of individuality and for disengaging this individu-ality from the Inconscient. Individuality allows one to participate in the evolu-tionary process. This is true of the "national ego" as well. The sense of nationhood provides a certain greater unity than that of individual selves, fam-ilies, and regions. When ego and the assertion of individuality and separateness (egoism) hinders, or at least does not promote, the evolutionary process that is the intention of the universe, it becomes the content of evil in Aurobindo's viewpoint. The refusal of any element of the evolution to evolve, the overasser-tion of any stage in the process as if it is the end point of the process, is to be rejected but not because the stage or element itself is unreal or without value. What is rejected is its refusal to be a part of the process and to integrate with higher stages of the evolution. The following summarizes the problem of these individuating products of the evolution, though Aurobindo is speaking here of the tendency of the national ego to become egoistic:

> Unfortunately, it is the nature of every self-asserting tendency or principle in the hour of its growth, when it finds circumstances favourable, to over-assert itself and exaggerate its claim, to carry its impulses to a one-sided fruition, to affirm its despotic rule and to depress and even trample upon other tenden-cies and principles and especially on those which it instinctively feels to be the farthest removed from its own nature. (25:386)

Here we find the critique of "one-sidedness" again where a "one-sided," fruition or result is egoism. One development in the process of the evolution of consciousness is taken as the end point, the final fruit, instead of a temporary development which should not be scorned or exclusively clung to, but should be integrated into all that will follow in the evolution.

To take Mind consciousness, then, as the final product—to take its logic, its theories, its limitations in rationality, even its law of contradiction, as what limits knowledge—is egoism and ignorance. It turns a mere stage of consciousness into the final development. Stuck in the "particulars" of divided reality, it refuses to move beyond Mind's way of knowing to participate in the evolution that lies ahead. It may even refuse to accept the idea that two notions contradictory on the level of Mind (such as immutable Being and ever-changing Becoming) can both be true on higher, more integral levels of knowledge that thereby have their own "rationality." Not so the higher consciousness of the Spirit.

> But the Absolute, obviously, finds no difficulty in world-manifestation and no difficulty either in a simultaneous transcendence of world-manifestation; the difficulty exists only for our mental limitations which prevent us from grasping the supramental rationality of the co-existence of the infinite and the finite or seizing the nodus of the unconditioned with the conditioned. For our intellectual rationality these are opposites; for the absolute reason they are interrelated and not essentially conflicting expressions of one and the same reality. (18:377)

For Aurobindo, the egoism of Mind that limits itself to "mental theories" is a refusal to participate with Aurobindo in the evolution in which he believed he was participating through his own yogic realizations. Such mental egoism rejects the possibilities of higher knowledge, which Aurobindo believed he had experienced and which became authoritative. It becomes thereby ignorance.

> The particularizing faculty of Mind only becomes Ignorance when it separates itself from the higher principles of which it is a power and acts not only with its characteristic tendency, but also with a tendency to exclude the result of knowledge, to particularize first and foremost and always and to leave unity as a vague concept to be approached only afterwards, when particularization is complete, and through the sum of particulars. This exclusiveness is the very soul of Ignorance. (18:487)

Hence, positions that did not recognize what Aurobindo saw, were limited, one-sided, egoistic. They were effectively hindering the Divine plan of the universe.

Since he accepted the authority of his own experiences of this Divine plan and its higher levels of knowledge, he concluded that those who did not see this merely did not have the higher experiences necessary to see the more integral truth of Reality. Their viewpoints reflect little true spiritual experience and they are unworthy of the effort one might put into attempts to refute them. As early as 1910, even before his retreat to Pondicherry, Aurobindo spoke of the futility of arguing with those who frankly lacked the higher experiences needed to see differently. "We recognize that to argue with those who have only opinion but no realization," he said, "is a hopeless task, since it is only by entering into communion with the Infinite and seeing the Divine Force in all that one can be intellectually sure of its [the Divine Force's] conscious actions" (2:105–106).

Only with the yogic experiences Aurobindo had could one know the nature of the evolution and the consequent limitations of that stage of consciousness called Mind. Those who did not agree with his exposition of the integral nature of Reality would not disagree if only they had experienced the "communion with the Infinite" and had thereby seen the Divine Force and its evolution of consciousness. Aurobindo's experiences were the final authority in the judgment of other positions and that, of course, included Gandhi's. To argue mere "mental theories," which Gandhi's must have been by Aurobindo's standard, is useless. To argue with Gandhi would get one nowhere unless Gandhi was willing to open himself to the yogic experiences of Aurobindo.

GANDHI AND NONVIOLENCE DISMISSED EXPERIENTIALLY

It was Aurobindo's experiences, then, that stood behind his dismissal of the Mahatma's thought and strategies. From the earliest records of Aurobindo's activism, we find him involved with a broad range of models for change. Nonviolence is merely one strategy among others, and Aurobindo often viewed violence as the best and only appropriate and moral strategy. He identified experientially with those elements of Indian political leadership that advocated violent overthrow if necessary, and he did not hesitate to lead in the violent overthrow of British dominance. He argued that nonviolence at a time when violence was appropriate could even be a "sin against the divinity within." Nonviolence was certainly not, in his understanding, the teaching of traditional texts such as the *Bhagavadgita*, and violence was clearly a part of Indian tradition. His everyday experiences on the Indian political scene were experiences that rejected a Gandhian approach to British oppression. Even without his yogic experiences, his life was one opposed to a Gandhian claim for the primary morality of nonviolence.

Likewise his developing thought system would not accept any one activist strategy as exclusive. He had opted for the integration of the various "sides" in the matter and came to reject any one position as an egoistic exclusivism. To do otherwise than integrate all strategies was one-sided. Gandhi's exclusive emphasis on nonviolence was merely one example of this one-sided egoism.

Finally, since Gandhi did not recognize the integral nature of reality, including the necessity to integrate both violence and nonviolence, this was evidence that Gandhi was lacking in higher spiritual experience. In particular Gandhi lacked the yogic experience of higher levels of Consciousness that Aurobindo accepted as true and crucial. This meant Gandhi's theories were limited to the partial understandings of the level of Mind. They were mere mental theories. There was, therefore, no use attempting to argue with them on a mental level at all, for the mental level was not the final judge of truth. It was limited. If one clung to its arguments, that in itself was egoism and Ignorance.

Though both Gandhi and Aurobindo would claim "experience" as their authorities, their experiences were quite different and Aurobindo understood Gandhi's as inferior, lower level. Thus, from his understanding of the yogic experience he accepted as true, Aurobindo could dismiss Gandhi and his theories as "mental theories built on a basis of one-sided reasoning and claiming for a limited truth a universality which it cannot have." Gandhi's theories were no better than other mental theories, and attempting to argue with them was a waste of time and energy because the Universe has already surpassed them, if only others could see that. Nonviolence was, for Aurobindo, no more than it was for Nehru or many of the others analyzed in this volume, a political strategy that was sometimes useful and sometimes not.

Maybe it was Aurobindo's previous experience in the midst of India's Nationalist movement; maybe it was his theories about the nature of Reality; maybe it was a commitment to his yogic experience; maybe it was the fact that unlike many other critics he never met Gandhi and was not charmed by his personality; maybe it was all of the above. In any case, while India and the world were enamored with Gandhi, his persona, his ideas, and his techniques, Aurobindo dismissed them quickly. Though he supported Indian independence, he was no longer ready to return to the Indian Nationalist movement Gandhi represented with his satyagraha.

Notes

1. See Gandhi's description of Aurobindo as "a humble devotee" and the Sri Aurobindo ashram as a place of peace and acceptance of all in *The Collected Works of Mahatma Gandhi* (Delhi: Government of India, 1971), 89:431–432.

2. Jawaharlal Nehru, Forward in Karan Singh, *Prophet of Indian Nationalism: A Study of the Political Thought of Sri Aurobindo Ghose, 1893–1910* (London: Allen and Unwin, 1963), 7.

3. Sri Aurobindo, *Birth Centenary Library* (Pondicherry: Sri Aurobindo Ashram, 1970), 16:432.

4. Ibid., 22:490–491.

5. Ibid., 486.

6. See Aurobindo's later account of this meeting in ibid., 26:25.

7. Peter Heehs, *Sri Aurobindo: A Brief Biography* (Delhi: Oxford University Press, 1989), 18.

8. Aurobindo, *Birth Centenary Library* 1:15.

9. Ibid., 12–13.

10. See Aurobindo's own later account in ibid., 26:23.

11. Heehs, *Sri Aurobindo*, 54–55.

12. Aurobindo, *Birth Centenary Library* 26:22. Aurobindo often spoke of himself in the third person.

13. Ibid., 24.

14. Ibid., 1:66.

15. Heehs, *Sri Aurobindo*, 37.

16. Ibid., 44.

17. Aurobindo, *Birth Centenary Library* 1:91–92.

18. Ibid., 97–98.

19. Ibid., 98.

20. See Robert N. Minor, ed., *Modern Indian Interpreters of the Bhagavadgita* (Albany: State University of New York Press, 1986) for a fuller discussion of the varieties of interpretations of the text and its battle, from allegorical to literal.

21. Aurobindo, *Birth Centenary Library* 22:492. See Robert N. Minor, "Sri Aurobindo as *Gita*-yogin," in *Modern Indian Interpreters of the Bhagavadgita*, ed. Robert N. Minor (Albany: State University of New York Press, 1986), 61–87.

22. Aurobindo, *Birth Centenary Library* 1:98–99.

23. For further discussions of these matters, see Robert N. Minor, *Sri Aurobindo: The Perfect and the Good* (Columbia, Mo.: South Asia Books, 1978); and Robert N. Minor, *The Religious, the Spiritual, and the Secular: Auroville and Secular India* (Albany: State University of New York Press, 1999).

24. Aurobindo, *Birth Centenary Library* 22:7.

25. Ibid., 32.

26. On this topic see Robert N. Minor, "Sri Aurobindo and Experience: Yogic and Otherwise," in *eligion in Modern India*, 3rd ed., ed. Robert D. Baird (Delhi: Manohar, 1989), 452–479.

27. For a full discussion, see Robert N. Minor, "The Response of Sri Aurobindo and the Mother," in *Modern Indian Responses to Religious Pluralism*, ed. Harold Coward (Albany: State University of New York Press, 1987), 85–104.

28. For fuller discussions of these levels in the context of Aurobindo's ontology as well as other aspects of Integral Yoga, see Stephen H. Phillips, *Aurobindo's Philosophy of Brahman* (Leiden: E. J. Brill, 1986); and Minor, *Sri Aurobindo: The Perfect and the Good.*

29. See, for example, Aurobindo, *Birth Centenary Library* 28:167–168.

5

Tagore and Gandhi

T. S. RUKMANI

INTRODUCTION

The history of the world is measured by the history of individuals who contributed significantly to furthering the quality of life on planet earth. In the twentieth century we find two Indians, Rabindranath Tagore and Mohandas Karamchand Gandhi, who made their mark on world history. Both were born in the last quarter of the nineteenth century: Tagore in 1861 and Gandhi in 1869. They lived during the momentous years of India's struggle for independence from colonial rule. C. F. Andrews, a friend of both Gandhi and Tagore, once remarked that "Tagore is essentially a modern; Mahatma Gandhi is the St. Francis of Assisi of our own days."[1] The German philosopher Hermann Keyserling said, "Rabindranath is the greatest man I have had the privilege to know. There has been no one like him anywhere on our globe for many centuries."[2] Albert Einstein said of Mahatma Gandhi, "Generations to come, it may be, will scarce believe that such a one as this ever in flesh and blood walked upon this earth."[3] One of them, Tagore, was the winner of the Nobel Prize for literature in 1913, and the other, Mahatma Gandhi, has the distinction of winning freedom for India through nonviolent satyagraha.

This chapter touches briefly on the relationship that Tagore and Gandhi had with each other during the years 1915 to 1941 (the year that Tagore passed away), in the context of the Freedom movement in India. As Gandhi's life is covered in the Introduction to this volume, I start this chapter with a brief outline of Tagore's life.

Rabindranath Tagore

Tagore, the senior to Gandhi by eight years, was born into an aristocratic Bengali family. His grandfather Dwarkanath (1795–1846) was one of the wealthiest men in Bengal at the time and had business dealings with the British.[4] He died in London in 1846 during one of his travels. Tagore's father, Debendranath Tagore, was closely connected with the Brahmo Samaj movement started by Raja Rammohan Roy. Tagore's first lessons in the philosophy of religion, the freedom of the spirit, and the importance of truth were all learned at the feet of his father.[5] Tagore grew up in a joint family with his seven brothers. Dwijendranath, his eldest brother, was a poet, musician, philosopher, and mathematician and he had a big role in molding the intellectual and poetic capabilities of his brother Rabindranath. Satyendranath was the first Indian to pass the coveted Indian Civil Service examination instituted by the British, and his fifth brother Jyotindranath was, throughout his life, engaged in one or another Nationalist activity.

Women in Tagore's household were also pioneers of some sorts. His sister Swarnakumari, besides being the first woman novelist of Bengal, formed a women's organization engaged in literary activities.[6] His sister-in-law published a children's magazine called *Balaka*. Satyendranath's wife traveled with him even to England, unusual for a woman in those days.

Tagore's father prized Truth above all else and the following incident, after the death of Dwarkanath in London, reveals the character of Devendranath. When Dwarkanath's firm had to close down due to its liabilities, Devendranath, "called the creditors together . . . and announced [that] . . . he and his brothers voluntarily renounced claims to the benefit of the trust until the last penny of the liabilities had been paid."[7] He not only paid off all the debts, but even "made good all the charities and donations which his father had promised before he went abroad." Tagore would say of his father, "A passive acceptance of the correct and the proper did not satisfy him; he wanted us to love truth with our whole hearts."[8]

His early schooling was but a formality. The rich literary atmosphere at home, combined with private tutoring, helped Tagore's hidden talents to blossom. Tagore says, "One great advantage which I enjoyed in my younger days was the literary and artistic atmosphere which pervaded our house."[9] He wrote his first verse when he was just eight years old and his first narrative poem, eight cantos long, at fourteen. He wrote poems, plays, fiction, and essays throughout his life and took to painting at the age of sixty.

Tagore was a widely traveled man and his winning the Nobel Prize for literature in 1913 catapulted him onto the international arena. There were lecture tours at many places and universities and he was conferred honorary doctorate degrees by many universities, including Oxford. He founded the now famous Vishwabharati University at Santiiketan, an institution started to realize the dreams of this singular individual who though born an Indian was above all an internationalist.

Tagore's literary efforts greatly overshadowed the other sides of his personality. The world knew him only as the poet and forgot his other contributions. He protested against the arrest of Bal Gangadhar Tilak in 1898 and publicly condemned it in a paper he wrote on the occasion.[10] He played an active role in the Bengal Swadeshi movement in 1905; he was concerned with the plight of the deprived, particularly the peasants and his heart went out to the "hungry, naked and homeless in their own land."[11] He had initiated programs of community development based on cooperative principles; he helped the peasants build their own schools and hospitals, roads and water tanks,[12] a Co-operative Farmer's Bank, and, along with setting up his ideal school Santiniketan in a rural area, also founded an institution called Sriniketan, "a nucleus for experiment in large-scale community development."[13] Thus, almost two decades earlier than Gandhi, Tagore had experimented with these community development ideas.

Tagore's contribution through his writings as a social critic was also invaluable. *The Castle of Conservatism* attacks dogma and "empty ritual" and is against orthodoxy that "strangles the growth of an individual."[14] He uses his female characters as "vehicles for an explicit and radical critique of the caste system, untouchability, religious hypocrisy" and so forth.[15] Many of his novels, such as *The Rifled Nest*, *Mote in the Eye*, and *Spot of Destiny*, address social issues. According to Roy, Tagore is the first writer in modern India "who brought women out of the kitchen and . . . into the parlor where they argue with men and exchange ideas."[16] He thus anticipated Gandhi in building a social consciousness in society. He cherished the independence of the self and freedom of the mind above all else. The following lines from *Gitanjali* quoted by astrophysicist S. Chandrasekhar when accepting the Nobel Prize in 1983 at Stockholm, expresses this one obsession throughout his life:

Where the mind is without fear and head held high;
Where knowledge is free;
Where words come out from the depth of truth;
Where tireless striving stretches its arms towards perfection;

Where the clear streams of reason has not lost its way
into the dreary desert sand of dead habit
Into that heaven of freedom, my Father, let my country awake.

(Chandrasekhar changed the last line to: Into that haven of freedom let me
awake.)[17] Tagore continued to compose poems until the very end of his life.

Tagore And Gandhi: Phase I

Gandhi's reputation as a nonviolent fighter for human rights in South Africa
had received publicity in India and had already earned him the respect of
Tagore. So when C. F. Andrews and W. W. Pearson set out for South Africa
in 1913 to see for themselves the unique experiment that Gandhi was trying
there, Tagore sent his best wishes to Gandhi through them "for the success
of his mission."[18] It was through Andrews that Gandhi formed his first impression of Tagore. This was the beginning of a lifelong admiration Gandhi
and Tagore had for each other.

When Gandhi finally left South Africa and closed down his Phoenix
ashram there, Tagore offered to accommodate those inmates in Santiniketan
until Gandhi could find his own place. The first contact was thus made but
Gandhi himself would meet Tagore in person only in March 1915 when he
spent six days at Santiniketan. The first differences between Tagore's personality and Gandhi's surfaced at this time. In a letter to Maganlal Gandhi, the
caretaker of the boys, Gandhi wrote, probably in response to Maganlal's description of the life at Santiniketan, "I had always felt, and it now appears that
there is no institution today in the world to excel Phoenix in its ideals or its
way of life."[19] Tagore's boys free like little "Ariels" jumping around contrasted with "Gandhi's little saints, too wise and sober for their age." Tagore
loved them, but Gandhi wished "they were not so completely nice."[20]
Gandhi, during his short stay, continuing his experiments in South Africa,[21]
tried to teach Tagore's children and teachers how to run their own kitchen
and keep the ashram clean. Tagore tolerated the new experiment but it did
not last long. The day it was introduced, March 10, is remembered as Gandhi
Day every year when the teachers and students do all the work themselves.

Gandhi also did not flinch at pointing out the special treatment ac-
corded to Brahmin boys in the ashram dining room.[22] Tagore abolished that
practice because it was against his own sense of social justice. That picture of
Gandhi as a man wanting to impose his way of life on others, "with a truly

dictatorial combination of maternalism and paternalism,"[23] must surely have left its impression on Tagore's mind in this first encounter.

The satyagraha tactics used by Gandhi in South Africa was tried initially in India to address issues not directly involved with India's Independence movement. He used it to get rid of the "indenture system of labor" and in getting relief for the Chanparan farmers against the compulsory planting of "indigo."[24] "The Champaran inquiry was a bold experiment with Truth and Ahimsā" as Gandhi stated in his autobiography.[25] After many such campaigns, satyagraha was finally adopted as a means for India's Independence struggle by the Indian National Congress in 1920. By now Gandhi had also consolidated his position in the country as a whole. This, in turn, helped the Indian National Congress, which until then was more or less an elitist organization, to become broad-based.

Nonviolent satyagraha took may forms in India like nonviolent noncooperation, civil disobedience, fasting, *swadeshi* (self-sufficiency), and using cloth only produced in the country which, in turn, led to widespread propagation of spinning and weaving and the *charkhā* (spinning wheel) regeneration and its corollary, the boycott of foreign cloth, strike/*hartal* (day of prayer), and even nonpayment of unjust taxes. In Ahmedabad in 1918, Gandhi had already used fasting during a strike by mill hands, which also became a part of satyagraha. It seems that Gandhi's experiences with the poor and exploited in the land, as well as the firsthand experience he had gained in his travels across the country, in a third-class coach of the railways, had convinced him that "India's welfare lay in a revival of the village and its traditions of craftsmanship, particularly those of spinning and weaving."[26] Though Tagore and Gandhi were united in their aspiration for the Independence of the country, they could not see eye to eye in the application of the principle of noncooperation for achieving swaraj.

GANDHI AND TAGORE: PHASE II—THE ROWLATT ACTS

After his brief stay at Shantiniketan, there was not much contact between Gandhi and Tagore until 1918/1919. Though Gandhi's earlier satyagraha protests did not bring him into direct confrontation with the British government, it was the Rowlatt Acts that "sought to perpetuate the extraordinary repressive powers conferred on the Government during the war, for doing away with ordinary legal procedure and for authorizing imprisonment without trial,"[27] that eventually changed Gandhi's perception of the British from a reasonable power to one that believed in all forms of repression. This finally provoked Gandhi to come out openly with his Civil Disobedience movement. The Jallianwalla Bagh massacre of April 13, 1919, where General Dyer fired point-blank on an unarmed crowd in an enclosed square that had gathered to protest the Rowlatt Acts, is an important landmark in the Tagore/Gandhi relationship.

Tagore had already had some minor differences with Gandhi. His letter to Gandhi in answer to his query about the use of Hindi-Urdu as the national language in India shows his reservations about Gandhi's views.[28] Tagore, while agreeing in principle with the idea, pointed out that it could create a problem for those from the south and would be impractical as "our politicians will find it extremely difficult to express themselves adequately in this language." But at this time of crisis, occasioned by the Rowlatt Acts, Tagore was wholeheartedly behind Gandhi. When Gandhi was arrested on April 8, 1919, under acts, Tagore wrote him an open letter calling him Mahatmaji for the first time, proclaiming that he had come to his motherland "to lead her in the true path of conquest."[29]

The Jallianwalla Bagh massacre brought out Tagore's strongest protest when he resigned his knighthood in a letter to the viceroy dated May 29, 1919. "The very least I can do for my country," says Tagore, "is to take all consequences upon myself in giving voice to the protest of the millions of my countrymen who for their so called insignificance are liable to suffer a degradation not fit for human blessings."[30] He did this even before Gandhi returned his own honors, such as the Kaiser-i-Hind Zulu War and Boer War medals, in August 1920 as part of noncooperation.

In letters written at this time, Tagore and Gandhi voiced admiration for each other. "We need all the moral force which Mahatma Gandhi represents and which he alone in the world can represent,"[31] says Tagore. Gandhi, in turn, lauds Tagore: "This great poet is a priceless gem of India. No one can deny that his poetry is full of spiritual wisdom, ethical ideas and other noble elements."[32] But the temporary truce was over and the differences between Gandhi and Tagore, held in abeyance during the height of the Rowlatt Acts, started surfacing again in the aftermath of the acts.

ALL-OUT NON-COOPERATION AND TAGORE'S RESPONSE

When Gandhi launched his all-out Non-cooperation movement in 1920, Tagore was away from the country and came back in July 1921 hoping to breathe "the buoyant breezes of this new found freedom." Instead he was disturbed at the "oppressive atmosphere" in the land that was intolerant of opposition, on the one hand, and fear to speak out one's mind, on the other hand. Soon after he attacked noncooperation in the now famous speech at the Calcutta University Institute called Satyer Ahvan or "The Call of Truth."[33] But even before that frontal attack Tagore had written from abroad his misgivings about the noncooperation stance of Gandhi. Noncooperation for Tagore was "political asceticism." He recalls his Swadeshi movement days in these letters of March 5, 1921 and March 13, 1921.[34] Gandhi writing in *Young India* said, in connection with education through English, that "Caitanya, Kabir, Nanak, Guru Govindsingh, Shivaji and Pratap were greater men than Ram Mohan Roy and Tilak." He was arguing for the benefits of learning through one's own language rather than through the medium of English. Tagore was not pleased with this comparison of Roy to Caitanya and others and wrote to a friend from Zurich protesting rather strongly against these remarks. He went to the extent of calling Gandhi "enamoured of his own doctrines, which is a dangerous form of egotism that even great people suffer from at times."[35] He referred to Rammohan Roy again in a letter of May 17, 1921, as "the first and the greatest who realized" the Upanisadic truth of unity. Thus, when Tagore spoke at the Calcutta University Institute, he was giving vent, not only to some genuine misgivings about noncooperation but also to some pent-up frustrations in not being able to understand the workings of the Mahatma's mind.

Both Tagore and Gandhi were "internationalists" at heart; but the circumstances that governed their individual "internationalism" were very different. Tagore had gone through his nationalistic phase during the Bengal Swadeshi movement and had found closure to that phase of his life. For him the idea of Nation was a powerful anesthetic that leads to "moral perversion."[36] He had learned firsthand how mass support can deteriorate into mob fury and had come to believe that only a change of heart, through proper cultivation of the mind, can lead to true internationalism. He was convinced that there was only one history that mattered for humans for "[a]ll national histories are merely chapters in the larger one."[37]

Gandhi, a man of the moment, could concentrate on national issues single-mindedly, without in any way becoming a "narrow Nationalist." While he was an internationalist having no boundaries and "keeping the windows of his home open for all cultures to be blown in," he could work for issues within a "national boundary" without being diverted by their international ramifications. He believed that "without being nationalist none could lay claim to internationalism."[38] Thus he could advocate noncooperation measures like the burning of foreign cloth that found no favor with internationalists like Tagore and Andrews. When Andrews pointed out the subtle racial overtones of the word *foreign* in "burning foreign cloth" and how it promoted "selfish nationalism," Gandhi explained it away.[39] Gandhi, the internationalist, was for peace and goodwill anywhere in the whole world and can thus qualify as a "nationalist having an international outlook"; but it was different from the internationalism of the mature Tagore. More than anything else Gandhi was a consummate politician which Tagore was not.

Moreover, at this juncture Tagore, who had conceived of his international Visvabharati University at Santiniketan in 1918, was giving shape to his own inclinations as an internationalist. The university came into being in 1921 and the Sanskrit motto chosen by Tagore—"Where the Whole World Would Meet in One Nest"—stood for a place where the best was cultivated from all over the world. Thus, when Gandhi was growing in nationalism and was advocating noncooperation, Tagore was immersed in bringing together the best in the East and the West at his Visvabharati. As Nobel laureate he belonged to the world; as an internationalist he refused to be bound by the narrow walls of nationalism. "What an irony of destiny," as Romain Roland says, "that he should be preaching co-operation between Occident and Orient at one end of the world, when at that moment, non-cooperation was being preached at the other end."[40]

Noncooperation came in many forms. Boycott of foreign cloth led to burning foreign made cloth, and to spinning and weaving of homemade *khadi* (home-produced cloth); the students were encouraged to boycott government schools; professionals such as lawyers were encouraged to withhold their services and "surrender their titles and honorary offices."[41] Tagore, who had first-hand experience of what science and technology had done for progress in the West, was particularly disturbed by the call to students to quit schools and colleges. In an essay titled "Cultural Fusion" read at a meeting on August 15, 1921, at the Calcutta University Institute even before his famous "The Call of Truth" speech at the same institute, Tagore voiced his fears of India turning its back on science and scientific cooperation with the West. He advocated cooperation between the East, with its message of "spirituality" and the West, with its "revitalizing power of science." Thus he was a supporter of cooperation between India and the West and found Gandhi's non-cooperation a difficult pill to swallow. Tagore was also convinced that India's problems were mainly social and not political and was thus not enthusiastic about Gandhi's non-cooperation for political purposes.[42] Tagore, along with many others, was appalled by Gandhi's all-out non-cooperation.[43] Before Tagore gave his famous "The

Call of Truth" speech, Gandhi answered some of Tagore's fears in an article in
Young India called "The Poet's Anxiety."

"The Poet's Anxiety" And "The Call Of Truth"

In "The Poet's Anxiety" Gandhi justified his Non-cooperation movement both
to the poet and to others as "a protest against an unwitting and unwilling participation in evil."[44] In his "The Call of Truth" Tagore wrote to Gandhi about
his fears of mob violence taking over: "The danger inherent in all force grows
stronger when it is likely to gain success, for then it becomes temptation."[45]

This speech, full of idealism, was probably the only bitter attack on
Gandhi by Tagore. He calls attention to the expansion of the soul from
within to make the country "of our birth more fully our own." Recalling his
experience during the Bengal Swadeshi struggle of 1905 he mentions how fu-
tile the picketing, burning, and other non-cooperation actions were then and
implying it will not be different now. Responding as an aristocrat to the exhi-
bition of angry feelings of the mob, he was cautioning people against react-
ing emotionally for "emotion by itself, like fire, only consumes its fuel and
reduces it to ashes; it has no creative power." The wild excitement he saw in
the people only shouted to him, "it did not sing to me," he said.[46]

He praised the Mahatma in this speech as the embodiment of Truth,
and as one who has felt "so many men of India to be his own flesh and blood.
. . . All honor to the Mahatma, who made visible to us the power of Truth."
Gandhi had claimed that India could gain swaraj within a year at the Congress
session of September 1920. Tagore refers to this claim and says the "gain . . .
is indicated by name, but is not defined." Thus "the object of the temptation
has been magnified through its indefiniteness, while the time and method of
its attainment have been made too narrowly definite." Tagore felt that the
Mahatma was trivializing swaraj as something to be won through shortcuts.
"For this task . . . the economist must think, the mechanic must labor, the ed-
ucationist and statesman must teach and contrive. In a word, the mind of the
country must exert itself in all directions." He expects Gandhi to give a call
for all the "forces of the land to be brought into action. . . . Freedom is in
complete awakening, in full self expression."[47]

Tagore was not able to see, because of his frustration, the greater sym-
bolism of the spinning wheel. "Where . . . is the argument that in our country
swaraj can be brought about by everyone engaging for a time in spinning?"
The command to burn foreign cloth, which could have "gone to women

whose nakedness is actually keeping them prisoners," calls for opposition and a valiant fight as it is bad economics. Tagore was not against the revival of India's handicrafts because he himself had worked for it in the past. But he failed to understand that through the symbol of spinning and weaving Gandhi, who was greatly influenced by John Ruskin's idea of true political economy which is "the proper management of the nation's labor,"[48] "communicated values of spiritual dynamism, of the importance of manual labor, of solidarity between the rich and the poor, of the protest against the tyranny of modern machinery (technology) and the economic exploitation of the poor by the rich."[49] Tagore, the idealist, believed that "what is harmful to the world is harmful to each one of us." But he should have known that in the community of nations that comprise the world, there is place only for equal partners.

Gandhi combined in himself a religious zeal along with infinite patience and a feel for the dramatic. A man of the masses, he derived his strength from the electrifying following he received from them. Tagore whose genius was in writing and not in action could espouse a cause for some time but could not sustain it for long. He also had the advantage of giving vent to his emotions in literary works, which he did after every quarrel he had with Gandhi and earlier after his withdrawal from the Bengal Swadeshi movement. "Tagore was no Gandhi; he lacked the latter's infinite patience . . . his genius for strategy and his unrivalled gift of leadership."[50]

Tagore was reliving his Bengal Swadeshi movement days and could see history repeating itself. No one believed that swaraj would be achieved in a year. An incorrigible idealist that Gandhi was, he knew the pulse of the people and "was obliged on occasions to over-dramatize a situation and exaggerate certain aspects of it to rouse adequate mass fervor."[51] Gandhi, as Erik Erikson said, "heard the clamor of the people when he listened to his inner voice."[52] Gandi succeeded initially for "[c]ountry folk as well as townsmen, shopkeepers and substantial farmers[;] laborers in tea gardens as well as lawyers, teachers and students heard and responded to Gandhi's call for a new sort of political campaign."[53] As Tagore had feared, the undesirable manifestation of pent-up rage did lead to violence of speech and action until Gandhi had to call off the Non-cooperation movement in February 1922.

THE GREAT SENTINEL

Gandhi responded to Tagore's "The Call of Truth" in *Young India* by calling him "The Great Sentinel."[54] He practically agrees with Tagore's assessment saying, "It is good, therefore, that the poet has invited all who are slavishly mimicking the call of the charkhā boldly to declare their revolt," but denies that there is any blind obedience on a large scale to his leadership. He also bemoaned the fact that the educated did not understand the truth underlying spinning and weaving. Gandhi's response was that of the average Indian. He speaks on behalf of the honest worker who starved because there was "no work to buy food with." Tagore and his elder brother, Bara Dada, were zamindars and Gandhi may be hinting at that when in his reply he says, "India lives in her seven and a half lakhs villages, and the cities live upon the villages. . . . The city people are brokers and commission agents for the big houses of Europe. . . . The cities have co-operated with the latter in the bleeding process that has gone on for the past two hundred years."[55]

Tagore could not but be reminded of his grandfather's association with the British, in earlier years, in this passage. It is quite possible that Gandhi himself had that in mind when he wrote it. There was a connection between swadeshi, that is, producing enough cloth "for the wants of India and distributing it," and swaraj, that is, independence; "boycott of foreign cloth was a means of relieving the chronic underemployment in the hungry millions." For Gandhi any economics that hurt "the moral well being of an individual or nation are immoral and therefore sinful." Gandhi passionately defends his non-cooperation hitting hard at Tagore's misgivings: "In burning my foreign clothes I burn my shame, I must refuse to insult the naked by giving them clothes they do not need instead of giving them work which they solely need."[56] In answer to the poet's description of swadeshi and noncooperation being narrowly nationalistic, Gandhi declares it to be "a message to the world." He ended this "proud and poignant" reply with some verses from the *Bhagavad Gita*. Rolland has aptly pointed out the contrasting visions of these two great men when he says that Tagore "lives in eternity but the demands of the present are imperious."[57]

Before writing "The Great Sentinel" Gandhi visited Tagore in Calcutta on September 6, 1921, in the presence of C. F. Andrews whom both respected and loved. Gandhi came to seek support from Tagore for his movement.[58] Tagore as proof of his reservations pointed to a scene outside his home: "Come and look over the edge of my verandah"—Gandhi looked down—"and see what your non-violent followers are up to. They have stolen cloth from the shops . . . they have lit a bonfire in my courtyard and are howling round it."[59] Gandhi as reported by Leonard K. Elmhirst reminded Tagore of his own participation in the Bengal Swadeshi movement and said, "My swaraj movement is the natural child of your swadeshi." When

Gandhi requested him to take to spinning he is reported as smiling and saying, "Poems I can spin, songs I can spin, but what a mess I would make, Gandhiji, of your precious cotton."[60]

MUKTADHARA AND THE CHARACTER VAIRAGI DHANANJAYA

This exchange between the poet and the Mahatma was widely publicized both within the country and abroad. Tagore retired soon after this, and sought refuge in his literary works. One of the finest works he wrote at this time (early 1922) was called *Muktadhara* (Free Current). Earlier, after the Bengal Swadeshi movement, he wrote *Prayascitta* (Atonement) wherein the character Vairagi Dhananjaya reminds one of a Gandhian figure. He is a prototype of the Gandhian Satyagrahi but written from Tagore's viewpoint in the year 1909, when Gandhi was only a name. That only shows how closely the earlier "Swadeshi Tagore" resembled the "Non-cooperation Gandhi." Even his characterization of Nikhil in his 1915 novel *Ghaire Bhaire* (The Home and the World) bears an uncanny resemblance to Gandhi.

Dhananjaya in *Muktadhara* was created after Tagore knew Gandhi very well and after their disagreement over non-cooperation. *Muktadhara* revolves around the story of the king of Uttarakut, Ranajit, controlling the waters of Muktadhara from irrigating the lands of Shivatarai, a neighboring country. Dhananjaya, as Tagore himself says, was taken from his earlier play *Prayascitta*, written in 1909. As the word *atonement* implies, Tagore was perhaps making amends for his withdrawal from the Bengal Swadeshi movement and in the character of Dhananjaya (which he would perhaps have liked to be) was painting a character who, as an unrelenting "champion of truth and nonviolence," was the ideal opponent to political despotism.

His fascination with the Gandhian character who fights totalitarian despotism through nonviolent satyagraha and who instructs the common folk to value "personal honour and integrity" above everything else makes him come back to this character in *Muktadhara*. Ranajit is made to express his (Tagore's) own fears of applying nonviolence to politics before it got internalized into one's own depth of mind. It looks as though Tagore is going through a lot of self-examination and sometimes doubting whether he could perhaps be making a mistake in condemning Gandhi's "methods." Both Tagore's fears and Gandhi's idealism are depicted well in this play. Tagore's Dananjaya expresses what Gandhi stood for better than Gandhi himself. Dhananjaya also conveys "the ambivalence he felt within himself about the strategy . . . of non-violence and how good intentions can develop into blind rage."[61] While the character Vairagi Dhananjaya resembles Gandhi very closely, King Ranajit seems to represent both the repressive foreign ruler, as well as one who presents counterarguments to Dhananjaya's noncooperative tactics somewhat like Tagore himself.

Even though the quality of the play suffers in translation, I give below some extracts from Marjorie Sykes's translation of the play, so that the reader gets to "hear" Tagore himself, in his own words.[62] In the following exchange with the citizens of Shivatarai, tormented by the ruler of Uttarakut, Dhananjaya gives voice to "Gandhi's" values of surrender to the God within and the greater strength of nonviolence.

> *Citizen:* Master, the king's brother-in-law, Chandapal beats us past all enduring.
>
> *Dhananjaya:* So you are still unable to master this violence? It still hurts you?
>
> *Ganesh:* It's not to be borne! My hands are itching to get at him!

In answer to Ganesh wanting to beat Chandapal back:

> Dhananjaya: Can't you show him what non-beating is? That needs too much strength I suppose. Beating the waves won't stop the storm. But hold the rudder steady, and you win.

Dhananjaya advocates nonviolence against violence much like Gandhi when he says, "Strike at the root of violence itself. . . . As soon as you can hold up your head and say that it does not hurt, the roots of violence will be cut." Tagore's fears of Gandhi leading an uneducated, emotionally charged mob, who have no will of their own and who follow Gandhi blindly, is hinted at:

> *Citizen:* We understand *you*, but your words we don't understand. . . . But we understand *you*, and so we shall have an early crossing.
>
> *Dhananjaya:* If you can't make my words your own, you will be drowned.
>
> *Citizen:* We have found shelter at your feet, so we must have understood somehow.

Dhananjaya: It is only too plain that you have not understood. Your eyes still see red, and there is no song on your lips. . . . You either flee to avoid the blow, or fight to ward it off; it is all one. Whichever you do, you merely follow the flock—you do not see the shepherd. [He goes on to tell the Shivatarai citizens that they are only clinging to him in blind faith.] You men all cling to me; the more you hold on, the less prospect there is of your learning to swim.

In another context, Ranajit questions Dhananjaya:

Ranajit: So it is you who have roused these people to madness? . . . Will you pay the taxes or not?

Dhananjaya: No, Maharaja, we will not pay.

Ranajit: You will not?

Dhananjaya: We cannot give you what is not yours.

Ranajit: Not mine?

Dhananjaya: Our excess food is yours; the food of our hunger is not.

Ranajit points out the fury of an uneducated mass of people and tells Dhananjaya that he is misleading them.

Ranajit: Your assurance merely drives their fear underground and covers it up. The moment there is a crack it will burst out seven times stronger. Then they will be lost.

Ranajit also hints at the blind worship people offer Dhanajaya as if he is their God.

Citizen: Haven't you seen our god, our god incarnate, . . . Dhananjaya?

Ranajit: You are their god now. . . . When they come to pay the king's taxes, you stop them. But when they pay the god's worship at your feet, (do) you feel hurt?

Dhananjaya: If only I could run away from it all. They spend all their worship on me. Gandhi himself had shunned away from people touching his feet and flocking to have his darshan as the Mahatma.[63])

There is reference to Ranajit, very much like Tagore, being in two minds in the following statement of his minister.

Minister: He talked to the Vairagi so long because he was in two minds about it. He could neither enter the camp nor leave it.

Tagore was conscious of his restless nature and the opposing pulls in himself which he describes in a letter: "I sometimes detect within myself a battle ground where two opposing forces are constantly in action, one beckoning to peace and cessation of strife, the other egging me on to battle. . . . Hence this swing of the pendulum, between passionate pain and detachment . . . between an itch to entering the lists and a longing to remain in thought."[64]

Many more situations and statements in *Muktadhara* call to mind both Tagore and Gandhi, as well as the political climate of those days, and can be read profitably for an understanding of the struggle that Tagore was waging within himself for a clearer perception of Gandhi. Gandhi seems to have read *Muktadhara* because there is a reference to it in the *Collected Works.*[65]

TAGORE AND GANDHI: THIRD PHASE

Gandhi visited Tagore in May 1925 at Santiniketan and tried to argue his case for the charkhā and spinning of homemade cloth but Tagore criticized "The Cult of Charkhā" in one more article published in *Modern Review* in September 1925. He speaks against the intoxicating effect of persuasion that can "produce a convenient uniformity of purpose, immense and powerful." Its mass appeal cannot be taken for the soundness of the method being followed, he argued. "Human nature has its elasticity, and in the name of urgency, it can be forced towards a particular direction far beyond its normal and wholesome limits." This, he believed, was what Gandhi's cult of spinning and weaving and promise of swaraj was doing to the people and the country. He harks back to Gandhi's calling Rammohan Roy a pygmy in "The Cult of Charkhā" as well.[66]

Gandhi wrote "The Poet and the Charkhā" in reply to "The Cult of the Charkhā" in *Young India* (5 November 1925) and also responded to the public reactions to their earlier exchanges in it.[67] Rumor that jealousy gave rise to their disagreements is set at rest and Gandhi has great praise for the poet who "lives in a magnificent world . . . of ideas." He believes that the poet has not understood the Charkhā movement as Gandhi presented it. "Just as, if we were to live we must breathe, not air imported from England nor eat food so imported, so may we not import cloth made in England." The Charkhā movement will also help in building programs of community service, he argued. The only thing that seemed to have hurt Gandhi much was Tagore's reference to Rammohan Roy being spoken of as a pygmy by Gandhi. Gandhi denies his calling him a pygmy and clarifies the context in which he had spoken of Roy. There is no evidence to show that Tagore and Gandhi ever came to reconcile themselves on the issues of spinning and weaving or on the boycott of schools and colleges by students or of burning foreign cloth.

The sound and fury generated by this correspondence between two of the greatest Indians at the time died down for awhile. Gandhi was arrested in 1922 and sentenced to six years imprisonment but was released in 1924 for health reasons. He remained in the background until 1928; and when he led the salt satyagraha march in 1930, Tagore was away from the country. He wrote against it in a letter to the *Manchester Guardian* and in another letter to the *Spectator* "he referred to Gandhi's new technique of revolution."[68] In Tagore's letters to friends and relatives he continued to comment on Gandhi's actions but these did not receive much publicity.[69] He wrote against the charkhā ,[70] disagreed with Gandhi on the question of birth control,[71] had reservations about the Poona Pact that Gandhi had achieved through his fast in 1932,[72] opposed his May 1933 fast,[73] and did not see eye to eye with Gandhi on the caste system.[74] In "The Shudra Habit" published in *Modern Review* in March 1927, Tagore criticized the *varnasrama dharma* (caste laws) that Gandhi defended.[75] He also expressed himself in his works and *Rakta Karabi* (Red Oleanders) reverts back to his theme of individual freedom.

Gandhi and Tagore came together in the early 1930s. Gradually, Tagore was more and more identified with the freedom struggle and found that he agreed with Gandhi on a number of issues. In this he was also helped by the hardened attitude of the British government. Gandhi wrote in 1931 on the occasion of the seventieth birthday of Tagore: "In common with thousands of his countrymen, I owe much to one who by his poetic genius and singular purity of life has raised India in the estimation of the world."[76] Gandhi's commitment to Hindu–Muslim unity and his fight against untouchability further touched Tagore's heart. Gandhi had got into the habit of seeking Tagore's blessings before entering a major course of action. He did that before resuming Civil Disobedience in January 1932 and before starting his fast at Yeravada in September 1932, against separate electorates. Tagore even contributed some writings and some translations for Gandhi's *Harijan* during this period.[77] Tagore visited the Sabarmati ashram in Ahmedabad in January 1930 and the earlier misunderstandings were well nigh forgotten. He visited Gandhi in Yeravada jail in Poona and was present when Gandhi broke his fast on September 26, 1932.

On January 15, 1934, Bihar was rocked by a severe earthquake. Gandhi who was working for the cause of the Untouchables at the time attributed the earthquake to "a divine chastisement sent by God for our sins . . . for there is a vital connection between the Bihar calamity and the untouchability campaign." When Tagore read Gandhi's statement he, along with many others, like Jawaharlal Nehru, was genuinely distressed and he severely condemned the illogicality of Gandhi's statement.[78] Gandhi, however, did not relent and stuck to his unscientific claim. But, unlike the lengthy charkhā and noncooperation debates, Tagore was content to let the issue go. Gandhi's conciliatory tone saying "I cannot prove the connection of the sin of untouchability with the Bihar visitation" may also have helped. There was also an exchange of letters between the two "regarding the election of Subhas Chandra Bose to the position of President of the Indian National Congress and his resignation in 1939."[79]

In 1934 Tagore was seventy-three years old and was getting increasingly anxious about the future of Viswabharati. There were no assured funds from the government for this private institution and Tagore was using money raised from his royalties and from staging plays for maintaining it. He finally appealed to Gandhi who at once responded with a substantial amount.[80] Tagore also requested Gandhi to become a life trustee on the Viswabharati committee in 1937, which he politely declined.[81]

In February 1940 Gandhi, with Kasturba, again visited Santiniketan which would prove to be his last meeting with Tagore. Gandhi called this visit a pilgrimage: "I have come here leaving behind me all the cares and burdens of politics, simply to have Gurudev's darshan and blessings. I have often claimed myself to be an accomplished beggar. But a more precious gift has never dropped into my beggar's bowl than Gurudev's blessings today."[82]

Tagore gave a letter to Gandhi before he left, which said in part, "Accept this institution under your protection, giving it an assurance of permanence if you consider it to be a national asset."[83] Gandhi's love and deep affection for Tagore, despite their occasional differences, made sure that he would honor this last wish of Gurudev.[84] He succeeded in getting the government of India to declare it a national university and to assume full financial responsibility for it. Today Viswabharati stands as a fitting memorial to the vision and free spirit of Rabindranath Tagore.

Tagore passed away on August 7, 1941, and Gandhi paid a touching farewell to his dear Poet: "In the death of Tagore, we have not only lost the greatest poet of the age, but an ardent nationalist, who was also a humanitarian. In Santiniketan and Sriniketan he has left a legacy to the whole nation, indeed to the whole world."[85] Earlier, in 1938, Tagore had written of Gandhi: "I have since learnt to understand him . . . not by the theories and fantasies of the creed he may profess, but by that expression in his practice which gives evidence to the uniqueness of his mind."[86]

CONCLUSION

The differences between Tagore and Gandhi have provoked different comments. Louis Fischer thought the two were totally opposite in nature: "Gandhi was the wheat field and Tagore the rose garden . . . Gandhi the emaciated ascetic with shaven head and face, Tagore the large white maned, white bearded aristocrat-intellectual with a face of classic, patriarchal beauty."[87] Others, such as Rajendra Verma, Krishna Kripalani, and G. D. Khanolkar, could see the differences as differing points of view over specific issues. Romain Rolland describes them as "fatally separated in their feeling as a philosopher can be from an apostle, as St. Paul from a Plato."[88]

The legacies that Tagore and Gandhi have left behind are indeed very different. On the international scene, Gandhi is ranked as one of the one hundred prominent individuals of the twentieth century. Tagore does not figure in that counting. In India the well-known magazine *India Today* lists Gandhi as an icon of the twentieth century along with Patel, Nehru, and others, while Tagore is mentioned as an icon of art and culture and bracketed with film actors and musicians. Gandhi never won an international award, but his philosophy of nonviolence and noncooperation has had a wider impact worldwide, and was used among others by world leaders such as Martin Luther King Jr. and Nelson Mandela. Gandhi's "spinning and weaving movement" led to a regeneration of a number of indigenous handicrafts and the Khadi cottage industries today provides employment for a huge population. Tagore's "zeal for the development of the Indian arts," in turn, played a large role in the renaissance of Indian culture and art. Gandhi is known to a number of people around the world, while Tagore is highly respected in literary and artistic circles and as a Nobel laureate for literature. Tagore's Santiniketan and Sriniketan stand as permanent landmarks in the fields of education and social reform. Independent India paid its highest tribute to Tagore when it chose his song as its national anthem. Gandhi's legacy is more obvious, while Tagore's is more subtle.

Yet the difference in temperament between Gandhi and Tagore was real and did not allow them to compromise. It is best expressed by Tagore himself in these words:

> It is extremely difficult for me to have to differ from Mahatma Gandhi in regard to any matter of principle or method. . . . For what could be a greater joy than to join hands in the field of work with one for whom one has such love and reverence? . . . The difference in our standpoints and temperaments . . . makes the Mahatma's field of work one which my conscience cannot accept as its own. That is a regret that will abide with me always.[89]

According to Jawaharlal Nehru, "Both Gurudeva and Gandhiji . . . were one hundred percent India's children, and the inheritors, representatives and expositors of her age long culture. . . . The surprising thing is that both of these men . . . should differ from each other so greatly! No two persons could probably differ so much as Gandhi and Tagore!"[90]

NOTES

1. Krishna Kripalani, *Rabindranath Tagore: A Biography* (London: Oxford University Press, 1962), 248.

2. Ibid., 287, fn. 21.

3. Klaus Klostermaeir, *A Survey of Hinduism*, 2nd ed. (New York: State University of New York Press, 1994), 447.

4. Rabindranath Tagore, *My Reminiscences* (New Delhi: Rupa and Co., 1922), 2–3.

5. Kripalani, *Tagore*, 52.

6. G. D. Khanolkar, *The Lute and the Plough*, trans. Thomas Gay (Bombay: The Book Centre Private, 1963), 84.

7. Kripalani, *Tagore*, 28.

8. Tagore, *My Reminiscences*, 77.

9. Ibid., 90.

10. Kripalani, *Tagore*, 176–177.

11. Ibid., 168.

12. Ibid, 150.

13. Ibid., 149.

14. Khanolkar, *The Lute and the Plough*, 157–158.

15. William Cenkner, "The Feminine in the Works of Rabindranath Tagore," in *Rabindranath Tagore: American Interpretations*, 2nd ed., ed. Ira G. Zepp Jr.) (Calcutta: Writer's Workshop, 1991), 108–109.

16. Ibid.

17. Krishna Dutta and Andrew Robinson, eds., *Selected Letters of Rabindranath Tagore* (Cambridge: Cambridge University Press, 1997), 527.

18. Kripalani, *Tagore*, 236.

19. *The Collected Works of Mahatma Gandhi* (hereafter *CW*) (Delhi: Government of India, 1971), 12:559–560; 22:365–367.

20. Kripalani, *Tagore*, 245–246.

21. T. S. Rukmani, "Mahatma Gandhi and Women," in *Gender in World Religions*, ed. Arvind Sharma, Pamela D. Stewart, Katherine K. Young, Paul A. Nathanson (Montreal: McGill University, 1994), 5:1–27.

22. Kripalani, *Tagore*, 247.

23. Erik Erikson, *Gandhi's Truth* (New York: Norton., 1969), 241.

24. M. K. Gandhi, *Gandhi: An Autobiography* (Boston: Beacon Press, 1965), 400–403.

25. Ibid., 416–425.

26. David McI. Gracie, ed., *Gandhi and Charlie: The Story of a Friendship* (Cambridge, Mass.: Cowley Publications, 1989), 54.

27. Judith Brown, *Gandhi: Prisoner of Hope* (New Haven, Conn.: Yale University Press, 1989), 128–136.

28. *CW*, 14:162–163; 163, fn. 2.

29. Ibid., 15:496, app. I.

30. Kripalani, *Tagore*, 266; *CW*, 15:346, and fn. 1.

31. Kripalani, *Tagore*, 290, fn. 25.

32. P. C. Roy Choudhury, *Gandhi and His Contemporaries* (New Delhi: Sterling, 1972), 216.

33. R. K. Prabhu and Ravindra Kelekar, eds., *Truth Called Them Differently (Tagore–Gandhi Controversy)* (Ahmedabad: Navjivan Publishing House, 1961), 41–73; *Modern Review* (October 1921): 423–433; and *CW*, 21:287, and fn. 1.

34. Prabhu and Kelekar, *Truth Called Them Differently*, 19–23; and *CW*, 20:539–541.

35. Prabhu and Kelekar, *Truth Called Them Differently*, 28–29.

36. Mool Chand, *Nationalism and Internationalism of Gandhi, Nehru, and Tagore* (New Delhi: M. N. Publishers, 1989), 131.

37. Ibid., 138.

38. *CW,* 28:129.

39. Gracie, *Gandhi and Charlie,* 97–98.

40. Romain Rolland, *Mahatma Gandhi,* trans. Catherine Groth (New York: Century, 1924), 102; and Kalyan Kundu, Sakti Bhattacharaya, and Kalyan Sircar, eds., *Rabindranath Tagore and the British Press, 1912–1941* (London: The Tagore Centre, 1990), 113.

41. *CW,* 16:60–61; 18:279–284; 19:102–107; 22:225–226; 40:67–68.

42. Rajendra Verma, *Rabindranath Tagore: Prophet against Totalitarianism* (Bombay: Asia Publishing House, 1964), 561.

43. Brown, *Gandhi,* 155.

44. *CW,* 20:161–64.

45. Prabhu and Kelekar, *Truth Called Them Differently,* 15.

46. Dutta and Robinson, *Selected Letters,* 259.

47. *The Modern Review* (October 1921): 423–433.

48. Anthony Parel, ed., *Gandhi: Hind Swaraj* (Cambridge: Cambridge University Press, 1997), xl.

49. Ibid., liv.

50. Kripalani, *Tagore,* 201.

51. Ibid., 290.

52. Erikson, *Gandhi's Truth,* 397.

53. Brown, *Gandhi,,* 164.

54. *CW,* 21:287–291.

55. Ibid.

56. Ibid.

57. Rolland, *Mahatma Gandhi,* 109; and Kripalani, *Tagor* , 296.

58. Kripalani, *Tagore,* 292; and *CW,* 21:83, 165–166.

59. Kripalani, *Tagore,* 292.

60. Ibid., 293.

61. Ira G. Zepp Jr., "The Feminine in the Works of Rabindranath Tagore" in *Rabindranath Tagore: American Interpretations,* 2nd ed., ed. Ira G. Zepp Jr. (Calcalutta: Writer's Worship, 1991), 184.

62. Marjorie Sykes, trans. *Three Plays: Rabindranath Tagore* (London: Oxford University Press, 1970), 9–72.

63. *CW,* 21:3.

64. Sisirkumar Ghose, *Rethinking Tagore: Three Lectures* (Mysore: University of Mysore, 1982), 4.

65. *CW,* 25:84.

66. *CW,* 28:482–484.

67. Ibid., 425–430.

68. Choudhury, *Gandhi and his Contemporaries,* 217.

69. Dutta and Robinson, *Selected Letters,* 359–360, 364–366.

70. Ibid., 322.

71. Ibid., 320–321.

72. Ibid., 417, 430; *CW*, 55:311–312, 349 (fn. 1); 451–452.

73. Dutta and Robinson, *Selected Letters*, 424–427; *CW*, 55:92 and fn. 1.

74. *CW*, 27:172–173.

75. *The Modern Review* (March 1927): 273–275.

76. Choudhury, *Gandhia and His Contemporaries*, 218.

77. *CW*, 53:363; 55:92; Dutta and Robinson, *Selected Letters*, 422, 424.

78. Verma, *Rabindranath Tagore*, 62; Dutta and Robinson, *Selected Letters*, 536–538.

79. *CW*, 69:96–99, app. 6 and 12.

80. Kripalani, *Tagore*, 380–381; Choudhury, *Gandhi and His Contemporaries*, 220.

81. *CW*, 64:381, 410–411.

82. Ibid., 71:220–221.

83. Ibid., 290–291.

84. Ibid., 76:117.

85. Ibid., 74:218.

86. Dutta and Robinson, *Selected Letters*, 538–540.

87. Louis Fischer, *The Life of Mahatma Gandhi* (New York: Harper and Brothers, 1950), 128.

88. Quoted in Kripalani, *Tagore*, 293.

89. Ibid., 321; *CW*, 28:482–484.

90. Kripalani, *Tagore*, 399.

Part II

Critiques of Gandhi by Groups

6

The Hindu Mahasabha and Gandhi

Ronald Neufeldt

Introduction

The recent violence against Christians in Gujarat, Madhya Pradesh, and Orissa has resulted in a prolonged debate over the wisdom and effects of proselytization and conversion. Not surprisingly, Gandhi's negative views concerning proselytization have at times been quoted with favor by spokespersons for groups such as the VHP (Vishva Hindu Parishad).[1] Such co-opting of the views of Gandhi might lead one to believe that he and the Hindutva forces in his day got along, that there was a sort of meeting of minds between them. Nothing could be further from the truth. If one takes groups such as the Hindu Mahasabha and the Rashtriya Swayam Sevak Sangh as representing the thinking of the Hindu Right, or Hindu nationalism in Gandhi's day, they were poles apart from Gandhi in their thinking on most issues, and in their vision for an independent India.

My concern in this chapter is to analyze the critique of Gandhi by the Hindu Mahasabha particularly as this is represented in the writings of V. D. Savarkar, the president of the Hindu Mahasabha from 1937 to 1942. Arguably it is under the leadership of Savarkar that the Hindu Mahasabha exhibits its most explicit and virulent critique of Gandhi. Savarkar's book *Hindutva*, in effect, became the foundation for the ideology of the Hindu Mahasabha and the Hindutva forces from the period of Bhai Parmanand's presidency of the Mahasabha (1933–1937) to the present. While the ideas for Hindu nationalism and anti-Congress tendencies in the Hindu Mahasabha predate the presidency of Parmanand, as Kenneth Jones points out, it was under the presidency of Parmanand that these ideas were made explicit as driving forces in the Hindu Mahasabha.[2] These ideas had been expressed as early as 1923 by Savarkar in his *Hindutva* and by B. S. Moonje, who preceded Parmanand as president of the Mahasabha and who had pushed for a

militant Hindu nationalism in opposition to the Congress.[3] Once militant
Hindu nationalism and an anti-Congress stance became explicit in its pro-
gram the Hindu Mahasabha became a political party in opposition to the
Congress. At issue were Congress, or Gandhist, approaches to the British,
India's fight for Independence, the business of nation building, and the place
of minorities on India's political and religious landscape.

While my focus in this chapter will be the critique of Gandhi or Gandhism as this is presented in *Hindutva* and in *Hindu Rashtra Darshan* (the
collection of Savarkar's Presidential Addresses to the Hindu Mahasabha), it
should be kept in mind that both Moonje and Parmanand had actively supported Savarkar's views during their respective presidencies. In effect, the
ideas of Savarkar became official ideology and policy for the Hindu Mahasabha arguably before Savarkar assumed the presidency. It should also be
noted that the Hindu Mahasabha had not always been anti-Congress or anti-
Gandhi. Accordingly, before dealing with Savarkar and his critique of Gandhi
I wish to provide a brief overview of the shifts in Mahasabha policy from support of Congress and Gandhi to opposition to Congress and Gandhi.[4]

THE HINDU MAHASABHA BEFORE SAVARKAR

According to Kenneth Jones the Hindu Mahasabha began in 1915 with the All
India Hindu Conference held at Hardwar. It is the case that Hindu Sabhas had
sprung up as early as the late nineteenth and early twentieth centuries in response to British colonialism, the founding of the Muslim League, and concern
over the secular nationalism of the Congress.[5] These no doubt served as models for the All India Hindu Mahasabha. B. N. Pandey, for example, sees the beginning of the Hindu Mahasabha in the establishment of the Hindu Sabha in
northern India in 1910.[6] Certainly Motilal Nehru, in a letter to Jawaharlal
Nehru, expressed the opinion that the establishment of the Hindu Sabha 1910
was an all-India affair that would turn out to undermine Congress concerns.

> Another new feature of the Congress week has been that it has given birth to
> an All India Hindu Sabha which in my opinion will not only minimize all
> chance of the Hindu-Mohammedan Committee doing any good but sap the
> foundation of the Congress itself. I opposed the formation of this Sabha as
> strongly as I could and had the satisfaction of bringing round to my view
> men like B. N. Bose and S. N. Banerjee, but the great majority of the so-
> called leaders in upper India, especially those of the Punjab, all worked
> themselves to a high pitch and could not be made to listen to reason.[7]

Nehru's concerns notwithstanding, the Hindu Mahasabha in its early years was not anti-Congress in orientation. For example, the All India Hindu Conference held in 1915 was concerned with promoting and protecting Hindu interests. However, there is nothing in the goals of the conference of the later militant and anti-Congress approach of the Hindu Mahasabha. These goals were:

1. to promote greater union and solidarity among all sections of the Hindu community and to unite them as closely as parts of one organic whole;

2. to promote education among members of the Hindu community;

3. to ameliorate and improve the condition of all classes of the Hindu community;

4. to protect and promote Hindu interests whenever and wherever it may be necessary;

5. to promote good feelings between Hindus and other communities in India and to act in a friendly way with them, and in loyal co-operation with the Government;

6. generally to take steps for promoting religious, moral, educational, social and political interests of the community.[8]

That the Hindu Mahasabha wished to cooperate not only with the British government but also with the Congress is indicated by the decisions made at the 1921 meeting at Hardwar. The name of the organization was formally changed to Akhil Bharat Hindu Mahasabha and the constitution was changed to align the organization with Gandhi's Non-cooperation movement.[9] However, reports of anti-Hindu riots, looting, forced conversions, rape, kidnaping, killing, and desecration of Hindu temples coming from Malabar, Multan, and Saharanpur from 1921 to 1923 resulted in a call for support of *suddhi* to reclaim Hindus lost to Islam at the 1923 and 1924 meetings, a call supported by the then-President Pandit Malaviya.[10]

Nonetheless, the growing anxiety over the future of the Hindu communities in the 1920s did not push the Mahasabha into taking an overt political stance against Congress and Gandhi. Indeed, Lajpat Rai, president from 1925 to 1927, given his commitment to an Indian nationalism beyond the boundaries of religious communities, was against having the Mahasabha enter the political arena. His concerns were the need for Hindu unity, the removal of untouchability, and the improvement of the conditions of Hindu women. To be sure, he called for unity among Hindus, but given his commitment to Indian nationalism, this appeal did not carry the political meaning that such appeals were to have later in Hindu Mahasabha rhetoric.[11]

While outright opposition to Congress did not materialize until 1932, a more militant approach for the Hindu Mahasabha was initiated by Moonje who assumed the presidency from 1927 to 1933. He saw no point to Congress politics, particularly in the business of protection for the Hindu community in the face of Muslim aggression and the suppression of Hindu rights in Muslim princely states.[12] This more militant stance was converted into an explicit support for Hindu nationalism and an overt political stance against Congress under the presidency of Parmanand. Under his leadership the Mahasabha took the stance that India was to be a Hindu country with one language, one religion, one culture, and suddhi was converted to a weapon of conversion regardless of one's heritage.[13] This set the stage for the ascendancy of Savarkar and his ideas as the driving force of the Hindu Mahasabha.

It is noteworthy that there is little comment from Gandhi on the Hindu Mahasabha until 1927, the year that Moonje assumed the presidency. While Gandhi found himself in disagreement with Moonje over issues such as untouchability, suddhi, and nationalism, he also supported the idea of organizing the Hindu community.[14] By 1933 Gandhi's attitude became less ambiguous, in that he referred to Mahasabha tactics as vicious.[15] In a letter written in 1941 he stated that "very few, if any, members of the Hindu Mahasabha are believers in non-violence."[16] Singled out in particular were Moonje, Parmanand, and Savarkar. For his part Savarkar saw Gandhi as a significant, albeit misguided, adversary in the struggle for India's independence.

SAVARKAR AND THE HINDU MAHASABHA

The relationship between Savarkar and Gandhi was a long one going back to Savarkar's student years in England from 1906 to 1910. Savarkar had come to England in 1906 on a scholarship established by Shyamji Krishnavarma. Krishnavarma had come to England in 1879 for liberal arts and legal studies. In England he became involved in agitation for home rule, establishing a Home Rule Society in London in 1905 and *The Indian Sociologist*, a journal dedicated to the cause of Home Rule.[17] Krishnavarma also established a number of scholarships and fellowships to assist promising young Indian men to come "to Europe and America for training in the theory and practice of violent revolution."[18] Savarkar came to England with the help of the one of these scholarships—the Shivaji Scholarship—having been recommended for the scholarship by Bal Gangadhar Tilak. In England Savarkar stayed at India House, a residence established by Krishnavarma for Indian expatriates and a recruiting place for the revolutionary cause. Gandhi himself stayed at India House on a visit to England in 1906 and shared a platform with Savarkar in 1909, an occasion on which he introduced Savarkar. In a letter written in 1921 Gandhi referred to this meeting and to Savarkar as a revolutionary.[19]

This reference to Savarkar's revolutionary activity points to an early disagreement between Savarkar and Gandhi, a disagreement that was to color their relationship and Gandhi's attitude to the Hindu Mahasabha in the two decades before Gandhi's assassination. In support of their activities both Krishnavarma and Savarkar took the view that the *Gita* and the *Ramayana* taught *hiṁsā* (violence) rather than *ahiṁsā* (nonviolence). Gandhi took the opposite view arguing for ahiṁsā rather than hiṁsā.[20]

The revolutionary activities of Savarkar and his supporters eventually led to the assassination of Sir William Curzon-Wyllie, the ADC of the secretary of state for India, in 1909 by one Madan Lal Dhingra and the assassination of A. M. T. Jackson, the British collector of Nasik. Savarkar and his revolutionary society, the Abhinava Bharat, were implicated in both assassinations. Indeed, if Dhananjay Keer is to be believed Dhingra was not only an ardent follower of Savarkar, but may have been encouraged by Savarkar to assassinate Curzon-Wyllie.[21] In March 1910 Savarkar was arrested in London and sent to Bombay for trial.[22] There he underwent two trials, one for his revolutionary activities and the other for aiding and abetting the murder of Jackson. The result was two sentences of transportation for life in the Andaman Islands.[23]

A groundswell of opinion in favor of the release of Savarkar eventually resulted in his transfer from the Andamans to the Alipore jail, then to the Ratnagiri jail and finally to Yeravda. Savarkar was eventually released conditionally in 1924. He was not to travel outside the confines of the Ratnagiri district without permission and was not to engage publicly or privately in political activity for a period of five years.[24] In this respect, it is perhaps ironic that it was during his time in the Ratnagiri jail that Savarkar wrote *Hindutva*, a work that was political through and through and that was also to have a lasting political effect on the thinking and policies of the Hindu Mahasabha. His unconditional release came in 1937, the year he assumed the presidency of the Hindu Mahasabha.

Savarkar's return to India and his eventual release reinitiated contact with and debate between him and Gandhi over the means to achieve independence and the shape of independent India. According to Keer, there was only one meeting between the two, and that occurred in 1927.[25] Nonetheless, they were keenly aware of each other's views and activities and addressed them in their respective speeches and writings. The issues that dominated the debate were the issues of nonviolence and the relationship of the majority to the minorities in India. In both of these debates the issue of nationalism or the shape of the nation became an item of significant disagreement between the two warriors in the fight for an independent India. It is to these issues that I now turn.

HINDUTVA

I begin with a brief discussion of the main themes found in *Hindutva,* a text written in 1923, but destined to become the point of reference for much of what has been called "Hindutva" since then. It is here that we see articulated the ideas Savarkar expanded later in his presidential addresses to the annual meetings of the Hindu Mahasasabha. As the title of this work indicates Savarkar was interested in addressing what Hinduness means or, if I may state it in another way, who a real Hindu is. In the process, he addressed themes such as Hinduism, indigenousness, nationalism, minorities, and nonviolence, ideas to which he returned in his presidential addresses.

Hindutva, Savarkar claimed, is broader than the spiritual or religious history of India. It signifies the whole history of India, embracing "all departments of thought and activity of the whole Being of our Hindu race."[26] It is intrinsically tied to the word *Hindu* or the idea of Hindu consciousness. This is an idea or a consciousness that is as old as the civilization that was fashioned in India by the ancient Aryans, and is therefore, at least as old as the *Ṛg Veda* (*H* 8). The Aryans, he claimed, used the word *Hindu* in the sense of civilization or nation. Savarkar's rendition of the spread of Aryan civilization reads like an expression of manifest destiny: "Tribe after tribe of the Hindus issued from the land of their nursery and led by the consciousness of a great mission and their Sacrificial Fire that was the symbol thereof, they soon reclaimed the vast, waste and but very thinly populated lands" (*H* 10). The point of this account is, of course, to counter two claims made about the origin and meaning of the term *Hindu*: First, it refers primarily to a religious tradition or family of traditions based on the Vedas, and second, it is that this usage is of relatively recent origin. Savarkar's claim is fundamental to his argument for a Hindu Rashtra. He seemed to feel that the claim of antiquity gave to the idea of a Hindu Rashtra a sense of truth and inevitability.

The account, however, begs an important question: Why was the term not in common use in the ancient texts? He argued that the name was forgotten as new colonies and a variety of peoples were incorporated into the Aryan or Hindu culture. As this happened the term *Hindu* was replaced by regional terms. However, this changed with the coming of Rama, whose advent signaled the real birth of the Hindu people. Here, too, we see the expression of a manifest destiny, but now a destiny fulfilled.

> At last the great mission which the Sindhus had undertaken of founding a nation or a country, found and reached its geographical limit when the valorous Prince of Ayodhya made the triumphant entry in Ceylon and actually brought the whole land from the Himalayas to the seas under one sovereign sway. The day when the Horse of Victory returned to Ayodhya unchallenged and unchallengeable, the great white Umbrella of Sovereignty was unfurled over the Imperial throne of Ramachandra, the brave, Ramachandra the good, and a loving allegiance was sworn, not only by the Princes of Aryan blood but Hanuman, Sugriva, Bibhishana from the South—that day was the real birth of our Hindu People. (*H* 11–12)

The world over the people of India came to be known as "Hindus" and the land was known as "Hindusthan" (*H* 15). Moreover, the language of this developing nation was Hindusthani, one of the eldest derivatives of Sanskrit, rather than a modern imposition (*H* 41). There is in this account an appeal to an idealized past, an appeal that Anderson and Damle have noted in their account of Hindu revivalism in general.[27]

The experiment in nation building, Savarkar claimed, was almost undone by the rise of Buddhism (*H* 17–22). Here one meets with criticisms leveled later at Gandhi, sometimes in almost bitter fashion. The problem with Buddhism was its teaching of ahimsā. In Savarkar's view ahimsā was entirely unsuited for the rough and tumble world of political ambition and national and racial distinctions that drive people to do battle with each other. Ahimsā may do for a future universal human state based on universal righteousness (*H* 38) but not for the realities of the present time. The "mealy-mouthed formulas of ahimsā" simply invited invasion from hordes who could not appreciate the finer points of Hindu civilization (*H* 19). Savarkar, in fact, implied that at times Buddhism acted as a fifth column for foreign Buddhist powers that had designs on India (*H* 25).

Thankfully, the resources for the revival of the nation were at hand. They could be found in the Vedas, the system of *varnas* (hereditary occupational groupings), the Law of Manu, and the ancient records of the Indian people kept alive in the Epics and the Puranas. Savarkar's language here is instructive:

"So the leaders of thought and action of our race had to rekindle their Sacrificial Fire to oppose the sacrilegious one and to reopen the mines of Vedic fields for steel, to get it sharpened on the altar of Kali, 'the Terrible so that Mahakal—the Spirit of Time' be appeased" (H 21). The recovery of national pride resulted in one hundred years of peace and plenty broken finally by the invasion of the Muslims. Savarkar argued that the invasion served as never before to unite Hindus into a nation. The seers, statesmen, and martial heroes who rallied the people did so by appealing to Hindutva and Hindusthan. It is noteworthy that among the heroes listed the pride of place belongs to warriors and they are credited not just with the protection of the Hindu civilization but also of Hindu religion (H 45–46).

The distinction between the two terms was a deliberate one because Savarkar wanted to argue for a nationalism based on Hindu culture. Hindu civilization referred to the whole of the history of the Hindu race, while Hindu religion referred to Hinduism or those ideological systems based in some sense on the Vedas. Savarkar made the point that a person can be a Hindu without believing in the Vedas (H 81). But to be a Hindu means more than simply being a resident of India or Hindusthan (H 82). This may be a good starting point but it is not enough, for it would allow adherents of alien religions to claim that they are Hindus. Who then can claim the term as one's own? There are a number of possibilities. One may come to be recognized as a Hindu through one's defense of Hindu culture, through intermarriage, or through adopting India as motherland and holyland. But there is one important qualification: To be Hindu one must subscribe to an indigenous dharma. A foreign dharma simply will not work.

> A Hindu marrying a Hindu may lose his caste but not his Hindutva. A Hindu believing in any theoretical or philosophical system, orthodox or heterodox, provided it is unquestionably indigenous and founded by a Hindu may lose his sect but not his Hindutva—his Hinduness—because the most important essential which determines it is the inheritance of Hindu blood. Therefore all those who love the land . . . as their fatherland consequently claim to inherit the blood of the race that has evolved, by incorporation and adaptation . . . can be said to possess two of the most essential requisites of Hindutva. (H 90–91)

Savarkar went to great lengths to point out that love for India as fatherland is not enough. If it were, Christians and Muslims could be called "Hindus" and this he did not want to allow. They may love India as a fatherland, they may even observe caste rules, but India is not a holyland for them in the sense that Hindu dharma has ceased to be a salvific dharma for them. By adopting a new religion they have cast their lot with a different cultural unit and have ceased to have a loving attachment to Hindu civilization and dharma (*H* 100–101). Savarkar's language on this issue is instructive. It is the language of adulteration. Indian Christians and Muslims have become infected by an alien adulteration.[28]

This raises two significant issues. One is the business of dual loyalties, something Savarkar saw as destructive of any attempt at nation building. His view was that any minorities who love India as fatherland only cannot be completely loyal to India. The second issue is the business of conversions. As will become clear, Savarkar supported the program of suddhi, but for him this meant more than simply a religious conversion. It meant the removal of the adulteration that had occurred through the acceptance of an alien dharma.

While territory played an important role in Savarkar's explanation of Hindutva, as will became evident in his presidential addresses, one cannot stay there. To do so is the stuff of the Gandhists. As Hansen has pointed out in his study of Hindu nationalism in modern India, there are two important coordinates in Savarkar's Hindutva: territoriality and culture.[29] It should be added that this is culture with a special meaning. Hansen sees the tenets of Savarkar's nationalism as follows: the primacy of territory, the antiquity of and emotional attachment to the name Hindusthan, the unity of language (Sanskrit followed by Hindi), a corporate whole held together by shared blood and race, and a territory invested with salvific significance.[30] While I would agree with Hansen on the essentials, I would argue that the business of shared blood and race is somewhat more complex than it might appear at first glance. Otherwise, the discussion of adoption and assimilation makes no sense.

Savarkar did not address Gandhi or Gandhism directly in his explanation of Hindutva, but the issues raised were no doubt aimed at Gandhi or Gandhism. Indeed, Savarkar's biographer, Keer, suggests that *Hindutva* was, at least in part, an intense reaction to Gandhism, particularly with respect to the treatment of the antinational demands of the Muslims.[31] The themes addressed in *Hindutva* were expanded in Savarkar's presidential addresses, and in this expansion critical comments, at times scathing, were directed at Gandhi and Gandhism, particularly with respect to nonviolence and Gandhi's vision for the nation.

NONVIOLENCE

As we have seen in his articulation of Hindutva, the use of violence is a recognized and significant factor in the business of nation building, particularly for the sake of a just cause. There are, after all, echoes of manifest destiny in

Hindutva. These do not in themselves move in the direction of the justification of violence, but coupled with Savarkar's critique of ahiṁsā in Buddhism and its disastrous effect for India and in his account of the martial heroes who protected Hindu religion and dharma, these echoes take on a martial coloring. Clearly, Savarkar saw the Hindu Mahasabha as inheriting the challenge and obligation to regenerate and protect *Hindudom*, a term that is synonymous with the independence of *Hindusthan*. Part and parcel of this challenge and obligation is the recovery of the martial heritage, or the idealized past of the Hindus. If this is not clear in his appeal to the examples of martial heroes such as Shivaji, Teg Bahadur, Gobind Singh, and Jaysingh,[32] and his appeal to the epics in *Hindutva*, it becomes abundantly clear in his presidential addresses.

In the second presidential address delivered at Nagpur in 1938 he accused the British of robbing the Hindus of their martial heritage, a heritage of which it is the duty of Hindus to reclaim. That they once had it is evident from the fact that the Muslims found that they could not, in the end, vanquish the Hindus. He had high praise for the martyrs to the Hindu cause: "Thousands of our martyrs embraced death as 'Hindus' to vindicate the honour of the Hindu religion. Thousands upon thousands, princes and peasants alike, revolted and rose as Hindus under Hindu flags and fought and fell in fighting against their non-Hindu foes. Till at last Shivaji was born, the hour of Hindu triumph was struck, the day of Muslim supremacy set."[33] The approach of nonviolence to the political realities of the day was simply not on for Savarkar. Gandhi and the Congress leaders who had criticized "Shivaji and Pratap as misguided patriots because they conquered by the sword" rather than conquering by love (*HRD* 102) simply did not understand the inherent ambition of the Muslims to conquer (*HRD* 104).

That the recovery of the martial heritage of the Hindus was a priority for Savarkar and the Hindu Mahasabha is clear from Savarkar's proposals for the Hindu Mahasabha program delivered at the twenty-first session of the Mahasabha held in Calcutta in 1939. Among the proposals is one that would compel all universities, colleges, and schools to make military training compulsory and to secure the entry of students in naval, air, and land forces (*HRD* 115). This was a far cry from Gandhi's conception of appropriate education, which would have run in the opposite direction, that is, in the direction of ahiṁsā. Anderson and Damle make the point that the style of the Hindu revivalists tended to reflect an aggressive Kshatriya worldview.[34] Savarkar certainly reflected this outlook in his opposition to Gandhi.

It is in this vein that Savarkar approached India's participation in the war. For him participation was not a question of loyalty; rather, it was a question of providing military training for the Hindu youth. The sanest policy he believed was to befriend the side that serves India's interests best (*HRD* 146). It is in this context that we find some of the most scathing denunciations of Gandhi's program of ahiṁsā as Savarkar understood it. In his view Gandhi's program was "based on the monomaniacal principle of absolute non-violence (*HRD* 149) and was immoral and antihuman in the sense that it did not confront incorrigible aggression with armed resistance. He accused Gandhi of misinterpreting the ahiṁsā of the Buddhists and the Jains, of proposing a rabid ahiṁsā, an absolute ahiṁsā instead of the relative ahiṁsā that he believed had been proposed by Buddhists and Jains (*HRD* 152). Against Gandhi, Savarkar proposed the survival of the fittest arguing that absolute nonviolence is not only devoid of saintliness but is, in fact, monomaniacal senselessness (*HRD* 152). The sword, he held, was the first savior of human kind (*HRD* 151).

> What held good in man's struggle with the brute world continued to be true throughout his social struggle, the struggle of clan against clan, race against race, nation against nation. The lesson is branded on every page of human history down to the latest pages that nations which, other things equal, are superior in military strength are bound to survive, flourish and dominate while those which are militarily weak shall be politically subjected or cease to exist at all. (*HRD* 152)

Thus his call for military training at the hands of the British. The war was to be welcomed as a golden opportunity for providing to India's youth the military training necessary to allow her to protect her borders and to help her recover her rightful heritage, the heritage that was in danger of being sold for a mess of pottage, the teaching of absolute nonviolence. He wanted sense, not saintliness but, he argued, buying into militarism does not make India any less saintly than would buying into the absolute nonviolence of Gandhi. The language he used to argue for a recovery of martial heritage of the Hindus is at one and the same time the language of conversion, the language of recovery of an idealized past, and the language of male machismo: "It is in this spirit that I want all Hindus to get themselves re-animated and re-born into a military race. Manu and Shri Krishna are our law givers and Shri Rama the commander of our forces. Let us relearn the manly lessons they taught us and our Hindu nation shall prove again as unconquerable and conquering a race as we proved once when they led us" (*HRD* 154).

That machismo is at issue is clear from Savarkar's concern about ridicule. He argued that buying into Gandhi's program will get India only ridicule. In response Savarkar exercised ridicule of his own.

> If but India believes and acts in the spirit of such absolute non-violence maintaining no army, no navy or no airforce, no nation shall invade her and even if some armed nation did invade her they could easily be persuaded to fall back as soon as they are confronted by the unarmed army of our Desika Sevikas singing to the tune of the spinning-wheel musical appeals to the conscience of the invading forces. When things have come to such a pass that such quixotic souls are sent as accredited spokesmen by the credulous crowd to the round table conferences and even in foreign lands such sense-less proposals are seriously advanced by them in the name of the Indian nation itself in so many words to the merriment of the foreign statesmen and the general public in Europe and America—the time has surely come to take this doctrinal plague quite seriously and to counteract it as quickly as possible. (*HRD* 153)

In part this counteraction was a call to the Hindus to recover their martial heritage. In part it was to hold up Gandhi's principle of ahiṁsā to ridicule, conflating in the process the teaching of ahiṁsā and the symbol of the spinning wheel. Sanghatanists were called to whip up the military enthusiasm of Hindus, for this was seen to be in the best interests of the Hindus. These interests demanded that India participate in the war, for participation would bring the needed industrialization and militarization of India (*HRD* 155). That this had not happened was laid at the feet of Gandhi and his "spineless school of non-resisters" in Congress (*HRD* 155). The call for militarization and the building of a military–industrial complex became an integral part of the Hindu Mahasabha platform from 1939 to 1941. One finds repeated references to the need for militarization, military training of the youth, and a supporting industrial complex in the resolutions of the Mahasabha.[35]

Savarkar's strong words and Gandhi's equally sharp and strong response would suggest that here we have an issue between the two that was not negotiable. In Gandhi's opinion, very few, if any, of the members of the Hindu Mahasabha believed in nonviolence.[36] Indeed, he saw the commitment to violence as a justifiable part of the drive for independence as a commitment to the law of the jungle or goondaism.[37] In his own words, he would "rather die than barter the ideals of truth and non-violence for independence."[38] For his part, Savarkar saw Gandhi's commitment to nonviolence as a weak-kneed response to a situation in which the philosophy of nonviolence did not belong.

The world, after all, had not yet arrived at the stage where issues of race and national self-interest could be transcended in the development of a universal human state. The nonviolence of Gandhi was, in his view, immoral. Savarkar was consistent in seeing violence as a morally right response in certain circumstances. And, given his appeal to the Vedas, Manu, the Epics, and martial heroes of the past, to deny this was to deny the historical heritage and birthright of Hindus.

THE NATION

Equally as scathing as his comments about ahiṁsā were Savarkar's criticisms of Gandhi's ideas concerning the future shape of the nation or country. Clearly, Savarkar's critique of ahiṁsā is relevant here since he saw the teaching of ahiṁsā as entirely unsuited for the political realities that India had to deal with. There are, however, other issues involved in the shape of the nation, namely, the concept of nationalism itself, the place of minorities in the future nation, and the business of minority rights.

It is clear from Savarkar's *Hindutva* that the terms *nation* and *nationalism* were to be understood in the sense of race and blood. Race and blood, however, seemed to be construed in a broader sense than one might expect. One could become Hindu and be seen as having Hindu blood by way of assimilation or adoption. The terms *race* and *blood* should not, therefore, be taken in the literal sense. They refer to the adoption of a way of life, a whole civilization, and the willingness to defend that civilization. This Savarkar argued is quite different from Gandhi's understanding of nation.

For Savarkar, to be a nation or a people meant to have a common culture, a common language, a common history, a common religion and to claim "this Bharatbhoomi from, the Indus to the Seas as his Fatherland and Holyland" (*HRD* 8–10). This is the meaning of the term *Hindusthan*, a term that supposedly has its roots in the Vedas and was appealed to over and over again in the defense of Hindu dharma throughout India's history. The independence of India was, for Savarkar, synonymous with the establishment of Hindusthan and to have Hindusthan is to have the political independence of Hindus. This is the meaning he gave to *svarajya* (swaraj). It is a meaning shot through with a kind of machismo that Gandhi would have found abhorrent. Furthermore, Savarkar's use of the term *svarajya* was quite different from the twofold meaning given to the term by Gandhi: spiritual self-rule and political independence. Hansen, in his study of Hindu nationalism in modern India, makes the point that for Gandhi "the pursuit of God was the pursuit of swaraj for the nation, communities, and individuals."[39]

The definition of svarajya as the political independence of Hindus meant that Savarkar saw the notion of territorial independence alone as woefully inadequate for India's future. India once had territorial independence under Aurangzeb, but this had meant death for Hindus—thus the uprisings of patriots such as Shivaji. "To the Hindus independence of Hindusthan can only be worth having if that insures their Hindutva—their religious, racial and cultural identity" (*HRD* 17). To use a territorial term, the Congress idea of nation, an Indian nation, was acceptable, but only if this meant that there would be no special provisions made for minorities. Hindus must be given their due as a majority. The principle must be one man, one vote (*HRD* 18).

In principle Savarkar saw the idea of territorial unity as deeply flawed. It was, first, a product of the denationalization of India that had occurred through the introduction of Western education (*HRD* 37–39). Second, Muslims of India had never bought into the idea of a territorial unity. They wanted a nation but it must be a nation built on cultural, religious, and racial unity, in other words, a Muslim nation. Savarkar accused Congress of pushing a brand of pseudo-nationalism and of being anti-Hindu (*HRD* 73). He argued that Congress nationalism is a communal nationalism because it recognizes a majority and a minority. This flies in the face of the principle of "one man one vote," irrespective of race, caste, and creed (*HRD* 94–95). The result of the thinking of the Congress leaders is, he argued, a policy that promotes communalism and appeasement, but which Gandhi and the Congress leaders think is eminently nationalistic.

> I want you to realize the mentality and the ideology of these Hindu leaders who still happen to be at the helm of the Congress. Neither Gandhiji or Pandit Nehru, nay even Subhas Babu or Mr. Ray, who, although they do not contribute in any way to some of the above vagaries of the Gandhist school, are still votaries—can I call it victims—of the school of thought which says in so many words, "Give to the Moslems so much that they could not wish to ask for anything more." They sincerely believe that to be the crux of Nationalism and wisdom. (*HRD* 100)

As in the case of the call for militarization, the condemnation of the appeasement of Muslims as antinational and the call for Hindusthan found their way into the formal resolutions of the Hindu Mahasabha.[40]

From Gandhi's side, to equate nation or nationalism with the terms *Hindu* and *Hindusthan* was to opt for a communal vision of India. As early as 1928 he had argued with Dr. Moonje, the vice president of the Hindu Mahasabha over the proper name for the nation. He stated, "Afghans don't expect Hindus to be Mussalmans, but they expect them to be like Afghans, that is like the inhabitants of Afghanistan. The corresponding term, therefore, is Indian. For the service of India, Mussalmans, Jews, Christians should be Indians as Hindus should be Indians."[41] Whether culturally or religiously, India was not to be described as a Hindu nation. It was on this account that Gandhi wrote to the secretary of the Hindu Mahasabha objecting to the use of the national flag on Hindu temples. The Indian nation was to be open to all irrespective of race or creed.[42] For Gandhi, the origin of a religion made little difference in the project of nation building. Independence had to be independence for the masses, whether of the Hindu, Muslim, Sikh, Christian, Parsee, or Jewish variety. As Gandhi understood it the Hindu Mahasabha was a sectional organization, interested in winning benefits only for a particular community at the expense of other communities.

At issue here is the business of dual loyalties, a concern Savarkar had raised in *Hindutva* and that he addressed at length in his presidential speeches. For him it was simply impossible to be loyal to the Indian state, on the one hand, and to have a loyalty to a nonindigenous religion, on the other hand. As much as he tried to downplay the importance of religion in defining Hindu and Hindutva, here he chose not to ignore it; rather, he emphasized it.

> Whatever may happen some centuries hence, the solid fact of today cannot be ignored that religion wields mighty influence on the minds of men in Hindusthan and in the case of Mohammedans especially their religious zeal, more often than not borders on *fanaticism*! Their love towards India as their motherland is but [a] handmaid to their love for their Holyland outside India. Their faces are ever turned towards Mecca and Medina. But to Hindus Hindusthan being their Fatherland as well as their Holyland, the love they bear to Hindusthan is undivided and absolute. (emphasis in original; *HRD* 14–15)

Technically religious allegiance was not an issue as long as it did not lead to dual loyalties. One could be an atheist, a Buddhist, a Sikh, or a Jaina and still be a Hindu in the sense in which Savarkar attempted to define the term. These were, after all, judged to be Hindu in a cultural sense. The Muslims, however, were a different matter. Given the character of the Muslims, the Gandhian program of appeasement simply would not work. Muslims in Savarkar's view could not buy into even territorial allegiance given their theology, theoretical politics, and stage of development. They were still at the stage of intense religiosity (read fanaticism) and a concept of the state that divides the world into Muslims and non-Muslims. A faithful Muslim could not swear loyalty to any state that is ruled by non-Muslims, but a faithful Muslim "is called upon to do everything in his power by policy or force or fraud to convert the non-Muslim there to the Muslim faith, to bring about its political conquest by a Muslim power" (*HRD* 49). Muslims, Savarkar claimed, have a "secret urge goading (them) to transform India into a Moslem state" (*HRD* 89).

To make matters worse, Muslims were increasing their population at an alarming rate, putting in danger the Hindu majority (*HRD* 50). Indeed, the minorities were to be treated with suspicion in proportion to their numbers and their similarities to the Hindus. The Parsees were acceptable because they were most akin to the Hindus and had made India their home. Christians were culturally similar and had no extraterritorial designs but did proselytize. The Jews were not a threat given their small numbers (*HRD* 56). Muslims, given their fanaticism and their practice of forced conversions, were not to be trusted at all. The appropriate response to the proselytizing activities of Christians and Muslims was to engage in an aggressive policy of suddhi rather than the Gandhian program of appeasement and its misplaced optimism about Hindu–Muslim unity. In Savarkar's view this was the dream of naive politicians: "As it is, there are two antagonistic nations living side by side in India several infantile politicians commit the serious mistake in supposing that India is already welded into a harmonious nation, or that it could be welded thus for the mere wish to do so. These our unthinking friends take their dreams for realities" (*HRD* 24).

Clearly Gandhi was meant in the comment about infantile politicians, given his defense of Muslims and his objections to the kind of characterization of Muslims seen in Mahasabha propaganda. For Savarkar's part the need of the hour was not compromise or appeasement or the apologetic attitude of the Congress leaders, but to breathe life into the suddhi campaign. Given his definition of Hinduism and his call to reestablish the organic Hindu nation, the call for aggressive suddhi could only mean a call to increase the number of Hindu voters to counteract the growth of the Muslim population. If there were indeed two nations as Savarkar argued, then as far as he was concerned the only way to assure the reestablishment of the Hindu nation on its proper footing was an aggressive campaign of reconversion.

Gandhi, like the Hindu Mahasabha, took a dim view of the business of proselytization, particularly among the Harijans. Accordingly he called on leaders of different religions not "to compete with each other for enticing Harijans into their fold."[43] Gandhi was equally as apprehensive over the call for an aggressive suddhi campaign and condemned as vicious attempts by the Hindu Mahasabha to associate his name with suddhi activities.[44] Not only did he not share Mahasabha concerns over boosting the Hindu population through suddhi, he condemned it as yet another form of conversion. A sense of this can be seen in Gandhi's response to the Hindu Mahasabha appeal for a memorial for Swami Shraddhanand of the Arya Samaj.

> For my part I still remain unconvinced about the necessity of the *shuddhi* movement, taking *shuddhi* in the sense it is generally understood. Shuddhi of sinners is a perpetual inward performance. *Shuddhi* of those who can be identified neither as Hindus nor as Mussalmans or who have been recently declared converts but who do not know even the meaning of conversion and who want to be known definitely as Hindus is not conversion but *pray-aschitta* or penance. The third aspect of *shuddhi* is conversion properly so called. And I question its use in this age of growing toleration and enlightenment. I am against conversion whether it is known as *shuddhi* by Hindus, *tabligh* by Muslins or conversion by Christians. Conversion is a heart-process known only to and by God.[45]

By the same token Gandhi took as dim a view of Savarkar's concerns over dual loyalties and his distrust of the minority communities, particularly of the Muslims. As he understood it the Hindu Mahasabha was intent on subordinating the interests of other communities to their own, rather than protecting the interests of the minorities. He accused the Hindu Mahasabha of giving the Muslims a bad rap, of arguing that Hindus and Muslims cannot live together because most Muslims cannot be trusted.[46]

At issue here is a sharp difference about the meaning of assimilation. Gandhi did speak of absorbing "Christians, Muslims and others, as one indivisible nation, having a common interest,"[47] but the absorption he spoke of was to a higher cause, transcending the reality of the discrete communities, not subordinating these communities to another. Hansen refers to this as a romantic Orientalist idea that moves in the direction of a spiritual unity.[48] According to Anderson and Damle assimilation for Gandhi meant "a brotherhood or a confederation of communities," moreover a confederation dedicated to the nonviolent pursuit of truth.[49] Savarkar rejected both the Gandhian idea of assimilation and the nonviolent foundation on which this assimilation was built. Assimilation for him meant assimilation to a single cultural community, and the need of the hour was not nonviolence but the energism that came from the reappropriation of the martial heritage of the

Hindus. Gandhi's idea of Muslim–Hindu unity was, in Savarkar's opinion, a pipe dream.

CONCLUSION

Savarkar and Gandhi did agree on one thing: the need to struggle for and achieve independence from England. In this struggle they acknowledged each other as fellow patriots. But this was about as far as the agreement went. They disagreed sharply on the means to achieve independence, what the nation should be called, the place of minorities in the nation, and the vision for the fundamental character of the nation. The points at which there was apparent agreement are most instructive in underlining Savarkar's and the Mahasabha's opposition to Gandhi.

Both called for support of the British war effort. However, they differed sharply in the reasons for that call. For Gandhi support of the British in the war effort was a moral issue, a question of allegiance. For the Hindu Mahasabha, particularly under the leadership of Savarkar, support for the British was a utilitarian issue only. Savarkar rejected entirely the idea that India should support the war effort because India owed something to the British. To him this was mere sentiment. Participation in the war effort would assist in the industrialization of India, in the creation of ready-made armed forces, and in the recovery of the long-forgotten spirit of Hindu militancy. While Gandhi took an allegorical approach to the *Gita*, preferring to see the battle as a reference to the internal struggle between good and evil, Savarkar and those who thought like him were prone to glory in the martial aspects of the *Gita* and the Epics, seeing these as evidence for a Hindu machismo that needed to be recovered, particularly in the fight for independence and in relationship to India's Muslim neighbors.[50]

The two opposed religious proselytization, again for entirely different reasons. While Gandhi was opposed to proselytization, he was not opposed to the sharing of and dissemination of religious views. For Gandhi there really was no need for proselytization and conversion because fundamentally all religions, properly understood, taught much the same message. Nonetheless, Gandhi mistrusted Christian missionaries, seeing them as tools of British imperialism. Gauri Vishwanathan has suggested that this mistrust allowed Hindu Nationalists to make common cause with Gandhi on this issue: "In his deep scepticism about the work of missionization, Gandhi imbued Indian nationalism with a Hindu ethos that laid the groundwork for an identitarian notion of Indianness. His resistance to conversions simultaneously affirmed a Hindu past which had the power to assimilate different communities and produce a sense of oneness."[51]

Even if the support for the Hindutva program was unwitting, as Vishwanathan suggests, it must be pointed out that the concerns of Hindu Mahasabha in opposing proselytization were miles removed from Gandhi's concerns. For Savarkar and the Hindu Mahasabha, the opposition to proselytization and conversion was driven by an alternative vision for the Indian state in which the number of Hindus was of paramount importance in both a religious and a political sense. This was to be a Hindu state in which all citizens viewed India as fatherland and holyland. In such a vision there could be no room for dual loyalties, a loyalty to India, on the one hand, and a loyalty to an "alien" religion, on the other hand. There is in this language the fear of conspiracy against India, whether this is of the Christian variety or of the Muslim variety. Such language was quite foreign to Gandhi who chose to speak in terms of Indian nationalism and an India that takes seriously the concerns and even demands of its minorities. He believed in the possibility of a pan-Indian civilization that recognized multiple diversities and identities. Sumit Sarkar has argued compellingly that Gandhi's ahiṁsā "involved not just non-violence, but the assumption that human communication was possible even across the sharpest divides."[52] In short he believed in the possibility of breaking down barriers. The Hindutva ideology of Savarkar and the Mahasabha, in emphasizing India as both *pitṛbhūmi* and *puṇyabhūmi*, served to set up barriers rather than to break them down.[53]

NOTES

1. John C. B. Webster, "Gandhi and the Christians: Dialogue in the Nationalist Era," in *Hindu–Christian Dialogue: Perspectives and Encounters*, ed. Harold Coward (Maryknoll, N.Y.: Orbis Books, 1989), 81.

2. See Kenneth Jones, "Politicized Hinduism," in *Religion in Modern India*, ed. R. D. Baird (New Delhi: Manohar, 1995), 255–258.

3. Ibid., 253–255.

4. For this overview I rely heavily on Jones's treatment of the Mahasabha in "Politicized Hinduism." See also the treatment by Lise McKean, *Divine Enterprise, Gurus, and the Hindu Nationalist Movement* (Chicago: University of Chicago Press, 1996), 71–96.

5. Jones, "Politicized Hinduism," 243.

6. B. N. Pandey, ed., *The Indian National Movement, 1885–1947: Select Documents* (New York: St. Martin's, 1979), 4.

7. Quoted in Ibid., 18–19.

8. Jones, "Politicized Hinduism," 145.

9. Ibid., 247.

10. Ibid., 248–250. Malaviya assumed the presidency of the Hindu Mahasabha from 1923 to 1925.

11. Ibid., 252–253. *Śuddhi* was originally a campaign initiated by the Arya Samaj for the reconversion to Hinduism of those who had at one time left the Hindu fold for another religious community.

12. Ibid., 253–255.

13. Ibid., 255–258.

14. See Gandhi's May 14, 1927, letters to Chinai and Moonje in *The Collected Works of Mahatma Gandhi* (New Delhi: The Publications Division, Ministry of Information and Broadcasting, 1983), 33:322, 324. See also his letter to Moonje dated December 16, 1928, in *Collected Works*, 38:231–232. (Hereafter cited as *CW*.)

15. See Gandhi's letter to Nehru in *CW*, 56:167.

16. *CW*, 73:311.

17. Dhananjay Keer, *Veer Savarkar* (Bombay: Popular Prakashan, 1988), 29–30.

18. M. K. Gandhi, *Hind Swaraj and Other Writings*, ed. Anthony J. Parel (Cambridge: Cambridge University Press, 1997), xxv–xxvi.

19. *CW*, 20:104–105.

20. *CW*, 32:102.

21. Keer, *Veer Savarkar*, 52–53.

22. See ibid., 71–80.

23. See ibid., 81–92.

24. Ibid., 164.

25. Ibid., 175–177.

26. V. D. Savarkar, *Hindutva: Who Is a Hindu?* (New Delhi: Bharti Sahitya Sadan, 1989), 4. Hereafter references to this work will be cited parenthetically in the text as *H* followed by page(s).

27. Walter K. Anderson and Shridhar D. Damle, *The Brotherhood in Saffron: The Rashtriya Swayam Sevak Sangh and Hindu Revivalism* (New Delhi: Vistar Publications, 1987), 11.

28. See Savarkar's discussion in *H*, 91–92.

29. Thomas Blom Hansen, *The Saffron Wave: Democracy and Hindu Nationalism in Modern India* (Princeton, N.J.: Princeton University Press, 1999), 77.

30. Ibid., 78.

31. Keer, *Veer Savarkar*, 162.

32. See Savarkar's discussion in *H*, 47–70.

33. V. D. Savarkar, *Hindu Rashtra Darshan*, (Bombay: Veer Savarkar Prakashan, 1992), 33. Hereafter references to this work will be cited parenthetically in the text as *HRD* followed by page(s).

34. Anderson and Damle, *The Brotherhood in Saffron*, 11.

35. See Sobhag Mathur, *Hindu Revivalism and the Indian National Movement: A Documentary Study of the Ideal and Policies of the Hindu Mahasabha, 1939–45* (Jodhpur: Kusumanjali Prakashan, 1996), 110–111, 119, 121, 136.

36. See Gandhi's response to the secretary of the Bengal Hindu Mahasabha who had suggested a satygraha campaign against actions taken by the Muslim League minster of Bengal in *CW*, 73:311.

37. Ibid., 74:9, 75.

38. Ibid., 88:90.

39. Hansen, *The Saffron Wave*, 45.

40. See Mathur, *Hindu Revivalism*, 108–110, 112, 118, 183, 237.

41. *CW*, 38:231–232.

42. Ibid., 74:350.

43. Ibid., 63:235.

44. Ibid., 56:167.

45. Ibid., 32:515.

46. Ibid., 89:287.

47. Ibid., 56:384.

48. Hansen, *The Saffron Wave*, 45.

49. Anderson and Damle, *The Brotherhood in Saffron*, 20.

50. See Parel, *Hind Swaraj*, xxvii; and *CW*, 32:102.

51. Gauri Vishwanathan, "Literacy and Conversion in the Discourse of Hindu Nationalism," *Race and Class* 42, no. 1 (2000): 3.

52. See Sumit Sarkar, "Indian Nationalism and the Politics of Hindutva," in *Making India Hindu*, ed. David Ludden (New Delhi: Oxford University Press, 1996), 274. Yogendra K. Malik and V. B. Singh make a similar argument in *Hindu Nationalists in India: The Rise of the Bharatiya Janata Party* (New Delhi: Vistar Publications, 1994), 1–27.

53. For an excellent treatment of the consequences of the ideology of Savarkar and the Hindu Mahasabha, see McKean, *Divine Enterprise*, 71–96.

7

Gandhi and the Christian Community

TIMOTHY GORRINGE

Although there is an ancient church within India that dates back to at least the third century c.e., and although there were Portuguese, Jesuit, and Lutheran missions that long predated British rule, it remains true that the expansion of Christian numbers in India was in large part bound up with the Empire. For this reason, from the 1830s onward, *Christian* came to be indelibly associated with *colonial*. This meant that no Nationalist could take an impartial view of Christianity, and, conversely, both missionaries, and the church as a whole, stood divided on "the national question." When the Montague Commission was collecting evidence on Indian self-rule in 1917 the Christian community published a pamphlet with the title "Indian Christian Objections to Self-Government in India." Indian Christians were, to begin with, alarmed at the prospect of losing the privileges that came with British rule. In 1940 Nehru noted in the newspaper that was the organ of the Indian Christian community, *The Guardian*, "a tendency for Indian Christians to consider themselves as a class apart and cut off from the great majority of the Indian community." There was, he said, "a certain psychological friction" between Indian Christians and others, caused by "the political association of Christianity with foreign domination."[1] Independence, he was sure, would cure this problem. Gandhi believed that becoming a Christian "denationalized" a person. "The moment a person turns Christian," he wrote in the same year, "he becomes a 'sahib log.' He almost changes his nationality. He gets a job, a position which he could not otherwise have got, he adopts foreign clothes and ways of living. He cuts himself off from his own people and begins to fancy himself a limb of the ruling class."[2] This was clearly Gandhi's deeply felt view, and generous friendships with missionaries never changed it. The American missionary Stanley Jones reports a conversation with Gandhi in which he sketched out a picture of an Indian Christian church without a distinct political identity, existing only as a moral, spiritual, and social entity. Gandhi supposedly responded that in such a case "most of the objections to Christianity would fade out of the mind of India." However, when Jones published the conversation a denial was issued on Gandhi's behalf.[3]

There is no doubt that many missionaries were, to some extent, to blame for the "psychological friction" Nehru speaks of. "Christian missions have fought shy of the national question until recently" wrote Eddy Asirvatham in 1938. "The prevailing point of view amongst them is that the British Government has on the whole been a good government and that, whatever its faults . . . it deserves our sympathy in the constant efforts it is making at present to confer self government upon the people of India. . . . They easily forget that no foreign government ever rules a subordinate people out of purely altruistic motives."[4] Stephen Neill, bishop of Tiruneveli during the latter years of the raj, confirms this. The attitude not only of British missionaries but of those of other countries, he wrote, was conservative.

> They greatly valued the peace and order brought by the British raj, the uninterrupted tranquillity in which they could carry on their work. . . . A number of missionaries felt themselves . . . attracted by the Indian liberals, men who had drunk deeply at the founts of the English liberal traditions, and were prepared to move slowly in the direction of a genuine democracy. . . . Indian Christians tended still to be little interested in politics. They belonged for the most part to the communities which had been trained over many centuries to think that their first duty was to obey.[5]

"A number" of missionaries were attracted by Indian Liberals (a euphemism for Nationalists). Were the majority? There were certainly missionaries who so identified with the raj that they reproached Gandhi with being a troublemaker and could not understand why he did not appreciate the blessings of British rule.[6] In 1922 the editors of the *Madras Christian College Magazine* "sought in vain for anything positive or constructive" in Gandhi's program, concluding that he was "an anarchist at heart" and even "an apostle of lawlessness."[7] S. K. George was of the view that Christian missionaries were not too happy about Gandhi's testimony to the essential soundness and practicality of Christian teaching "because he is not a Christian in their sense of the term."[8] Others wondered whether Gandhi had sufficiently appreciated from the New Testament the fact that nonviolence ended up in death, and that it was therefore not a policy which could be recommended.[9]

There was, therefore, on the part of some missionaries, and perhaps of the wider Christian community, some distrust of Gandhi or hostility toward him. On the other hand, many Christian leaders, both Indian and expatriate, were committed to the Nationalist struggle, and therefore to Gandhi, from a very early stage. People such as K. T. Paul, general secretary of the YMCA in India, sought Gandhi out, won his friendship, and passionately embraced nationalism. Opposition to this stance by missionaries in Calcutta finally compelled him to resign his job, just two years before his death.[10] Bishop Azariah of Dornakal, the best-known and the most effective of the Indian bishops, wrote in his Diocesan magazine in September 1942, after Gandhi's arrest for the "Quit India" agitation, "With trembling conviction Indian Christians see that they must be on the side of India's freedom. If China, Japan, Persia and Turkey can hold up their heads as independent nations in the eye of the world their motherland should certainly have the same status. With millennia of culture and civilization . . . with its invincible God-consciousness—their dear India, they feel, deserves to be free India."[11] The following year the president and secretaries of the All-India Christian Council telegraphed the viceroy: "Respectfully request Government to release Gandhi unconditionally in order to further reconciliation. This will be widely favoured by Christian opinion supportive to Government."[12] "Supportive" here did not mean that British rule was endorsed. The same conference had passed a resolution giving its "unqualified support" to the idea of a free and independent India, and looked to the time, after the war, when "all empire ideologies should be eliminated as a menace to the future peace of the world."[13]

What especially distinguished the Christian response to Gandhi was the tendency to interpret him primarily as a religious personality, and indeed to understand him in relation to Christ.[14] Even though Gandhi met his death at the hands of a Hindu chauvinist, many Hindus understood Gandhi in the same way, if Stanley Jones is to be believed. Among Jones's Hindu interlocutors were those who saw in Gandhi a second Christ:

Again and again Hindus rise in my meetings and ask if I do not think that Mahatma Gandhi is a Christlike man. I usually reply that I cordially differ from him in a good many things, nevertheless do think in some things he is a very Christlike man indeed. I have had them reply that they would go much further: they believed he was the incarnation of Christ. A Hindu gave utterance to the same thought when listening to a preacher preaching in the bazaar in North India on the second coming of Christ: "Why do you preach on the second coming of Christ? He has already come—he is here—

Gandhi" . . . the point is that Gandhi is their ideal, and they are identifying that ideal with Jesus.[15]

What we may call the "religious reading" of Gandhi was shared by missionaries and Indian Christians alike. The Indian lawyer and lay theologian P. Chenchiah, for example, described the Independence struggle as a quest for national salvation. Traditional religion, he wrote, has sought the salvation of the soul but led by Gandhi, we seek the soul of the nation. The faith of Mahatmaji involves three principles:

> (1) That religion, religious discipline, religious power, are intended to build up free states and societies and individuals. In other words, that religion should not exhaust itself in promises about the future, in dogma and ritual. It should not discard life. If it does not serve life it should be discarded. (2) That Jesus in his teachings on the Sermon on the Mount and his sufferings on the Cross, placed in the hands of men a new weapon of defence and offence far more powerful than force and coercion and oppression. (3) That the use of Ahiṁsā requires a well tempered and disciplined mind. It is the weapon of the courageous and not of the weakling.[16]

Indian Christians, said Chenchiah, were "intensely concerned" with Gandhi's project to fashion a national program on the principles of the Sermon on the Mount, "compendiously described as the doctrine of Ahiṁsā." Gandhi tried to detach Christian principles from the person of Jesus and make them instances of social and political reconstruction. Far from this being a problem, "The Christian church in India has been following this movement with hope, joy and fervent prayer as the first application of Christian principles to units larger than the individual. . . . The Indian Christian sends his prayer to the throne of grace that he will succeed."[17] Chenchiah had no desire to claim Gandhi for the church. He saw in him a "mixed product of the Gospel of Christ and the message of the Gita. Both Jesus and Sri Krishna may recognise in him a disciple."[18]

Another Indian Christian whose career suffered for his support of the national cause, and of Gandhi in particular, was S. K. George. He was forced to resign from his teaching position in Calcutta in 1932 for supporting civil disobedience, and could not thereafter find a job within the church. Like Chenchiah he saw Gandhi's satyagraha as "Christianity in action." "Not to recognise in him the greatest ally of essential Christianity in India," he wrote, "the greatest worker for the kingdom of God in the world today, is to betray gross inability to discern the working of God's Spirit."[19]

He put Gandhi alongside Lao Tse, the Buddha, and Socrates (his order) as "a peak of human achievement which it would be folly for the race to ignore."[20] In seeking to describe him he went first to Isaiah 53, the Suffering Servant passage, and then to Rudyard Kipling's *If*. Looking not only to India, but to what was happening in Germany in 1939, he believed that if democracy and justice were to survive it could only be through religion. "The way to it may be shown by Mahatma Gandhi, the way of suffering love, love resisting evil, bearing upon itself the consequence of evil, but refusing to yield to it, or to repay evil with evil, but overcoming it."[21] Even more than Chenchiah, George is not concerned with a Christian critique of Gandhi, but with what Christians have to learn from him. "He goes far beyond the Christian and Groupist preacher," he wrote, "in organizing resistance to collective injustice; but unlike the secularist the power with which he would challenge entrenched injustice is the power of the Spirit, the power of love."[22]

We have seen that there were missionaries, perhaps even the majority, who were hostile to Gandhi, or skeptical of him. There were a number, however, who were very close to him, and some were even disciples. Foremost among these was the person Gandhi described as "more than a brother to me": Charles Freer Andrews.[23]

Andrews had come to India with the Cambridge Brotherhood in 1904, and at once drew attention to himself by attacking British racism. So celebrated did he become for this stand that Gopāl Krishna Gokhale asked him to go to South Africa in 1913 to join Gandhi's struggle. Andrews answered the call, and this began a unique friendship. Like Gandhi, Andrews was an activist, engaged in struggles not only in India but in Fiji and Africa as well. Although he believed that contact with Britain had been of benefit to India, support for the Independence movement was completely natural to him.[24] "Independence," he said in an address to Calcutta students in 1921, "complete and perfect independence for India, is a religious principle with me because I am a Christian."[25] Andrews and Gandhi were, then, political allies, but their friendship was based on religion not on political affinity.

When we look at Andrews's *What I Owe to Christ*, published in 1932, we find ourselves engaged in a structure of feeling that has more in common with the thirteenth-century Franciscans than it has with the present day.[26] Andrews was intellectually first rate. He was offered fellowships at three Cambridge colleges, and could easily have had an academic career. He was also politically well informed, and no naif.[27] In his sermons he frequently attacked racism and imperialism. He practiced what liberation theologians were later to call "solidarity with the poor," and spent his life in pursuit of freedom for indentured labor, and for overcoming all racial and caste division. And yet his writings are absolutely free of the rhetoric of political militancy. In them there are no villains and he knows no hermeneutic of suspicion. He saw only good in others and this generosity of spirit led him to the most total love and support for both Rabindranath Tagore and Gandhi, with both of whom he performed *pranam* on his first meeting—to the horror of his British guides in South Africa.[28] He differed from Gandhi on a number of points, as we shall see, but his "spirit of love," to use William Law's phrase, must be understood as the essential presupposition for their conversation. Andrews was perhaps Gandhi's closest friend. After Andrews's death Gandhi wrote, in *Harijan*, "Nobody knew Charlie Andrews as well as I did. Gurudev was *guru*—master—to him. When we met in South Africa we simply met as brothers and remained as such to the end. There was no distinction between us. It was not a friendship between an Englishman and an Indian. It was an unbreakable bond between two seekers and servants."[29] To one another they were "Mohan" and "Charlie." "Our hearts met from the first moment we saw one another," Andrews wrote, "and they have remained united by the strongest ties of love ever since."

> To be with him was an inspiration which awakened all that was best in me, and gave me a high courage, enkindled and enlightened by his own. . . . In him, from the very first, I felt instinctively that there had come into the world, not only a new religious personality of the highest order, moving the hearts of men and women to incredible sacrifice, but also a new religious truth, which yet was not new, but old as the stars and the everlasting hills. His one message was that long-suffering and redeeming love is alone invincible.[30]

Andrews saw in Gandhi a living out of true Christianity. Gandhi, he said, took "the true Christian position—suffering wrongdoing patiently and overcoming evil by good." Gandhi's personality was "so entirely 'Hindu,' and yet so supremely 'Christian.' It seemed to point to an organic unity, beneath the outward differences of religion, which needed to be traced, if mankind was ever to become one in spirit."[31] Gandhi lived out the Sermon on the Mount. "What he called Satyagraha, or Truth Force, was obviously Christian."[32]

It was precisely this profound friendship that enabled Andrews to disagree deeply with Gandhi from time to time, the closest we get to a full-scale, sympathetic, Christian critique. Analyzing their discussion over twenty years one can find five points of conflict.[33] First, and most important, Andrews never accepted Gandhi's views on caste. "I have always recognised," wrote Gandhi in 1920, "that there are fundamental differences between you and me on the caste question. . . . Caste I consider a useful institution if properly regulated. Untouchability is an evil against God and humanity. I would purify the former, I would destroy the latter . . . rid this caste of its impurities, and you will find it to be a bulwark of Hinduism and an institution whose roots are embedded deep in human nature."[34] This was something Andrews, with his roots in the incarnationalism and labor politics of the Christian Social Union, could not accept. To Andrews, caste was every bit as bad as white racism. "We must honestly and fairly and squarely face the non-Brahman movement and all that it implies," he wrote to Gandhi. "This kind of thing appears to me every whit as bad as the religion of the 'white race' which is being proclaimed in Africa today."[35] Gandhi returned to the issue the following year:

> I look at the problem as an Indian and a Hindu, you as an Englishman and a Christian. You look at it with the eyes of an observer, I as an affected and afflicted party. . . . That Hinduism considers it a "sin" to touch a portion of human beings because they are born in a particular environment! I am engaged as a Hindu in showing that it is not a sin and that it is a sin to consider that touch [is] a sin. It is a bigger problem than that of gaining Indian independence but I can tackle it better if I gain the latter on the way.[36]

Gandhi's appeal to ethnic difference here is, of course, absolutely tendentious, as the disagreement with Ambedkar shows, and this is perhaps reflected in the tetchiness of his response to missions among Untouchables. The extremely high proportion of Christians from the Untouchable community led, even at this period, to real differences in view between Gandhi and Indian Christians. Gandhi's occasional lapses, when he urged that missions to Untouchables should not be pursued because Untouchables did not have "the mind and intelligence" to understand an appeal to the gospel, were incompatible with fundamental Christian presuppositions.[37]

Second, Andrews often shared with Tagore a hesitancy about Gandhi's degree of militancy. When Gandhi decided on the policy of noncooperation after the Amritsar massacre, Tagore disapproved. He felt that it generated an unhealthy spirit of violent nationalism. Andrews tried to mediate between Gandhi and Tagore, and wrote to him, of one of Gandhi's speeches:

> It is a great speech as he delivered it. It has all the call back to simplicity and frugality and sacrifice which makes his high appeal so powerful. But somehow it is, like war itself, a thrusting back into the bare primitive, not a grasping of the richness of the future which awaits mankind. It seems to miss all that art means and music means, and song. I know that Mahatmaji would

say "Quite so: but are we not at war?" I know there is truth there, and we
must be ready to strip life bare, at times. But *quite* bare? No![38]

In reply to this critique, Gandhi insisted that "[o]ur non cooperation is neither with the English nor with the West—it is with material civilization and its
attendant greed and exploitation of the weak. . . . The hungry millions ask for
one poem, invigorating food."[39]

Gandhi always made clear that he had hatred for no Englishmen, and
for no individuals.[40] His relations with the prison officials who "looked after"
him from time to time are incomparable models of courtesy and goodwill.
One of Andrews's few real disagreements with Gandhi was over the campaign
to burn foreign cloth. Andrews felt deeply for the Lancashire mill operatives,
who he knew were also poor. He wrote, "The picture of your lighting that
great pile of beautiful and delicate fabrics shocked me intensely . . . destroying in the fire the noble handiwork of one's fellow men and women, of one's
brothers and sisters abroad, saying it would be 'defiling' to use it—I cannot
tell you how different all this appears to me!" Gandhi defended himself
calmly and robustly. He wrote back to Andrews:

> The central point in burning is to create an utter disgust with ourselves that
> we have thoughtlessly decked ourselves at the expense of the poor. Yes, I see
> nothing wrong in making it a sin to wear cloth that has meant India's degra-
> dation and slavery. What I am trying to do is to perform a surgical operation
> with a hand that must not shake. I would respect the wonderful love put
> into cloth prepared by a sister in Europe, but I could not even then recon-
> cile myself to the use of foreign cloth even as one must not take at the hands
> of one's mother indigestible food given in ignorant love.[41]

Curiously, in another area, Andrews's pacifism appears as more consistent than that of Gandhi. Prior to the Amritsar massacre, and to British attitudes to the Turkish caliphate after the First War, which changed Gandhi's
views of the British Empire profoundly, Gandhi had been prepared to encourage recruitment for the war. This, wrote Andrews, "is one of the points where
I have found myself in painful disagreement." At the same time we have to
recognise that "there can be no two opinions concerning the entire nobility of
his . . . action in one great Passive resistance movement after another, wherein
he entirely abjured the use of any physical force to attain his spiritual end."[42]

Third, and related, Andrews joined with Tagore in warning of the danger of self-righteousness in campaigns of nonviolent resistance. In the same
letter protesting the cloth burning Andrews wrote, "Do you know I almost

fear now to wear the khaddar that you have given me, lest I should appear to be judging other people, as a Pharisee would, saying, 'I am holier than thou.' I never felt like this before."[43] In an echo of Paul's argument in Galatians, Andrews charged Gandhi with seeming to set up a new religion with spinning and wearing khaddar as the essential factor. "Why should I be specially concerned with whether so and so wears khaddar or foreign made cloth?" he wrote. "All I principally want to know is what the man is morally worth. Christ wanted us, in judging a person, to be guided by his heart and not by his outward appearance." Gandhi's answer, extraordinarily at this point, is "[t]here is a difference between Hindu and Christian ideas." Andrews went on, "You might as well say that if I ate a particular diet I would gain spiritually. I simply can't understand that." He instanced his mentor, Bishop Westcott, a meat eater, but still a truly spiritual man. Gandhi replied, "Hard cases make bad law. You can't preach to the generality of people asking them to eat what they like, and yet continue to believe that they are pure."

Andrews's objection to the "religion of spinning" was chiefly based on his picture of Tagore, sitting up at midnight to do his spinning. "We are all fitted for different kinds of work," he protested. "Why make the wearing of khaddar and spinning a *religious* duty?" Gandhi can only fall back on assertion: "Well, it must be a religious duty. Are you sure every Indian will occupy himself usefully in the service of the country simply if I cease to insist on making spinning a religious duty?"[44]

Andrews was similarly unsure about Gandhi's use of the fast. He was completely behind the 1921 fast, undertaken as "atonement" for Indian violence, but not of the 1932 fast "unto death," designed to block the granting of separate voting rights to Untouchables. The weapon of fasting, wrote Andrews on November 10, 1932, "if it is not uniquely used for a God-given opportunity will certainly be used by fanatics to force an issue that may be reactionary instead of progressive."[45] Andrews sought to understand Gandhi's fast on the lines of Jesus' going to Jerusalem, and forcing the issue. All the same, he wrote, "The method of fasting, committing suicide, still instinctively repels me."

Fourth, Andrews, though celibate and absolutely committed to poverty himself, could not accept Gandhi's tacit rejection of the body, which he felt verged on Manichaeanism. In *Hindu Dharma* Gandhi wrote:

Hinduism is undoubtedly a religion of renunciation of the flesh so that the spirit may be set free. It is no part of a Hindu's duty to dine with his son. And by restricting his choice of a bride to a particular group, he exercises rare self-restraint. Hinduism does not regard a married state as by any means essential for salvation. Marriage is a "fall" even as birth is a "fall." Salvation is freedom from birth and hence death also. Prohibition against inter marriage and inter dining is essential for a rapid evolution of the soul.[46]

Andrews, by contrast, affirmed the goodness of marriage, and disapproved of Gandhi's imposition of a vow of celibacy at his Sabarmathi ashram as "a slur on marriage." The human body, for Gandhi, was, said Andrews, "an evil, not a good. Only by complete severance from this human body can perfect deliverance be found."[47] In this he compared Gandhi to St. Paul. Although Andrews himself had had conscientious difficulties with the doctrine of the resurrection of the body he nevertheless maintained the central affirmation of the goodness of the body that follows from the incarnation. He also found himself more at home with "the less Puritan ideals of Santiniketan" (Tagore's ashram).[48]

Finally, Andrews differed with Gandhi on the possibility of conversion. It was part of Gandhi's understanding of *swadeshi* (self-sufficiency) that every person had their own religion, into which they were born, and where it was proper for them to remain. While Andrews was against mass conversion, and did not himself do evangelistic work, he wanted to insist on the possibility of conversion. He discussed the issue with Gandhi in 1937, and afterward wrote a long reflection on their conversation:

> Your talk on religion yesterday distressed me, for its formula, "All religions are equal," did not seem to correspond with history or with my own life experience. Also your declaration that a man should always remain in the faith in which he was born appeared to be a static conception not in accordance with such a dynamic subject as religion. Let me take the example of Cardinal Newman. Should he, because he was born in protestant England, remain a Protestant? Or again, ought I, in my later life, to have remained a rigid Anglo Catholic, such as I was when I came out to India? You again, have challenged Hinduism and said, "I cannot remain a Hindu, if untouchability is a part of it." . . .
>   Of course, if conversion meant a denial of any living truth in one's own religion, then we must have nothing to do with it. But I have never taken it in that sense, but rather as the discovery of a new and glorious truth which one had never before seen and for which we should sacrifice one's whole life. It does mean also, very often, the passing from one fellowship to another, and this should never be done lightly or in haste. But if the new fellowship embodies the glorious new truth in such a way as to make it more living and real and cogent than the old outworn truth, then I should say to the individual "Go forward"; become a member of the new faith which will make your own life more fruitful.[49]

The various interventions assembled in *Christian Missions: Their Place in India* make clear that Gandhi never took this point.[50] Swaraj meant for him that the religions of India were Hinduism, Buddhism, and Islam. He saw no need for Christianity and disliked missionary methods. The mass conversion of Untouchables seemed to him a way of exploiting weakness, a way of making "rice Christians." From his time in England on, many Christians had sought to convert him. Jones kept up the attempt. To him Gandhi wrote:

> I appreciate the love underlying your letter and kind thoughts for my welfare, but my difficulty is of long standing. . . . I cannot grasp the position by the intellect; the heart must be touched. Saul must become Paul, not by intellectual effort but by something touching his heart. I can only say my heart is absolutely open. I have no axes to grind. I want to find truth, to see God face to face. But there I stop.[51]

In many of his utterances Gandhi tended to emphasize religious and ethical principles over devotion to God. "I do not regard God as a person," he once wrote. "Truth for me is God, and God's law and God are not different things or facts, in the sense that an earthly king and his law are different."[52] In the same way he denied any interest in the historical Jesus, and was indifferent to the question whether Jesus truly lived and died. The essential thing for him was the truth of the Sermon on the Mount.[53] Although there is every reason to believe that Gandhi did in fact also follow the *bhakti marga*, and not just the *karma marga*,[54] this prioritization of principle over person goes a long way to explain the difference on conversion. In the 1937 letter Andrews goes on:

> Christ is to me the unique way whereby I have come to God, and have found God, and I cannot help telling others about it whenever I can do so without compulsion or undue influence. I honour Paul the apostle when he says, "Necessity is laid upon me. Woe is me if I preach not the gospel!" I feel the message which Christ came into the world to proclaim is the most complete and inspiring that was ever given to men. That is why I am a Christian.[55]

Christ, Andrews always insisted, was first and foremost a living presence for him. The center of his religious experience, write his biographers, "was an intense personal devotion to a living, human Christ; his prayers were intimate talks with a Great Companion, vividly, warmly present at his side, the Jesus of the Gospels." "With regard to the infinitude of God that lies beyond this," Andrews himself wrote, "I seem able at this present stage of existence to know nothing that can be defined. But the human in Christ, that is also divine, I can really know; and when I see this divine beauty, truth and love in others, it is natural for me to relate it to Christ."[56] It was this presence and person he shared, above all by his life.

Of these various differences the most momentous is that over caste, as the rise of the Dalit movement forty years after Gandhi's death has emphasized. Given the "religious reading" of Gandhi we have seen in this chapter, it must be said that Gandhi seems to have been misled by his own religious idealism.[57] He had no objection to cleaning latrines, and indeed urged everyone to do it. "A scavenger is as worthy of his hire as a lawyer or a President," he wrote in *Harijan* in 1937. "That according to me is Hinduism." But he deduced from this the consequence that "one born a scavenger must earn his livelihood by being a scavenger, and then do what he likes."[58] Gandhi felt that if scavenging and bread labor were part of every person's duty a new outlook would develop and caste barriers disappear.[59] He saw that, in the issue of nonviolence, it was unrealistic to expect everyone to live up to this ideal, but with regard to caste his idealism prevents him from seeing how structural factors, like employment in a certain trade, function to keep people poor and oppressed and effectively guarantee a much lower standard of life. In effect, his idealism meant that he endorsed karma. His contemporaries were right that he was a quite extraordinary human being. Chenchiah's claim that he shows us that only the religious impulse can save the world is another matter. At his death Andrews was making arrangements for Dietrich Bonhoeffer to come and see Gandhi. What a conversation would have come from that meeting, Gandhi read through "religionless Christianity"! As it is, the conversation is continued in the light of an ambiguous legacy.

NOTES

1. *The Guardian* (Madras), 4 January 1940. This was despite the British government's avowed neutrality in religious matters. D. Forrester, *Caste and Christianity* (London: Curzon 1979),64.

2. *The Guardian*, 18 January 1940.

3. E. Stanley Jones, *Mahatma Gandhi: An Interpretation* (London: Hodder and Stoughton, 1948), 88.

4. P. Devasahayam, ed., *Rethinking Christianity in India*, 2nd ed. (Madras: Hogarth, 1939), 292.

5. Stephen Neill, *The Story of the Christian Church in India and Pakistan* (Grand Rapids, Mich.: Eerdmans, 1970), 132. The description of

Christian communities as "trained to obey" is an oblique reference to the fact that most Christians were drawn from what were then known as "Untouchable communities."

6. An example is G. H. Macfarlane, discussed by Gandhi in *Young India* (2 February 1922). Also see *The Collected Works of Mahatma Gandhi* (hereafter *CW*) (New Delhi: Ministry of Information, 1958), 22:317ff.

7. *Madras Christian College Magazine*, 2, no. 1 (1922) cited in E. S. Alexander, *The Attitude of British Protestant Missionaries towards Nationalism in India* (Delhi: ISPCK, 1994), 85.

8. S. K. George, *Gandhi's Challenge to Christianity* (London: Allen and Unwin, 1939), 71.

9. The criticism was voiced in an editorial of the Anglo-Indian newspaper *The Statesman*, based in Calcutta. Cited in George, *Gandhi's Challenge*, 25. Gandhi responded that though he was not a Christian in the sectarian sense "the example of Jesus" suffering is a factor in the composition of my undying faith in non violence which rules all my actions. . . . Jesus lived and died in vain if he did not teach us to regulate the whole of life by the ethical law of love."

10. H. A. Popley, *K. T. Paul Christian Leader* (Calcutta: YMCA, 1938), 246. In his case, said Gandhi, his Christianity seemed to deepen his nationalism. What especially impressed Gandhi was that he always "stoutly opposed" demands for special concessions for Christians in the forthcoming constitution. That people such as Paul and George had to resign their jobs as a result of supporting a Nationalist agenda might suggest, of course, that the majority of the Indian Christian community was not behind Gandhi.

11. C. S. Milford, *The Church and the Crisis in India* (London: Edinburgh House Press, 1946), 14.

12. Ibid., 16.

13. Ibid., 10.

14. It is important to note that Gandhi himself understood the importance of India having a secular constitution. As Margaret Chatterjee points out, Gandhi never spoke out against secularization or secularism. See her *Gandhi's Religious Thought* (London: Macmillan, 1984), 5. Later she writes, "Secularism for him . . . (means) respect for all men and all faiths . . . (it) *depends* on men who care first and foremost, about their own faith" (120–121).

15. E. Stanley Jones, *The Christ of the Indian Road* (London: Hodder and Stoughton, 1926), 77.

16. Cited in Devasahayam, *Rethinking Christianity*, 131. The support of this group of Indian theologians was unaffected by the stinging rebuke the volume received from Gandhi, who said that it "left a bad taste in the mouth." The authors argued that mass conversion of Untouchable groups was defensible on the grounds that Hindu attitudes to caste were not easily going to

change. Gandhi replied that mass conversion of Harijans was in practice always bound up with offering material inducements. *Harijan* 3–4 (1937).

17. Devasahayam, *Rethinking Christianity*, 171.
18. Ibid., 190.
19. George, *Gandhi's Challenge*, 12–13. George said of Gandhi that it was he "who made Jesus and his image real to me" (dedication to the revised edition of *Gandhi's Challenge* [Ahmedabad: Navajivan Publishing House, 1960]).
20. Ibid., 22.
21. George, *Gandhi's Challenge*, 105–106. Stanley Jones agreed with this. In *The Christ of the Indian Road*, first published in 1925, Jones devoted an entire chapter to Gandhi as more than any other individual responsible for what he took to be a new interest in Christ in India. Jones felt that what was owed to Gandhi was, in particular, a new understanding of the cross:

> Gandhi's movement in its failure left a new spiritual deposit in the mind of India. The cross has become intelligible and vital. Up to a few years ago one was preaching against a stone wall in preaching the cross in India. The whole underlying philosophy of things was against it. The doctrine of karma, as ordinarily held, has little or no room for the cross in it. . . . But with teaching of Gandhi that they can joyously take on themselves suffering for the sake of national ends, there has come into the atmosphere a new sensitiveness to the cross. (91–92)

22. George, *Gandhi's Challenge*, 95 Contemporary Indian Christians continue this perspective. A Jesuit symposium on Dalit theology concluded that despite the problems Gandhi "stands as a guide, friend and philosopher to many who follow his footsteps in uplifting the depressed classes." P. Susai, S.J. "Gandhi's Response to the Depressed Classes," in *Emerging Dalit Theology*, ed. X. Irdayaraj (Madras: Jest/TTS, 1990), 99. Another Indian Jesuit has published *A Gandhian Theology of Liberation* (Maryknoll, N.Y.: Orbis Books, 1984). This book ends with Gandhi's challenge to Christianity: "Gandhi challenges Christians to the Christology of Jesus as servant rather than the Christology of the church about Jesus as Lord. . . . Gandhi calls us to learn the full meaning of vicarious existence from Jesus, and to apply it in our worship, belief, missionary action, and suffering" (127). So too in M. M. Thomas's chapter on Gandhi in *The Christian Response to the Asian Revolution* (London: SCM, 1966).
23. D. G. Tendulkar, ed., *Mahatma: Life of M. K. Gandhi* (New Delhi: Ministry of Information, 1951), 2:17.
24. Andrews argued the case for the way in which contact with Britain had rejuvenated Indian culture in *The Renaissance of India*, published in 1912.
25. B. Chaturvedi and M. Sykes, *Charles Freer Andrews* (New Delhi: Ministry of Information, India, 1947), 166.

26. The phrase *structure of feeling* was coined by Raymond Williams. He meant by it the sum of all those things which tell us what it is like to live in a particular society, "a very deep and very wide possession, in all actual communities, precisely because it is on it that communication depends." See his *The Long Revolution* (Harmondsworth: Penguin, 1965), 64–65. Andrews frequently compared Gandhi to St. Francis.

27. Cf. his letter to Gandhi on September 9, 1920, in which he writes, "Personally I am coming more and more to see that . . . capitalism is the alternative driving force of all this imperialist aggression." Chaturvedi and Sykes, *Charles Freer Andrews*, 156.

28. *Pranam* is the form of *namaskarma* (greeting), in which the disciple kneels before the master and touches his feet. Andrews described the reaction to his venerating Gandhi in this way in a letter to Tagore: "I can see him (one of the editors of the "white" press) still, holding up his hands in horror and saying, 'Really, you know Mr Andrews, really you know, we don't *do* that sort of thing in Natal, we don't *do* it, Mr Andrews. I consider the action most unfortunate, *most* unfortunate'. . . . They boil over with indignation that I—an *Englishman* mind you!—should have touched the feet of an Asiatic" (Chaturvedi and Sykes, *Charles Freer Andrews*, 98).

29. *Harijan*, 9 April 1940, cited in N. Macnicol, *C. F. Andrews: Friend of India* (London: James Clarke, 1944), 37.

30. C. F. Andrews, *What I Owe to Christ* (London: Hodder and Stoughton, 1932), 246–247. Andrews was known to the Untouchables as "Gandhi's brother" (Chaturvedi and Sykes, *Charles Freer Andrews,* 180). Gandhi wrote to Tagore in April 1918 that Andrews's guidance is "at times most precious to me" (*CW*, 14:375).

31. Andrews, *What I Owe to Christ*, 251–252, 190. With this remark we may compare the view of E. Stanley Jones in his *Along the Indian Road* (London: Hodder and Stoughton, 1939):

> I have the feeling that the greatest things in Mahatma Gandhi are Christian things. The fundamental note in his life—the overcoming of evil by good, of hate by love, of wrong by taking on oneself suffering, of conquering by a cross—is essentially a Christian note. . . . But after that is said, one must add, although Mahatma Gandhi is deeply Christianized, far more than most Christians, yet he is essentially a Hindu. The centre of his allegiance is not in the Gospel but in the Gita. (129)

32. Andrews, *What I Owe to Christ*, 277.

33. For three of the main differences between Gandhi and Andrews I am following M. M. Thomas, *The Acknowledged Christ* (London: SCM, 1969), 219ff.

34. Letter from Gandhi to Andrews, dated May 25, 1920, in *CW*, 17:534.

35. Chaturvedi and Sykes, in *Charles Freer Andrews,* 156.

36. Letter from Gandhi to Andrews, dated January 29, 1921, in *CW,* 19:288. Of course Gandhi's attitude to caste was always a minority view, notoriously in relation to Ambedkar. Today Dalit theologians disown Gandhi and regard his teachings as having done "enormous harm to this section of society." See B. Das, "Socio-Economic Problems of Dalits," in *Dalit Solidarity,* ed. B. Das and J. Massey (Dehli: ISPCK, 1995), 80. Writing in 1989, Abraham Ayrookuzhiel speaks of caste as the "cultural contradiction" of Hinduism. Gandhi did not admit this contradiction. "He romanticised the Indian cultural heritage and advocated the integration of Dalits within Hinduism. It has totally failed." See Abraham Ayrookuzhiel, "The Ideological Nature of the Emerging Dalit Consciousness" in *Towards a Common Dalit Ideology,* ed. A. P. Nirmal (Madras: Gurukul Seminary, 1989), 88.

37. In *Harijan,* 19 December 1936. In *The Guardian,* 7 January 1937, Gandhi wrote: "To approach the Palavas and Pariahs with their palsied hands and palsied intelligence is no Christianity." It remains a cause of indignation to Dalit theologians that Gandhi was against the conversion of Untouchables "to more egalitarian religions" (Das, "Socio-Economic Problems," 81).

38. Chaturvedi and Sykes, *Charles Freer Andrews,* 176.

39. Ibid., 177.

40. After a particularly ugly communal riot in Bombay in 1920 he declared a fast until "Hindus and Musalmans of Bombay have made peace with the Parsis, the Christians and the Jews." "There is only one God for us all, whether we find him through the Koran, The Zend Avesta, the Talmud, or the Gita," he wrote. "And he is the God of Truth and Love. I have no interest in living, save for proving this faith in me. I cannot hate an Englishman or anyone else. I have spoken and written much against his institutions, especially the one he has set up in India. I shall continue to do so if I live. But you must not mistake my condemnation of the system for that of the man. My religion requires me to love him as I love myself. I would deny God if I did not attempt to prove it at this critical moment." See Tendulkar, *Mahatma,* 2:69.

41. Letter from Gandhi to Andres, dated August 13, 1921, in *CW,* 31:499.

42. C. F. Andrews, *Mahatma Gandhi's Ideas* (London: Allen and Unwin, 1929), 133.

43. Chaturvedi and Sykes, *Charles Freer Andrews,* 177.

44. Letter from Gandhi to Andrews, dated October 15, 1924, *CW,* 25:232ff.

45. Chaturvedi and Sykes, *Charles Freer Andrews,* 264.

46. M. K. Gandhi, *Hindu Dharma: The Glory and the Abuses* (Ahmedabad: Navajivan Publishing House, 1978), 11. We can also note Gandhi's frequent warnings to friends, in his letters, to avoid any rich diet! On August 29,

1918, he wrote to Andrews, "In my opinion mutiny of the palate means mutiny of everything" (*CW*, 15:34).

47. Andrews, *Mahatma Gandhi's Ideas*, 343. Writing to Andrews on July 6, 1918, Gandhi referred to war as "a necessary evil, even as the body is" (*CW*, 14:477).

48. Andrews, *Mahatma Gandhi's Ideas*, 331.

49. D. O'Connor, ed., *The Testimony of C. F. Andrews* (Madras: CLS, 1974), 118. The appeal to the rights of the individual here is the crucial issue. Gandhi was still thinking in terms of membership of given communities. Another less important difference emerges in Gandhi's refusal to countenance "minority religions" when speaking of the equality of all religions. Jones argued that if the distinction held at one level it should hold all the way through, and that therefore Gandhi was implicitly conceding the right to rank religions. Jones, *Mahatma Gandhi*, 83–85.

50. M. K. Gandhi, *Christian Missions: Their Place in India* (Ahmedabad: Navajivan, 1941). The volume is a collection of letters and utterances by Gandhi on the subject.

51. Jones, *Along the Indian Road*, 140. Jones records Gandhi's remark about him that he was a sincere person, "but too convinced of the truth of his own opinions."

52. Cited in Thomas, *Acknowledged Christ*, 194.

53. M. K. Gandhi, *The Message of Jesus Christ* (Bombay: n. p., 1940), 35. Jones agreed that Gandhi "never seemed to get to Christ as a Person" (*Mahatma Gandhi*, 105).

54. *Karma marga* is the way of action, *bhakti marga* is the way of devotion. One thinks of Gandhi's composition of devotional hymns *(bhajans)* and of his preference for the hymn "When I Surveyed the Wondrous Cross," which he often asked Andrews to sing for him. Andrews insisted that Gandhi was a theist quite as much as he was. "To both of us this belief in God is as certain and immediate as our own personal existence" (Andrews, *Mahatma Gandhi's Ideas*, 34).

55. Chaturvedi and Sykes, *Charles Freer Andrews*, 310.

56. Ibid., 235.

57. So Susai, "Gandhi's Response to the Depressed Classes," 99.

58. Cited in Das, "Socio-Economic Problems," 81.

59. So Chatterjee, *Gandhi's Religious Thought*, 39.

8

The Mahatma and the Sikhs

Nikky-Guninder Kaur Singh

The relationship between Gandhi and the Sikhs is most ambivalent and intriguing. On the one hand, Gandhi respected the Sikhs and felt close to them. Since the Jallianwalla tragedy (April 13, 1919) to the last days of his life when he broke his fast on Guru Gobind Singh's birthday (January 18, 1948), Gandhi sympathized with Sikhs, praised them for their bravery, and admired their religious heritage. Particularly impressive is Gandhi's kinship with the Guru Granth and the spiritual message of the Ten Gurus. He calls himself a follower of Guru Gobind Singh, and repeatedly remarks that there is no difference between Hindus and Sikhs. Some time ago Dr. S. Radhakrishnan commented that Gandhi got the idea for his popular public prayer *(ishvara allah tere nama/mandira masdija tere dhama/sabko san-mati de bhagavana)* from Guru Gobind Singh's verse recorded in the Dasam Granth.[1] In Gandhi's own words, "The Ashram Bhanavali contains quite a few psalms from the Bible and *bhajans* from the Granthsaheb."[2] Even when Sikhs were outraged by the partition of Punjab, Gandhi made statements such as "The Granth Saheb and the Guru are as much mine as theirs" (*CW* 88:21). A month earlier he had remarked, "Why I had said to no one else than Master Tara Singh that I was the true heir of Guru Govind Singh and not he" (*CW* 87:201).

But Gandhi's feelings are not generally reciprocated by the Sikhs. They do not wholeheartedly claim him to be one of their own. If Gandhi regards Sikhism as his own religious tradition, why do Sikhs see him as the *other*? In contrast with Gandhi's statements, Sikh writings tend to disclose a chasm between the Mahatma and the Sikhs. There are rare exceptions, which portray him in positive light (such as S. S. Gandhi's paper[3]), but for the most part we either encounter silence—which in itself is indicative of an intense disappointment[4]—or we read critiques that range from mild to harsh.[5] There is also some envy on the part of Sikhs who feel Ram Singh Namdhari was the first spiritual revolutionary of India to organize Non-cooperation and Swadeshi movements in the Punjab against British imperialism. The Sikh leader, however, is eclipsed by Gandhi and remains forgotten. But the most vocal account has been Gurmit Singh's *Gandhi and the Sikhs*.[6] The only full-fledged text that deals with the Gandhi–Sikh relationship, it is a severe disparagement of the Mahatma. Gurmit Singh is incensed that Gandhi resisted Dr. Ambedkar's proposal that the Depressed Classes should convert to Sikhism. So his entire book is permeated with a hostility against Gandhi's comment cited in his first chapter: "It would be far better that scores of untouchables of India should be converted to Islam than that they should become Sikhs."[7] Subsequently, all of Gandhi's goodwill toward the Sikhs is viewed merely as biased sugarcoating by Gurmit Singh. A similar current flows through Shauna Singh Baldwin's widely acclaimed novel *What the Body Remembers*. In subtle prose, Gandhi emerges as a "shilly-shallying politician"—"a man who says he is all religions, Hindu, Sikh, Muslim, Christian, is a man of no conviction."[8] The hurt and betrayal felt by the Sikhs comes out strikingly throughout her novel: "The Mahatma raised the national flag of a free India and it did not have a strip of deep Sikh blue as he promised."[9] In contemporary Sikh circles Gandhi is blamed for the problems and tragedies that continue to ravage partitioned Punjab.

We are caught between the Mahatma's affinity for the Sikhs and the Sikhs's distance from him. Why this discrepancy? As far as I see, there is a fundamental variance in their response to religious difference and plurality, and for me that fundamental difference in attitude is the cause of the Gandhi–Sikh disparity. Gandhi is an inclusivist for whom Hindus, Buddhists, Jains, and Sikhs all flow into the vast ocean of Hinduism. He clearly perceives no difference between himself and the Sikhs. Whereas Sikhs, a minority population in India, tend to be mainly pluralists who perceive themselves as a distinct tradition—different from other religious traditions, and yet very much a part of the rich and colorful mosaic of Indian religions. The antithesis between their respective inclusivist and pluralist positions only leads to confusion and hurt. Gandhi is rejected: Sikhs do not want his affectionate spiritual embrace; Sikhs are suffocated: Gandhi shrouds their independence and identity. Each side is unable to understand the other.

Their fundamental difference becomes apparent in the 1924 correspondence between Mahatma Gandhi and the leaders of the Shromani Gurdwara Prabhandak Committee (SGPC) which will be the focus of this chapter. Since its establishment in 1920, the SGPC has wielded immense power in Sikh life, and its president is the Sikh equivalent of the pope. The committee sets up rules and regulations for Sikhs to follow throughout the world. The exchange between the Mahatma and the Sikh leaders five years after the Jallianwalla massacre comes at a crucial psychological juncture in the development of Sikh history.

At this point of their history, Sikhs are more in tune with themselves. Their political awareness heightens their sense of personal and religious identity. The emerging social and political polarization in their milieu further drives them to create an autonomous framework.[10] Sikhs begin to aspire for the practice of their rites of passage and their ceremonies in their own distinctive way. Sikh rite of marriage was legalized by the Anand Marriage Bill passed in 1909, after which Sikh weddings were no longer patterned on Hindu ritual. Sikh masses start to claim their shrines, the Gurdwaras: They wanted them under the collective control of the Sikh community and utilize the incomes derived from them for Sikh purposes. From the time of the gurus, Sikh shrines served as the central point for the community, creating and maintaining social, cultural, intellectual, and political links. But under the British, the overall governance, performance of rites of passage, and the land attached to Sikh Gurdwaras, passed into the hands of the Mahants (clergy-cum-managers) who deviated from Sikh practices. The Mahants had the support of the British, and did not care much for Sikh sentiment. Many of them, especially the Udasis, installed images of Hindu gods and goddesses in Gurdwara premises to attract Hindu worshipers.[11] The most glaring incident followed the Jallianwalla massacre: General Dyer, who had ordered the brutal massacre of hundreds of innocent men, women, and children right next to the Golden Temple, was honored shortly thereafter within its sacred precincts.[12] The official clergy of the central Sikh shrine conferred upon Dyer the "Saropa" (a mark of distinguished service for Sikh faith or for the good of humanity)—sending shock waves among the Sikh masses.[13] On October 12, 1920, students and faculty of the Khalsa College called a meeting to take immediate action to liberate the Gurdwaras from the control of Mahants.

Its natural consequence was the formation of the Sikh SGPC on November 15, 1920, with 175 members to manage and reform Sikh shrines. With many Gurdwaras shifting into their orbit, Sikh leaders found the need to organize a political party, and so the Shromani Akali Dal came into being in January 1921. As the political arm of the SGPC, the members of the Akali Dal promoted the ideas of the SGPC throughout the Sikh public, and the Gurdwara Reform movement itself came to be known as the "Akali movement." In many instances, the Akalis had it easy: The transition was smooth, but there were many others in which the Akalis had to go through a lot of trial and tribulation to bring Gurdwaras under the management of the SGPC. In a sequence of tragedies—the Nankana Holocaust (1921), Guru ka Bagh (1922), and Jaito

(1924: the immediate backdrop to the correspondence under study)—
hundreds of Akalis lost their lives. But each event made the Sikhs stronger and
more fervent. According to the eminent Sikh historian Khushwant Singh, "The
Akali movement was the first example of passive resistance organized on a mass
scale which proved wholly successful; the largest civil disobedience movements
launched by Mahatma Gandhi and organized by the Indian National Congress
were but pale imitations of the Akali achievement."[14]

So in 1924 Sikh emotions are intense. Sikhs have developed a strong
sense of their identity and are politically motivated. No more are the British
their *mai bap* (mother–father), no more will they be treated unfairly, and no
more will they have other Indians run their sacred spaces. The challenges and
victories of the Akalis incite them for more action and autonomy. In fact, in
their many tragedies and triumphs, Gandhi had been their source of strength
and motivation. At this point in their dynamic momentum, the Sikhs need
the backing of the Mahatma. However, as the SGPC correspondence reveals,
the Mahatma steps back. Was he afraid of them asserting their individuality?
Like a parent was he suddenly scared to see them mature? Did he have a separation anxiety? The more the Sikhs assert their individuality, the more
Gandhi wants to keep them in his sweeping Hindu fold. The literary exchange between them during the spring of 1924 is a turning point in the
Gandhi–Sikh relationship. As Mohinder Singh says in his standard work on
the Akali movement, "the Mahatma . . . suddenly withdrew his support."[15]
The correspondence makes a very interesting dialogue, for on the surface
there is congruence between the Mahatma and the Sikhs; but as we hear their
tone closely and read between the lines, we begin to sense their differences.
Surely the SGPC letter is not the word of all the Sikhs, and the Sikh attitude
to Gandhi in 1924 is by no means frozen in history. Yet the voice and the sentiments that we hear in that correspondence are expressive of mainstream
Sikh views at that time and mark a departure in the outlook of most Sikhs.
The SGPC is the representative body of the Sikhs; its letter addressed to
Gandhi is an important Sikh document that serves as a vital opening for our
understanding of the rupture between the Mahatma and the Sikhs, a rupture
whose impact is still felt on the Indian subcontinent today.

THE HISTORICAL CONTEXT

If we examine the historical context, Gandhi and the Sikhs have had a close
rapport. Unfortunately, their bond was forged under tragic circumstances

during the Jallianwalla massacre in Amritsar. Gandhi expressed great sympathy for the Sikhs—along with Hindus and Muslims—and he himself headed the committee appointed by the Indian National Congress to investigate the massacre and the martial law regime. Gandhi visited the bloodstained Bagh in the vicinity of the Golden Temple, and many congressmen and congresswomen followed his example. They visited the spot as pilgrims, touching the ground with their foreheads, some even using it as *bibhuti* (the sacred mark) on their foreheads (*CW* 16:372). Gandhi's compassion, in turn, inspired the Sikhs. They created a new organization, the Central Sikh League, consisting of Nationalists who were opposed to the Chief Khalsa Diwan's sycophancy to the British. Gandhi's sympathy and support drew the Sikhs into the Congress fold and made them active participants in the fight for freedom.

Gandhi also traveled to other parts of the Punjab that had suffered the tyrannical martial law regime following the massacre. He went to Gujranwala, Ramnagar, Akalgarh, and visited important Sikh places, such as the house where Ranjit Singh (the first Sikh emperor) was born, and other beautiful Sikh mansions and gardens now destroyed by the British. Gandhi describes in a haunting tone like T. S. Eliot's, "Today they are inhabited only by birds. The mansions slowly crumbling away. The garden looks like a wasteland" (*CW* 17:328). Gandhi was touched by the affection of the Punjabi villagers. When they showered him with flowers, he asked them for garlands of handspun yarn, which men and women enthusiastically began to create (*CW* 17:329–330).

Gandhi also visited the Khalsa College, the academic center of the Sikhs. He asked the students, and their teachers and friends, to renounce their loyalty to the British and become the loyal heirs of Guru Nanak. Gandhi urges the Sikhs to shatter their construction as British subjects and refuse assistance to the imperial masters. He wanted them to stop their aid to the British as they tried to crush the indigenous freedom movements in their colonies. He helped the Sikhs see through the falsity and injustice of the imperial rule: "The Government steals an anvil from you and compensates you with the gift of a needle" (*CW* 18:356). Gandhi's was a genuine attempt to make Sikhs politically conscious of colonial snares and seductions.

When the Akalis suffered a calculated barbarity at the hands of Mahant Narain Das in Nankana Sahib, Gandhi was most sympathetic toward the Sikhs and most appreciative of their heroism. The Sikhs were brutally shot, burned and butchered by Narain Das and his accomplices on Sunday, Febuary 20, 1921. Gandhi addressed huge gatherings on how the Mahant had "out-Dyered Dyer." Gandhi painfully enumerates his atrocious attacks on the Sikh holy book, on the innocent victims, and on the sacred shrine commemorating the birthplace of the founder, Guru Nanak: "Everything I saw and heard points to a second edition of Dyerism more barbarous, more calculated, and more fiendish than the Dyerism at Jallianwalla. Man in Nankana, where once a snake is reported to have innocently spread its hood to shade the lamb-like Guru, turned Satan on that black Sunday" (*CW* 19:399). Gandhi impresses upon the masses to remember the nonviolence of the physically strong Sikh martyrs. By positing "fearlessness" Gandhi merged the teachings of the Sikh gurus with his own ideals of patriotism. Those Sikhs who gave up their lives at Nankana, such as Dulip Singh and his companions, were, reminds Gandhi, "bound by the Congress pledge of non-violence" (*CW* 20:68). While making poignant testimonies of the Nankana tragedy, Gandhi simultaneously underscores the Congress–Sikh unity and musters support for his principle of nonviolence.

Sikh scholars have observed that during his visit to Nankana Sahib, Gandhi encouraged the Sikhs not to cooperate with the government regarding the official inquiry into the tragedy. Gandhi offered to serve as the president of the nonofficial inquiry committee if the Akalis adopted a formal resolution of noncooperation. He enjoined the Sikhs to expand their movement from the freedom of Gurdwaras to the freedom of India.[16] Thus the idea of noncooperation was instilled by Gandhi and became a crucial crusade for the Akali Sikhs.

At this stage of Gandhi–Sikh rapport, Gandhi even defends the *kirpan* (sword), one of the Five K-s of the Sikhs.[17] The Punjab government tried to divest the Sikhs of their sacred symbol by restricting its size. Gandhi denounced such repressive measures. He publicly cited the analogy made by the secretary of the Sikh Young Men's Association that "the sword is to the Sikh what the sacred thread is to the Brahmin." Championing the Sikh cause, Gandhi says, "Much as I abhor the possession or the use of arms, I cannot reconcile myself to forcible prohibition" (*CW* 20:406).

Not only did Gandhi sympathize with and champion for the Sikhs, he also celebrated with them. On November 7, 1921, the keys of the Golden Temple treasury were forcibly taken by the British, which deeply offended the Sikhs. The SGPC protested strongly, and asked the Sikhs to hold assemblies to condemn the action of the government. The Sikhs were forbidden to participate in any function connected with the forthcoming visit of the Prince of Wales, and instead encouraged to go on strike on the day of his arrival. Sikh leaders were arrested by the deputy commissioner, and so were many more. Dressed in black and singing hymns, the Sikhs gladly filled British jails. Under pressure of the growing agitation, the government gave in. On January 19,

1922, at a huge gathering at the Golden Temple, Sardar Kharak Singh, president of the SGPC, received the bunch of keys wrapped in red cloth—symbolic of an auspicious transition. The Mahatma sent Kharak Singh a telegram: "First decisive battle for India's freedom won. Congratulations." Gandhi's response must mean a lot to the Sikhs for almost every Sikh author proudly quotes it.

Again, when Sardar Kharak Singh was elected president of the Provincial Congress Committee, Gandhi was delighted. Kharag Singh (1867–1963) was a greatly respected leader of the Sikhs, and was known as their *betaj badshah* (the uncrowned king). Gandhi remarked that the Congress Committee had made an excellent choice: "It could not have done better. In honouring Sardar Sahib, the Committee has honoured itself. The election of Sardar Kharak Singh is also a delicate compliment paid to the Sikhs for their bravery, sacrifice and patriotism" (*CW* 22:441; March 1922). The Sikhs must have been elated to hear him praise them.

Such examples from the early relationship between the Mahatma and the Sikhs reveal mutual respect, admiration, and friendship. The Sikhs look up to the Mahatma and follow his advice. They are inspired by his message of noncooperation and nonviolence. And clearly, there is an emotional investment on both sides. The harmonious backdrop is crucial for our grasp of the magnitude of their rift. Had there been no initial bond between the Mahatma and the Sikhs, their misunderstanding and confusion would not have had much significance either.

THE LITERARY TEXT

Their correspondence during the spring of 1924 shows a downward trend in the Gandhi–Sikh relationship. Scholars regard this as a crucial moment in Sikh history when Sikhs desperately needed the Mahatma's help and guidance. However, Sikh historians say that "the Mahatma showed himself unable to form a correct assessment of the Akalis and their movement and suddenly withdrew his support to their cause."[18] The Sikhs at this time were victims of still more British repression, and the setting for the Gandhi–Sikh literary exchange is most dramatic. The Sikh Maharaja of Nabha, known for his nationalist tendencies and sympathy with the Akalis, had been deposed. The Sikhs protested against his deposition and the government reacted by declaring the SGPC an unlawful association on October 13, 1923. Sikh leaders and active members of the SGPC were arrested and tried on charges of sedition against the king. The situation worsened in the small town of Jaito, in the Nabha state, where a large group of Akali worshipers were arrested by the police during an *akhandpath* (uninterrupted reading of Sikh scripture) they had inaugurated. To vindicate their right to worship in the Gurdwara, and atone the sacrilege committed by the police, batches of twenty-five Akalis began to march daily from the Akal Takht. They would cover the distance of 190 kilometers between Amritsar and Jaito, but before they reached Jaito, they were taken into policy custody, beaten, and sent to a remote desert without food or money. Later, *shahidi jatha* (martyrdom batch) of five hundred in strength started to come from Amritsar. On February 9, 1924, Jathedar Udham Singh led the first one, and the news of the huge Jatha marching on foot from Amritsar to Jaito created great excitement in the countryside. Gandhi's letter to the SGPC is addressed less than a month later from Poona (March 4, 1924).

Its opening sentence is complex, brimming with what Friedrich Nietzsche would call Apollinian and Dionysian currents: "If I am entirely satisfied as to the nature and implications of the present Akali movement and the methods adopted to gain the end, I should have no hesitation in throwing myself heart and soul into it and even in burying myself in the Punjab, if it became necessary in order to guide the movement."[19] It has a rather long grammatical structure. It is at once both rational and passionate, logical and ecstatic, intimate and distant. The cautionary "If" at the outset braces the reader to be on guard. But the tense and tight precondition is immediately juxtaposed to an explosive burst: "I should have no hesitation in throwing myself heart and soul into it and even in burying myself in the Punjab." Gandhi requires satisfaction from the Akalis regarding the nature, implications, and methods of their movement, and in turn offers his heart and soul, and even his body, to guide them. His tantalizing and sensational effect is framed in five solid and systematic preconditions:

1. The strength of the Akalis.

2. A clear manifesto publicly stating the minimum.

3. Full assurance and, therefore, a document intended for publication signed by all the principal leaders or on behalf of the SGPC, giving a description of the methods which will clearly set forth all the implications of nonviolence.

4. That the movement is neither anti-Hindu nor anti any other race or creed.

5. That the SGPC has no desire for the establishment of Sikh Raj.

In a brief letter to "Sikh Friends," also dated March 4, 1924, Gandhi raises another issue and solicits response from the SGPC: "I learnt too, that a Hindu temple within the precinct of the Golden Temple had been destroyed by the Akalis and that the latter took their stand upon religion. In your letter, which you have promised, I would like you please to deal with all these questions" (*CW* 23:220). The fact that he will guide them if and only if his conditions are fulfilled, shows that the Mahatma at this juncture is not giving the Sikhs his support or approval. Overall his letter is distant, the tone authoritarian, and it is hard to believe that it is the same author who was sympathizing, advising, and defending the Sikhs just a short while ago.

How do the Sikhs reply? We have the letter dated April 20, 1924, signed by the secretary of the SGPC that discusses all of the issues raised by Gandhi (*Papers* 56–59). Each is carefully thought through, and answered in a balanced manner. The opening paragraph expresses their congruence and even joy: "We are glad that on these points our views coincide with yours and we can request at once to declare them on your behalf again, if you like" (*Papers* 56). My overall impression, however, is that the Sikhs are far from being glad. In fact, their balanced language betrays a feeling of violation. That the Mahatma does not understand them comes out strikingly in the following three dimensions.

1. *Gandhi does not know them.* In the course of the letter, the Sikhs imply again and again how Gandhi fails to understand what their movement is all about" "[I]f you study the facts about our movement" (*Papers* 56). "It appears that as yet you have not had the opportunity to go through the literature of the movement published by us and also that our representatives have not been able to adequately explain many important points" (*Papers* 62). "As you will see from the first chapter of the book the *Gurdwara Reform Movement*" (*Papers* 66). This two-pronged technique (whether their own representatives have not succeeded in explaining adequately or if Gandhi were to read just the first chapter of the book) is a polite way of making the singular point that Gandhi has no knowledge of who they are, what their experience has been, and what they are aspiring for. In other words, he is ignorant of the motions and emotions of their movement.

The letter discloses the frustration of the SGPC leaders that the inclusivist Gandhi—so very open on the surface—really does not see or hear their point of view. They are different from the Mahatma, and he needs to learn about their differences. No general cloudy knowledge of the Sikhs will do, and they urge the Mahatma to understand their unique position articulated in the first chapter of their publication on the Gurdwara Reform movement.

2. *Gandhi does not recognize them.* The SGPC letter reiterates Sikh identity. Gandhi's question about the removal of the Hindu icon from the precincts of the Golden Temple allows them an entry to assert their fundamentally contrary position. In fact, the SGPC generated from the impulse to reform all Sikh shrines, and so the removal of Hindu icons, practices, and ideologies was crucial for its members. All the tragic battles they fought against the Mahants and the British administrators were directed to retrieve the essentials of Sikhism. Brahmanic rites discarded by the gurus had entered into the Sikh way of life. The SGPC wanted to take control of all Sikh shrines precisely to remove all extraneous images and practices, and to reestablish Sikh elements in their sacred spaces.

The letter again is very polite in the way in which it asserts the aniconic nature of Sikhism. It begins by subtly confirming that the demolished was not a Hindu temple but the Hindu image of *Shiva-lingam.* As it continues, "The Sikhs are not idol-worshippers and the SGPC had always looked forward to an amicable removal of the image in consultation with Hindu leaders. In fact this matter had been broached with Pandit Malavyaji and Swami Shankeracharya, both of who had agreed with the Sikh view" (*Papers* 61–62). Apparently there is a "Sikh view" which is not Hindu. The SGPC members had been deliberating on the issue of the icon, and even had the support of Hindus they mention—Gandhi clearly not one of them. While apologizing for the damage done, they also categorically refuse any reinstallation process: "While we resent to be called idol-breakers, we dare not figure as idol erecters" (*Papers* 62). It is clear to me that the SGPC members do not find the need to explain the obvious fact that Akali, the name of their movement, derives from Guru Nanak's articulation of the Divine as *akal* (timeless). Their tenth guru, Gobind Singh, had underscored the formlessness and transcendence of the Divine in sublime poetry particularly in his hymn *Akal Ustati* (Praise of the Timeless One). The SGPC letter, however, resounds with exasperation: How could that One be installed into an icon? How could that One be symbolized in the male phallic image? How could Shiva's *linga* stay in Sikh holy precincts? The SGPC letter does not go into any historical or philosophical explanations; it does not attempt to prove or seek any justifications. Briefly but firmly, it rejects the doctrine of *avtarvad* (incarnation). Its terse style is effective for it carries a latent power, which forces the reader to recognize the separate experience and consciousness of the Sikhs.

The members do openly express their hurt and apology for the manner in which the Shiva-lingam was removed. It was done suddenly, stealthily, in the depth of darkness by "some irresponsible and misguided men, most probably Sikhs" with whom the SGPC claims to have no connection whatsoever. "When it was discovered the next morning, the S.G.P.C. hastened to condemn this action and expressed its deep regret in public and its readiness to make amends to injured Hindu sentiments in consistency with the principles of Sikhism" (*Papers* 62). Their pluralist locus is evident: The Sikhs feel the pain brought to their Hindu community. There is respect and empathy for the other as they seek to make amends, yet only in a way that would be consistent with the principles of Sikhism. So, short of reinstallation of the idol, "we were ready to make it up to our Hindu brethren in a hundred ways." While they stand rooted in their own tradition, the Sikh conception and perception is not posited as the one and only reality excluding all others. The statements made by the SGPC show them functioning in a multicultural India. The faith in their own religion does not prevent them from reaching out emotionally and meaningfully to their Hindu brethren. Section III of the letter ends with: "By a strange irony of fate the image was demolished on the same night, April 12, when about 1600 Akalis were patrolling the streets of Amritsar to protect the life and property of Hindus and their temples and *Thakardwaras*. This combination of circumstances pained the SGPC most" (*Papers* 62).

The words bring back the memory of Tegh Bahadur, the ninth Sikh guru, who gave up his life to the Mughal authorities for the upkeep of Hindu religious symbols: the *janeu* and the *tilak*. From the moment of its inception, Sikh faith rejects all external signs of social hierarchy that are retained in the sacred thread worn by the upper-class Hindu males, and a popular illustration is that of a defiant eight-year-old Nanak shattering his lovely janeu-initiation ceremony organized by his family and community. Yet, Guru Nanak's ninth successor died a martyr for the janeu, which signified the right of individuals to freely practice their own and different religions. The situation in 1924 is quite similar: The Sikhs do not want a Hindu icon on their own compound, but they will wholeheartedly defend the life, property, and temples of the Hindus. The Sikhs are not threatened by their Hindu neighbors; they are not their opponents. The Sikhs do not say that theirs is the only way of approaching the Divine, nor do they construct their own aniconic experience as an exclusive priority. Why else would sixteen hundred Sikhs be bravely patrolling the streets of Amritsar to protect Hindu temples that house icons and images? The SGPC takes responsibility and expresses deep pain and public apology for the way in which the Shiva-linga was removed from the Golden Temple. The answer to the question raised by Gandhi ends up being a plea that the Mahatma recognize the flow of "pluralism" in Sikh psyche and blood.

3. *Gandhi misinterprets them.* The SGPC letter urges Gandhi not to misinterpret their pluralist intentions as exclusivist. Over and over, they say, "Our movement is neither anti-Hindu nor anti-any other race or creed. Though essentially religious in spirit and objectives, it is thoroughly national in outlook. . . . The movement is purely religious and has no secular object or intention" (*Papers* 57).

Gandhi is suspicious about their motives, and requires assurances from the Sikhs, and the Sikhs in turn try their best to convince Gandhi that they have an entirely religious agenda. They explain that the travel to Jaito Gurdwara by the shahidi jathas was not a covert act for propaganda against the maharaja's removal but a pilgrimage to their sacred shrine for akhandpath, their religious rite, their legitimate right. Actually, the Guru Granth is the sole aural and visual icon for the Sikhs, and reading or hearing or reciting his passionate poetry is the Sikhs' sole ritual. So the interruption of akhandpath by the British authorities in Jaito was most sacrilegious to the Sikhs who in exchange vowed to carry out 101 uninterrupted readings. Their letter says, "It is our intention that when the Gurdwara is thrown open to us we should depart within a few days after establishing our rights and making necessary arrangements for the fulfillment of our vow of completing 101 Akhand Paths there" (*Papers* 59). The SGPC specifications to the Mahatma are clear: All that Sikhs want is their freedom and right to worship in their own way and in their own sacred space.

In fact, they reject any political or territorial aspirations: "The S.G.P.C. is a purely religious body and has no desire for the establishment of Sikh Raj" (*Papers* 57). This categorical statement is followed by an anguished cry: "It is most painful to us that it should have been necessary to have to make this explanation even to you." Obviously, the trust and faith that the Mahatma had in them is no more. Political and territorial exclusions of a Sikh kingdom are misread and misappropriated into their fundamental right for religious liberty. While the Sikhs wanted their akhandpaths in an *akhand* India (unbroken India) with Hindus, Muslims, Parsis, Jains, and Buddhists, their objectives in 1924 were misunderstood. That the government clouded and confused their issues did not matter to the Sikhs but that "even you found it necessary to ask for repudiation on our part of the charge of desiring a Sikh Raj and harboring ill-will against other communities" (*Papers* 61) was very painful to them.

What I found most touching in the SGPC response was their admission of love for particular Hindus, Muslims, and Christians. Whenever Gandhi would express his love for the Sikhs, it was always in the abstract. They were "Sikhs" akin to Plato's forms, and very seldom did we come across any real persons. But when the SGPC members defend their position against territorial goals, their attachment and love for individuals comes out strikingly: "If for no other reason the love of these friends [a whole list is given including Jawaharlal Nehru, Gidwani Onkarnand, Santanam, Kitchlew] and of Malvyaji, Swami Shankerachary, Ali Brother, Mr. C.F. Andrews and yourself would prevent us from becoming anti-Hindu or anti any other community or entertaining any dreams of dominating over communities" (*Papers* 58). It is also a telling illustration of their pluralist perspective. Obviously the SGPC does not erect a Sikh canopy and hug all the named above as though they were Sikhs. Nehru, Ali Brother, or Andrews are not gathered together into their singular Sikh worldview; they remain diverse and different—Hindu, Muslim, and Christian. And in spite of their differences, the Sikhs feel a close attachment to them all. While the Sikhs do not want anyone imposing "any restrictions on us as to the number of pilgrims, period of stay, and mode of worship in our Gurdwaras" (*Papers* 59), they clearly do not want to be severed from the richness and plurality of India.

The SGPC spells out their two minimum demands: law that would provide for a central, representative, and elected body of the Sikhs as the trustees of all historical Gurdwaras, and the freedom of their religious symbol, the kirpan or sword. Gandhi himself had supported these very causes, but with an ironic twist of circumstances, the Sikhs now have to convince the Mahatma about the importance of their essential religious principles. In case of problems arising from Gurdwara administrative restructuring, they accept arbitration. But they are adamant about their right to wear, possess, carry, manufacture, sell any size or form of kirpan, their traditional religious symbol (*Papers* 63). We may recall Gandhi citing the kirpan–janeu analogy. Unfortunately neither the Sikhs nor the Mahatma had it right. Whereas the sacred thread is exclusively worn by the upper-caste male, Guru Gobind Singh's sword is worn by all four castes, and by both men and women. How the sword represents the feminine dimension of knowledge and compassion is also left out in the patriarchal dialogues. Nevertheless, it must be hard for the Sikhs to convince somebody who had at one point quoted them word for word.

I think the most frustrating and agonizing aspect for the SGPC would be to reassure Gandhi about their nonviolence. This was something they strongly believed in. The Sikhs in huge numbers had sacrificed their lives for it; the Sikhs in so many past events had unflinchingly borne brutalities for it. Even the Mahatma had praised them for their pledge to nonviolence. How could he doubt them at this crucial moment? An eyewitness to Guru-ka Bagh atrocities, Reverend C. F. Andrews, poignantly recounts the Sikhs's courageous defense for the ideal of nonviolence:

The brutality and inhumanity of the whole scene was indescribably increased
by the fact that the men who were hit were praying to God and had already
taken a vow that they would remain silent and peaceful in word and thought.
. . . Apart from the instinctive and voluntary reaction of the muscles that has
the appearance of a slight shrinking back, there was nothing, so far as I can
remember, that could be called deliberate avoidance of the blows struck. The
blows were received one by one without resistance and without sign of fear.[20]

Ruchi Ram Sahni is another witness: "Mahatma Gandhi himself could
not have expected more faithful followers to carry out his non-violent non-
co-operative struggle in the face of the gravest provocation."[21] The SGPC letter itself does not remind or depict any particular events in which Gandhi had
witnessed Sikh bloodshed, their charred remnants, their brutally beaten flesh.
The authors do not seek any sympathy from the Mahatma. Perhaps the Sikhs
are too proud or too angry to acknowledge what was most obvious. They
seem to be following the old saying *qui s'excuse s'accuse* so they think it is beneath their dignity to prove themselves. Their letter reads, "The S.G.P.C. has
been holding this principle and has always enjoined it on itself and all those
who have accepted its lead. . . . Our experience of this method has strengthened our faith in it and our adherence to it" (*Papers* 57).

Clearly, the letter suggests that nonviolence (satyagraha, which really
means the power of truth) has been appropriated by the Sikhs. They are not
simply following the Mahatma, but making it a part of their own movement
and even modifying it to match their religious ideals. The Sikh voice of independence and autonomy begins to ring out loud and clear. They reject
Gandhi's two stipulations: limitation on the numbers of satyagrahis, and the
acceptance of arrest. The letter refuses to accept Gandhi's specification that
the satyagrahis be limited to "one or at the most two." From the SGPC's
point of view, this was an utter disregard for the significance of their fundamental institution of *sangat* (congregation) "believed to be the Guru incorporate" (*Papers* 66). Moreover, by limiting the numbers, Gandhi was
neglecting the religious principles behind the shahidi jathas in the Jaito struggle. Nor, as the letter boldly asserts, will the Sikhs submit to the cat-and-
mouse policy of their rulers. Gandhi did not want them to resist arrest in any
way; in contrast, the Sikhs avow to passively disobey the order of arrest while
maintaining their pledge to nonviolence: "There is to be absolutely no retal-
iation, but only more suffering is to be invited on ourselves by refusing to
obey the mere words of command for arrest. . . . It should be borne in mind
that we are not fighting for any ordinary worldly rights but for the most precious right of religious liberty not to win any new rights, but to retain those

already ours, without which our life is impossible" (*Papers* 68). Here we have a paradigmatic image of the Sikh pluralists. As Diana Eck argues, there is no such thing as a "generic pluralist," so their pluralism demands that they be fully committed and charged to face the struggles of the Sikh community. The letter proclaims over and over that Sikhs have no political or secular agenda; their sole objective is "the most precious right of religious liberty." The Sikhs dare to be their deepest self, and that involves their freedom to live the Sikh way of life in relationship with their contemporaries—Hindus, Muslims, Jains, Buddhists, Parsis, and Christians. The SGPC in 1924 is braced for what Eck calls the "pluralist challenge: commitment without dogmatism and community without communalism."[22]

So the correspondence addressed to Gandhi that begins with a note of congruence ends up showing us the two sides standing apart from each other. There is indeed a sharp shift from the passionate speeches in Nankana Sahib made on behalf of the Sikhs to Gandhi's letter dated March 4, 1924, demanding, soliciting, requiring assurances from the Sikhs in thought, word, and deed. Historians attribute Gandhi's change of mind either to his fears that Sikhs would turn violent or that they would break away from his movement. The awakening and new excitement among Sikhs could have been quite threatening: The lionhearted Sikhs were no longer fighting for the Raj; but they now had their own direction and purpose. We can never quite know what was really going on in the Mahatma's mind. Later in life, he nostalgically reminisces, "There was a time when in Nankana Sahib I was described as true friend of the Sikhs." The breach did take place. My sense is that their approaches to religious diversity came to a clash during the Jaito struggle.

THE RELIGIOUS SUBTEXT

Gandhi saw people of other religious traditions through an inclusivist lens. In a typical majority consciousness, he smoothly glided Sikhs into his grand panoramic vision of Hinduism, the eternal dharma. As early as March 1921 he was upset with Sikh leaders (most likely SGPC members, even though he does not name them) for articulating the difference and originality of the Sikh religion: Guru Nanak, of course, was a Hindu but, according to Sikh leaders, he founded a new religion (*CW* 19:421). Gandhi places a Hindu construction on Guru Nanak, and condemns Sikh leaders for claiming him as the founder of a new religion. Earlier in the same piece entitled "Sikh

Awakening" Gandhi thinks of Sikhs as a sect of Hinduism "but their leaders think that theirs is a distinct religion." Thus Gandhi explicitly denies the originality of Guru Nanak, and he is annoyed by all those Sikhs who posit him in non-Hindu categories. As far as I see, it is the Sikhs's separate identity that really bothers Gandhi and manifests itself in the spring 1924 Gandhi–Sikh correspondence. A few months later, Gandhi again says:

> My belief about the Sikh Gurus is that they were all deeply religious teachers and reformers, that they were all Hindus and that Guru Gobind Singh was one of the greatest defenders of Hinduism. . . . I do not regard Sikhism as a religion distinct from Hinduism. I regard it as part of Hinduism and reformation in the same sense that *Vaishnavism* is. I read in the Yeravda Prison all the writings that I could lay my hands upon regarding the Sikhs. (*CW* 28:263)

Not only Nanak, but all of the ten Sikh gurus are also solidly set into a Hindu framework. For Gandhi, Sikhism is a segment of the Hindu reformation movement, similar to *Vaisnavism* (a Hindu movement practicing devotion to Lord Vishnu). The Sikh gurus are religious reformers, and the unique revelation of Guru Nanak, crystallized by his successor gurus, is totally blurred by the Mahatma. Sure Nanak was born into a Hindu family, but he had a deep spiritual experience that was his and his alone. He is not a mere reformer. The Sikh faith is grounded on Nanak's vision, and developed on his distinctive personality and message. As Nripinder Singh insightfully writes, "To see Guru Nanak allied to, or participant within, an earlier ongoing tradition however rich and variegated is to misconstrue not only the mission of a man but also the phenomenon of prophecy and the religious experience of a multitude of people over a course of five centuries."[23] Likewise, the individual contributions of Guru Nanak's successor gurus, their socioethical vision, and their ideology are all usurped from the Sikh context and patched into the Hindu *Weltanschauung* (ideology).Gandhi's inclusivist horizon completely erases the autonomy and identity of the Sikhs.

Interestingly, Gandhi blames the so-called distinction between Hinduism and Sikhism on British propaganda. He argues that there is no genuine difference between Hindus and Sikhs, and this dangerous "poison" was simply fabricated by the British. He mentions reading historical accounts of the Sikhs by J. D. Cunningham, Gokulchand Narang, and Max Arthur Macauliffe while in jail. However, Gandhi disapproves of Macauliffe, precisely because of his emphasis on "Sikhism as a separate religion having nothing in common with Hinduism" (*CW* 25:155). Macauliffe's study of Sikhism, and his translation of sacred poetry, are greatly esteemed in the scholarly world; it is also believed that he was found by his servant reciting Guru Nanak's Japji on his deathbed. However, for Gandhi, Macauliffe's contribution is a distortion. He carried this vein of thought throughout his life, for later on he makes a similar criticism of yet another British scholar: "Formerly, there was no distinction between the Hindus and Sikhs. All the poison was spread by Thomas Macaulay who wrote the *History of the Sikhs*. Since Macaulay was a well-known historian, everyone swallowed what he said. The Granthsaheb of the Sikhs is actually based on the Hindu scriptures" (*CW* 88:280).

In a way, Gandhi even refuses to acknowledge that Sikhs may have had a self-awakening. Not only are the essentials of Sikh metaphysics and ethics dismissed by Gandhi, but also the creativity and dynamism of the various Sikh movements. The Singh Sabha tried to resurrect the message of the Sikh gurus. Bhai Kahn Singh Nabha tried to awaken the slumbering psyche of the Sikhs in his popular work *Ham Hindu Nahin* (We Are Not Hindus). The Chief Khalsa Diwan became a social and educational body to spread Sikh values. The Ghadr Party and the Babbar Akalis imprinted their fierce heroism on the minds of many Sikhs. The Sikh League tried to shatter the false consciousness of the imperial masters. And the contributions of the Gurdwara Reform movement led by the SGPC and the Akalis promoted Sikh self-awareness most profoundly.

Of course, we cannot overlook Gandhi's own contribution. He did send sparks of self-awareness among the Sikhs. Before his day, a few of the Sikh movements, the Chief Khalsa Diwan in particular, were under British patronage and actually helped to cover up for His Majesty's exploitations. Gandhi visited Punjabi villages, Sikh academic centers such as the Khalsa College, and Sikh shrines, and he succeeded in reinforcing political consciousness among the Sikhs. As the SGPC correspondence acknowledges, the Akali movement was inspired by Gandhi's noncooperation and his nonviolent satyagraha. Over the course of the years, the Sikhs became stronger and more confident in themselves. The support of Gandhi during their early battles and victories gave them authenticity and courage.

And that backfired at Gandhi. As the SGPC letter of April 9, 1924, reveals, with their newfound strength, the Sikhs begin to challenge Gandhi's inclusivism: The Mahatma does not know them, he does not recognize their identity, and he misinterprets their pluralist approach for exclusivism. They want to be recognized as Sikhs who are different from other Indians, nevertheless respected and loved for their difference. The Sikhs begin to scrutinize and test Gandhi's mono-colored spiritual umbrella. The Mahatma does not understand or refuses to understand them. He confuses their perspective with exclusivist tendencies, which proved to be harmful at that volatile period of Indian history. In his reaction, Gandhi becomes even more adamant about Hindu–Sikh oneness. We hear Gandhi reiterating his intrinsic idea:

> The two religions are fundamentally one. Even Guru Nanak never said that he was not a Hindu nor did any other Guru. If we read the Granthsaheb we shall find that it is full of the teachings of the Vedas and Upanishads. . . . .It cannot be said that Sikhism, Hinduism, Buddhism and Jainism are separate religions. All these four faiths and their offshoots are one. Hinduism is an ocean into which all the rivers flow. (*CW* 90:177)

In Gandhi's horizon the Vedas are the ocean that contains all religions. Sikhism, Hinduism, Buddhism, and Jainism have no boundaries as they flow and fuse into each other in the oceanic womb of Hinduism. Gandhi's view hides within it a hierarchical acceptance of plurality, with Hinduism at the highest. I would like to borrow Eck's image and apply it to Gandhi: Everyone is invited in his inclusivist vista, but he is the one who puts up the tent; Sikhs are gathered in, but in Gandhi's terms, within his Vedic framework, and as part of his Hindu system.[24]

My personal critique of Gandhi echoes the SGPC letter. Much as I am flattered by his intimacy with Sikhism, I am equally disturbed. Despite his constant praise of Sikh gurus and their verses, why doesn't Gandhi cite some directly? One of the rare exceptions that I came across was Guru Arjan's hymn *"koi bole ram ram, koi khudae"* (some utter Rama, some Khuda). Gandhi quoted a verse from it during the intense Hindu–Muslim–Sikh strife (*CW* 89:251). Guru Arjan's words expressing the unity of the Divine were indeed very pertinent to and valuable for the heart-wrenching times. This quotation expresses Gandhi's grief at the destruction of India and everything he believed in by communalism. As a Sikh I wish he had shown more instances of such direct knowledge of Sikh scriptures.

Why didn't Gandhi ever make special mention of the Sikhs during the Jallianwalla Bagh tragedy? April 13 was a special day for the Sikhs. They had gathered together in Amritsar for the Baisakhi celebrations (commemorating the Birth of the Khalsa) from various parts of the Punjab. More than half the victims were Sikhs but Gandhi never quite says that. His speeches enunciate that he was most effected by the blood of innocent Hindus, Muslims, and Sikhs—flowing and fusing together. His ardent critic Gurmit Singh even chides the Mahatma for not returning the Kaiser-i- Hind Medal awarded to him in 1915 (in contrast with Rabindranath Tagore who immediately gave up his knighthood).[25]

Did Gandhi really understand the Sikh religion? (The English word elicits a standing "under.") In a passage in which he is praising Guru Gobind Singh, Gandhi says, "He was a man given to charity, he was unattached, he was an incarnation of God" (*CW* 89:274). Guru Gobind Singh an incarnation of God? This would be anathema to the Sikhs![26] Gandhi's saturation in Vedic thought does not permit him to bracket out his own worldview and discover Sikh phenomena for itself. Guru Nanak's message of harmony was very conducive to Gandhi's India, but rather than drown him in his Vedic ocean, Gandhi needed to validate the "Sikhness" of the Founder.

The Sikhs in fact became victims of Gandhi's inclusivism. He seems to feel so close to the Sikhs that he simply does not hear their particular needs and demands. Gandhi is almost like a mother who seldom notices her child, and in a situation where she is responsible for someone else's child, the mother neglects her own to take care of the other. Our SGPC text communicates to the Mahatma that he has overlooked Sikh aspirations. Gandhi had reprimanded Sikh Leaguers for requesting representation in the prospective flag which is a telling example of his negligence:

> We must not be parochial, provincial, or clannish. Hindu and Mussulman colours are specially represented, not so much for the numbers they represent, as for the fact that they have remained apart for so long that their mutual distrust has been an effectual bar against the realization of national aspirations. The Sikhs have never had any quarrel with Hindus. And if one has the Sikh colour separately represented, why not the Parsi, the Christian, and the Jewish? I hope the Sikh Leaguers will see the unpractical nature of their suggestion.[27]

At that time in their history, the Sikhs accepted Gandhi's rebuke. After all, the Sikh League was born from Gandhi's own inspiration. Their political movement was young, and the Sikhs looked up to Gandhi for guidance. In all likelihood it was "unpractical" to see Hindu–Sikh differences. But by 1924 the Sikhs had gained self-awareness, and had their distinct course charted out. Almost a quarter-century following their correspondence, after the partition of India, in an independent India, having lost West Punjab, the Sikh Deputation visits Gandhi in Delhi—just a week before his tragic end. The venerated Sikh leader, Giani Kartar Singh, said on January 21, 1948, "Everybody cannot be a Mahatma Gandhi" (*CW* 90:471). His few words make explicit the Sikh rejection of the Mahatma, but this rejection was not something new that happened overnight in 1948. It had a long history that began with the quietly worded letter of the SGPC in 1924. That was the real point when the Sikhs left the Mahatma.

NOTES

1. S. Radhakrishnan, *The Principal Upanishads* (London: Allen and Unwin, 1953), 139.

2. *The Collected Works of Mahatma Gandhi* (Delhi: The Publications Division, Ministry of Information and Broadcasting. Government of India, 1967), 89:472. Hereafter cited in the text parenthetically as *CW* followed by volume and page(s).

3. See S. S. Gandhi, "Sharomani Gurdwara Prabhandak Committee and Congress," in *Proceedings of Punjab History Conference Twenty-second Session, March 25–27, 1988* (Patiala: Punjabi University, 1989), 252–270.

4. Harbans Singh, *The Heritage of the Sikhs* (Delhi: Manohar Publications, 1983).

5. Patwant Singh, *The Sikhs* (London: John Murray, 1999).

6. Gurmit Singh, *Gandhi and the Sikhs* (Sirsa: Usha Institute of Religious Studies, 1966).

7. Ibid., 17.

8. Shauna Singh Baldwin, *What the Body Remembers* (New York: Doubleday, 1999), 335.

9. Ibid., 83.

10. Dietrich Reetz, "Ethnic and Religious Identities in Colonial India (1920s–1930s)," *Contemporary South Asia* 2, no. 2 (1993): 111.

11. Khushwant Singh, *A History of the Sikhs* (Princeton, N.J.: Princeton University Press, 1966), 2:195.

12. Kailash Chander Gulati, *The Akalis Past and Present* (New Delhi: Ashajanak Publications, 1974), 24–25.

13. Ajit Singh Sarhadi, *Punjabi Suba: The Story of the Struggle* (Delhi: Kapur Printing Press, 1970), 19

14. Khushwant Singh in his foreword to Gulati, *The Akalis Past and Present.*

15. Mohinder Singh, *The Akali Struggle: A Retrospect* (Delhi: Atlantic Publishers and Distributors, 1988), 80.

16. See Singh, *The Akali Struggle*, 80.

17. The Five K-s are the physical symbols worn by Sikhs, both male and female: *kesha* (unshorn hair), *kangha* (comb to keep hair tidy), *kirpan* (sword), *kara* (steel bracelet), and *kaccha* (drawers).

18. Singh, *The Akali Struggle*, 81

19. *CW*, 23:218–220. Also collected by Ganda Singh, ed., *Some Confidential Papers of the Akali Movement* (Amritsar: SGPC, 1965), 53–55. Includes photographs of Gandhi's handwritten letters. Hereafter cited in the text parenthetically as *Papers* followed by page(s).

20. Quoted at length by Singh, *Heritage of the Sikhs*, 274–276.

21. Ruchi Ram Sahni, *Struggle for Reform in Sikh Shrines*, ed.Dr. Ganda Singh (Amritsar: SGPC, n.d.), v.

22. Diana L. Eck, *Encountering God: A Spiritual Journey from Bozeman to Banaras* (Boston: Beacon Press, 1993), 195.

23. Nripinder Singh, "Guru Nanak, Prophecy, and the Study of Religion," in *Studies in Sikhism and Comparative Religion* (New Delhi: Guru Nanak Foundation, 1989), 23.

24. Eck, *Encountering God*, 179.

25. Singh, *Gandhi and the Sikhs*, 55.

26. Guru Gobind Singh is categorical about identifying himself as the slave or servant of the Divine, and rejects all other appropriations. See his *Bicitra Natak*, in *Shabdarath Dasam Granth Sahib*, ed. Randhi Singh (Patiala: Punjabi University, 1985) 6:32–33.

27. *CW*, 20:107; and *Simla*, 17 May 1921.

9

Indian Muslim Critiques of Gandhi

ROLAND E. MILLER

What did Indian Muslims think of Mohandas Karamchand Gandhi? When Khan Abdul Ghaffar Khan (1891–1989), the stern Pathan leader who became known as the "Frontier Gandhi," left India on July 30, 1947, he said: "Mahatmaji has shown us the true path. Long after we are no more, the coming generations of Hindus will remember him as an Avatar."[1] At the other end of the spectrum of opinion Mohammed Ali Jinnah wrote to Gandhi on the eve of the fateful Nagpur Congress meeting, December 1920, "Your methods have already caused split and division in almost every institution that you have approached hitherto, and in the public life of the country not only amongst Hindus and Muslims but between Hindus and Hindus, and Muslims and Muslims, and even between fathers and sons."[2] Between these extreme views there are many other opinions, some of which fall into the definition of critiques. Is there a pattern to Indian Muslim critiques of Gandhi? And who are the Indian Muslims that we are considering?

I will quickly get the second question out of the way. For the purpose of this chapter I will restrict myself to Indian Muslims who knew and worked with Gandhi. Moreover, with the exception of Malayalam materials, I will confine myself to a selection of those who wrote in English or are translated.[3] My attempt to profile those viewpoints is conditioned by four factors. The first is the historical development of the Freedom movement which brought together Indian Muslims and Gandhi within a daunting complexity. The second is the developing nature of Muslim self-consciousness, both political and religious, and the psychological involvement of Indian Muslims in the wider events of the Muslim world. At the political level they took changing directions, and at the religious level the situation compelled them to explore unfamiliar theoretical possibilities. The third factor is the intimate nature of the personal relations that existed within a fairly confined coterie of leaders. Some of the relationships were deeply affectionate ones, while

others were abrasive. The final factor is that Gandhi's own pilgrimage was
very much a progressive one, and Muslims who found his position agreeable
at one stage did not so find it at other times. These factors in combination
meant that Indian Muslim views of Gandhi were marked by a "stutter-step,"
even a "flip-flop" quality, rather than by an even flow.

Accepting these limitations, let us examine the Indian Muslim (hereafter simply Muslim) critiques of Gandhi. They can be organized into four
major categories. The first I refer to as the mild disagreements of close colleagues that tend to be minor criticisms set within an overarching friendship.
The second category has to do with the theory of ahiṁsā, and the conviction
of Muslims that this could be maintained only as a policy and not as a creed.
The third category relates to the suspicion that Gandhi was leading India to
a kind of "Ram Raj" or Hindu state. The final category takes up the issue of
priorities, and the alleged shift in Gandhi's approach. Running through the
categories, but especially applicable to the final one, is Muslim uneasiness,
sometimes articulated, with Gandhi's personal style. That includes his unpre-
dictability, his stubbornness, his tendency to take unilateral and utilitarian
positions that in the Muslim perspective left them high and dry.

I will approach the critiques by way of the opinions of individuals, but
for the ahiṁsā discussion I will also utilize Gandhi's involvement with the
Mappila Muslims of Malabar.

THE FRIENDLY DISAGREEMENTS OF CLOSE COLLEAGUES

Muslim Respect For Gandhi And The Example
Of Hakim Ajmal Khan

The overall Indian Muslim respect for Gandhi resulted not only from the Indian cultural reverence for great leaders before whom one seeks *darshan*
(blessing) and whose failings one overlooks. In his case there was something
deeper, the conviction that Gandhi really cared for Muslims and sought justice on their behalf. More analytically, we can suggest that Muslim trust of
Gandhi was based on four things: his respect for religion and religious commitment, his regard for Muslims as full members of what he once called
India's "joint family," his peace-loving nature, and his honest friendship.

Hakim Ajmal Khan (1863–1927) typified the Muslim appreciation of
Gandhi. In his role as a Muslim leader he was a kind of father figure in positive Muslim–Hindu relations in India. A landowner, physician *(tibb)*, philan-

thropist, and the first chancellor of the Jamia Millia, he laid the groundwork for much of what was to follow. The manifesto that Hakim Ajmal Khan issued jointly with M. A. Ansari in 1922 indicates a Muslim perspective on Gandhi and the Swaraj movement:

> Our Hindu brothers are with us in the struggle . . . and they are our brothers in all truth, for the Holy Qur'an teaches that the friends of the faith are our brothers. . . . Our Hindu brothers are doubly so for they love our country as we do. . . . Together we will win Swaraj—a Swaraj that will enable us to secure justice for Islam. . . . Let us remain faithful in thought, word and deed, faithful to our cause, to our country, to the leader we have chosen— Mahatma Gandhi.

In unison they called upon Muslims "to follow Mahatma Gandhi unflinchingly."[4] But mingled with the approval of close colleagues, there were at times disagreements on specific points, and we see this in the views of Mukhtar A. Ansari and Abul Kalam Azad. We turn first to the lesser known but highly important figure of Ansari.

Mukhtar Ahmad Ansari: Disagreement Within Loyalty

A physician educated in Allahabad, Hyderabad, Madras, and Cambridge, England, for years the general secretary of the Congress; twice president of the All-India Muslim League (1918, 1922), and chancellor of the Jamia Millia after Hakim Ajmal Khan died, Ansari (1880–1936) was a core, perhaps *the* core, Muslim leader in the Freedom movement. Although his commitment to Gandhi's approach was real, he was a pragmatist, and he well typifies that familiar quality in Muslim leaders. He really believed in the power of persuasion, in working through problems together, and in the principle of give and take. I would suggest that this was at the root of some difficulties with both Gandhi and Jinnah, although his immense civility almost always controlled the expression of his opinions.

In regard to the continued tension that prevailed between the respective supporters of noncooperation and cooperation with the British he stated the following in his presidential address at the 1927 Congress assembly in Madras:

> For the achievement of our object we are not wedded to any particular policy nor do we consider any programme sacrosanct or binding forever. We have to judge the policy or programme by its suitability to our particular

social and political conditions, by its practicability, and by the results which
it is likely to give within a measurable limit of time. . . .
    It is not impossible that each community may even voluntarily forego
any portion of the enjoyment of its rights out of regard for the sentiments
and feelings of others.[5]

Ansari maintained this view to the end of his career. He was a healer, and he
expressed that basic orientation concretely when he led a Muslim Red Cres-
cent medical mission to Turkey in 1913.

Ansari's affection for Ghandiji was never in doubt. It was both a personal emotion and an ideological affinity. Mushirul Hassan suggests that
Ansari was captivated by Gandhi's personality, his idealism, his concern for
the downtrodden, and his leadership qualities. Thus Ansari referred to
Gandhi as "the acknowledged and intrepid leader of India who is never afraid
to speak the truth and who has, by his noble actions, endeared himself as
much to Mussalmans as to Hindus."[6] At a personal level Ansari also followed
Gandhi in regard to the principle of satyagraha, but it became the focus of
one of his critiques.

Ansari called satyagraha "a message of hope," and the most effective
method of agitation. It was also a populist approach well related to the religiosity of India. In company with others he suggested that the involvement
of Muslims in satyagraha was not only a moral necessity but a religious obligation involving the honor of Islam and the protection of the faith. When the
agitation turned to violence, however, he parted ways with Gandhi. While he
believed that satyagraha could still succeed where Gandhiji himself was in
charge or involved, it otherwise could not. "In these circumstances," he said,
"I consider the satyagraha movement to be practically impossible and wholly
unprofitable. . . . Except some isolated people, I consider Mussalmans generally absolutely unfit to act on the principles of satyagraha."[7] This conviction
helps to explain Ansari's critique of Gandhi's civil disobedience efforts in the
post-1930 period. At the root of the critique was his belief that the conditions
of satyagraha were not the same in 1930 as they had been in 1920. There was
far too much tension in the air, and the first priority had to be given to
improving Muslim–Sikh–Hindu relations.

Positive Muslim–Hindu relations were Ansari's enduring priority. As we
shall see in more detail in the final section, he could not agree with any down-
grading of that fundamental effort, even in the interest of the Freedom movement itself. His major critique of Gandhi related to the latter's shift in priority
from harmony first to independence first. In 1930 he wrote to Gandhi that
communal harmony is "the one and only thing."[8] A unity based on common

enmity will be lost when the enmity ends. A deeper bond must be forged. To this end he believed in the efficacy of consultation and dialogue: "I have all along pinned my faith in mutual adjustments through formal and informal conversations."[9] Such discussions can and will be fruitful because of the underlying unit of Muslims and Hindus. His fundamental position on that issue was similar to Azad's, and they set the tone for many others. He believed that the destiny of Indian Muslims was linked with all other Indians with whom they had everything in common except religion. In his view the choice between loyalty to nation or loyalty to faith, as it was sometimes put forth, was a false alternative. Not only were the two loyalties compatible, but Muslims must also join in a united effort with fellow Indians to struggle for freedom, and thereafter to work with the democratic polity that is best-suited for India's conditions, adopting "more or less secular lines in politics."[10] He made his own commitments quite clear on July 16, 1926, when he resigned from both the Muslim League and the Khilafat Committee.

P. C. Chaudhury summarizes Ansari's influence in these words: "It was practically through Dr. Ansari and Hakim Ajmal Khan that Gandhiji could get into the inner enclave of the orthodox and cultured Muslims of Delhi, and through them of Northern India.[11] They gave him real information on Muslim attitudes, and protected him when some Muslims broke away from him. Gandhi depended on Ansari's "unrivalled influence" with Muslims and spoke glowingly of the latter's "transparent honesty" with Hindus. At Ansari's death Gandhi said of him: "He was essentially a symbol of Hindu–Muslim unity with Hakim Saheb Ajmal Khan."[12]

Abul Kalam Azad: The Critique Of Silence

Hakim Ajmal Khan was six years older than Gandhi, and Ansari was eight years younger. We can think of them as Ghandi's contemporaries. Abdul Kalam Azad (1888–1958) was nineteen years his junior, making their relationship a marvel. Moreover, he was a Muslim religious scholar belonging to a class that did not ordinarily mingle with Hindu leaders. The wonder increases when we note the difference in their personalities. Both were ambitious, and to a degree flamboyant. But Azad was the reserved and private Quranic specialist, with an air of mystery, while Gandhi was the public icon of the masses.

Did the age differential play a role in the fact that Azad's critiques of Gandhi were not very explicit? Or was it his personality that took no delight in recrimination? Or was it the reality of their agreement in many fundamental issues? Yet we know that Azad disagreed with Gandhi, most notably in the final acceptance of India's division, a moment when Azad's silence spoke louder than words.

Abul Kalam Azad's public history is well-known. He developed from his precocious editorship of the revivalist Calcutta Muslim journals *al-HiLal* and *al-Balagh*, to his emergence as one of the acknowledged leaders of the Freedom movement. He became a stalwart leader in the Indian National Congress, serving as its president in 1923 and 1940, and thereafter. From his dashed hopes in 1947 he emerged to become free India's first minister of education. In the course of that career Azad went through major shifts in his point of view—from his early optimistic spirit of pan-Islamism to his final and consistent endorsement of the secular democratic approach for free India. His famous remark concerning a "Sabbath rest," which alluded to ten years spent in British jails, passes lightly over the extent of his suffering, which included the repeated losses of manuscripts of his scholarly works. He succeeded Dr. Ansari as leader of the Nationalist Muslims in the Congress, and "dragged the ulama"[13] into liberation politics.

Azad was not hesitant as others were in using the word *mahatma*, and he spoke openly of "the great soul" of Gandhiji.[14] He disagreed with the latter at times, but did so respectfully. In 1945 Gandhi wrote to Azad asking him to refrain from putting up inscribed plaques in honor of individuals who gave their lives in the 1942 agitation, on the grounds that it was not possible to know who really died for swaraj. He also asked Azad not to endorse a memorial for Begum Shah because she had not really done any public service. Gandhi ended the letter by saying: "If my advice does not appeal to you, you will please reject it. The love we hold for each other demands no less."[15] Azad accepted the advice in regard to Begum Shah, but rejected it in the case of the other memorials.

Azad agreed with Gandhi in most of the core issues of the Freedom movement. Hasan suggests that "even though religion and moral fervour bound the Mahatma and the Maulana in a common quest for swaraj, they did not share a common perspective on and outlook towards sociopolitical issues."[16] It could just as well be said that though the two had different religious contexts and vocabularies their common struggle for swaraj produced a surprising commonality of outlook on major issues. Thus Azad's critiques are related to specific issues or decisions rather than to underlying themes.

The Maulana's views on the priority of Harmonious communal relations, the importance of religious toleration, and the close relation of the spirit of religion and politics are well-known and will not be repeated here.[17] His ideas were embraced in a theology of unity that provided one of the two foundations for Azad's rejection of minority politics. The other was his sense of being Indian. Religiously he thought of himself as a Muslim, politically as an Indian. In his 1940 Congress presidential speech at Ramgarh he declared: "Nothing is further from the truth than to say that Indian Muslims occupy the position of a political minority. It is equally absurd for them to be apprehensive about their rights and interests in democratic India."[18] He expressed disdain for the thought that a Pakistan was needed to protect Muslim interests, contending that "Muslims are strong enough to safeguard their own destiny."[19] It was a personal tragedy for Azad that he could never convince the majority of his fellow Muslims about the merit of this view, particularly because at one stage he optimistically regarded himself as a possible Imam-designate for the entire Indian Muslim community.

Azad was critical of Gandhi's decision to attend the last two Round Table Conferences in London. He certainly did not want any diminution of the Nationalist Muslim view of the importance of Muslim–Hindu relations. Moreover, he did not care for Gandhi's return to nonviolent civil disobedience as a methodology. He himself believed in nonviolence as a policy and not as a creed. In the period of World War II Azad joined Nehru, Patel, and others in readiness to support the British war effort if they promised freedom for India in return. When Gandhi unhappily demurred, Azad managed to persuade the Congress leaders to give him a conciliatory reply reaffirming the ultimate primacy of nonviolent civil disobedience within an overall strategy.[20] It was Gandhi's reluctant acceptance of what he had called the "vivisection" of India that provided the greatest test for the Azad–Gandhi relation, however; that relation more than survived the test, sealed by Gandhi's self-giving advocacy on behalf of Muslims in the post-1947 conflicts.

When the day of Independence arrived, it is said that Abul Kalam Azad kept his lips firmly sealed. It was not his dream that had been fulfilled. The first line in his introduction to the second edition of the *Tarjuman* expresses what he must have felt: "The helplessness of man is noticeable in the fact that the plans he lays out scarcely attain perfection."[21]

THE INDIAN MUSLIM CRITIQUE OF AHIṀSĀ

In my discussion of Maulana Abul Kalam Azad I have introduced the issue of nonviolence. Azad did not accept Gandhi's ahiṁsā as "an absolute value." He held to the validity of defensive force and the idea of just war, and believed that the Prophet Muhammad provided the true example for the appropriate use of force. He wanted war eliminated as an instrument of national policy, but also affirmed: "We recognize that in certain circumstances a limited use of force may be necessary in order to prevent violence."[22] It is the figure of Mohamed Ali, however, who best exemplifies this critique.

Mohamed Ali: The Limitations of Ahiṁsā

Mohamed Ali (1878–1931) first met Gandhi in Aligarh in 1915, and he quickly wrote to Saifuddin Kitchlew (1884–1963): "It is Gandhi, Gandhi, Gandhi that has got to be dinned into the peoples' ear, because he means Hindu–Muslim unity, non-cooperation, swadharma and swaraj, while the rest are often petty communal or local, bodies most of them tinged with personal ambitions."[23] In 1925 he announced that he had identical views on the method for achieving freedom. "I am proud to regard him as my chief."[24] Soon thereafter he became critical of ahiṁsā.

A lively grandiloquent extrovert, influential journalist, and spirited leader of the Freedom movement Mohamed Ali obtained his B.A. at the age of eighteen, and with his elder brother Shaukat Ali's assistance studied at Oxford. On his return, preoccupied with other things, he failed his Indian Civil Service exams, provoking this sympathetic comment from a biographer: "Providence had earmarked him for a nobler task than to be merely a member of the I.C.S. The result was he could not pass it."[25] He did show his independent and radical side at an early age. In 1911 he started the English weekly *Comrade* and in 1914 he started the Urdu daily *Hamdard*, and they became the vehicles for his advocacy of the Ottoman caliphate. Their anti-British effort cost the Ali brothers four years in prison (1915–1919), but they emerged in triumph. Mohamed Ali's career reached its height as he became the president of the India National Congress, the Muslim League, and the Khilafat Committee. He fought to win Aligarh University and its students from support of the British to the Congress, and in 1920 with the help of Gandhi and others he convinced some to walk out and found the Jamia Millia, of which he became the first vice chancellor. In the end he could not free himself from the romantic Khilafat frame of reference as Azad and others did, and in the wake of its demise his role faded. He became embittered and broke with Gandhi in the late 1920s.

There were two issues over which Mohamed Ali differed seriously with Gandhi: his theory of nonviolence and his Hindu orientation. We will consider only the first issue at this point. Mohamed Ali stated his opinion of ahiṁsā in a speech at Faizabad, February 30, 1921, when he said that

Ghandiji and Muslims both stood for nonviolence, "he for reasons of principle and we for those of policy."[26] In 1923 in his presidential address at the Congress assembly in Canada he elaborated on his views, using some comments on Jesus to do so. He argues that Jesus' teaching of nonresistance to evil was due to the conditions of his time rather than to a fundamental objection to the use of force at all times. Mohamed Ali acknowledges the value of self-discipline, self-purification through suffering, and moral preparation for responsibility, but he says, "I am not a Christian believer in the sinfulness of all resistance to evils, and in their practice even if not in their theory the vast bulk of Christians and all Christian states are in full agreement with me." In fact, referring to Gandhi, he states that "it was reserved for the Christian government to treat as a felon the most Christlike man of our times."[27] Then Mohamed Ali presents his own theory:

> I believe that war is a great evil, but I also believe that there are worse things than war. . . . When war is forced on Muslims . . . then as a Musalman and follower of the Last of the Prophets I may not shrink but must give the enemy battle on his own ground and beat him with his own weapons . . . face it without stint and without cessation. . . . (But) when persecution ceases, and every man is free to act with the sole motive of securing divine good will, warfare must cease. These are the limits of violence in Islam.[28]

Why then associate with the Gandhian theory? To that question Mohamed Ali simply replies that the reasons are respect for Gandhiji and strategic awareness. The respect is reflected in these words: "I have agreed to work with Mahatma Gandhi, and our compact is that as long as I am associated with him, I should not resort to the use of force even for the purpose of self-defense."[29] But perhaps there was something deeper in Mohamed Ali than the sense of contractual obligation. It seems that he had been touched by an idea, by a principle. He spoke of "the greater love," suggesting that what we must live for and suffer for is a realisation in India of "the kingdom of God." Perhaps more convincing for fellow Muslims was his emphasis on the practicality of nonviolence. Because victory can be won without violence, its use would be a reproach. On the other hand, if nonviolent noncooperation should prove to be unsuccessful, there is still advantage in it. "I know that suffering willingly and cheerfully undergone will prove to have been the best preparation, even for the effective use of force." Referring to British oppression he declares: "In spite of my utter abhorrence of such violence I say with all deliberation that on the Day of Judgment I would rather stand before

God's White Throne guilty of all this violence than to have to answer for the unspeakable sin of so cowardly a surrender."[30]

The Mappila Rebellion, 1921: Critiques Rise From The Flames

The idea of ahiṁsā as a policy that could be adopted and discarded left the door open for local Muslim interpretation. The Mappila Rebellion illustrated how far grassroots Muslims were from accepting it as a controlling principle. The rebellion, however, also revealed Gandhi's selective utilitarianism in relation to Muslims, a critique that continues to be alive. In 1918 Gandhi had written to Mohamed Ali: "My interest in your release is quite selfish. We have a common goal and I want to utilize your services to the uttermost in order to reach that goal. In the proper solution of the Mohammedan question lies the realization of Swaraj."[31] In the case of the Mappilas there is a sense that Gandhi first aroused them and then abandoned them. On November 25, 2000, when I interviewed a revered leader of the Mappila intellectual renaissance and a former university vice chancellor he stated that there were three things that bothered Kerala Muslims about Gandhi: his stubbornness, his religious revivalism, and his virtual abandonment of the Mappilas.[32]

The Mappilas of Kerala, now constituting approximately 7.6 million and approximately 21.5 percent of the state, had experienced the negative impact of foreign rule long before the British arrived.[33] Vasco da Gama, landing in Calicut, Malabar, in 1498, had led the Portuguese incursion, introducing the age of European dominance. The Portuguese distorted a centuries-long period of harmony among Hindus, Christians, and Muslims, a process that I have described elsewhere.[34] The end result was a disaffected and volatile Mappila community, whose members were the victims of a repressive landownership system, were suffering from impoverishment, and were given to frequent violent uprisings against what they deemed to be oppression. The noncooperation movement in its Khilafat aspect dropped like a spark into this tinderbox. A key event was a conference of the Kerala Congress in Manjeri, Malabar,[35] April 28, 1920.

The conference brought the Khilafat movement to the attention of the Mappilas. In an action that some have regarded as the seed of the rebellion[36] activists passed a resolution supporting that movement, a decision opposed by Annie Besant and other moderates. In the short run it resulted in many startling expressions of Muslim–Hindu amity, but in the longer run the Khilafat agitation aroused the religious and emotional fervor of the Mappilas to a high degree. On August 18, 1920, Mahatma Gandhi and Shaukat Ali addressed a large public meeting at Calicut. Exhortations to join action against the British and rosy promises of quick results were in the air. While Gandhi urged Hindus to support Muslim demands for justice within the context of appropriate means,[37] Shaukat Ali was not so restrained, and those who were there recalled the stirring impact of his words.

Shaukat Ali (1873–1938), the first secretary of the Khilafat Committee, who operated in the shadow of his younger brother Mohamed Ali, deserves greater notice than he ordinarily receives for his leadership role. He was a bluff and hearty man rather than a reflective type, and was able to rouse people easily. Moved by his pro-Turkish sentiments and by governmental tardiness in granting Aligarh, his alma mater, university status, he left government service and went into opposition. Gandhi traveled extensively with him after his release from prison in 1919, and became very fond of him. He said of his companion: "There are many good and stalwart Muslims I know. But no Muslim knows me through and through as Shaukat Ali does."[38] Shaukat Ali, on the other hand, was quite outspoken on his disagreement with Gandhi in regard to ahiṁsā. Before coming to Calicut, in a speech at Shajahanpur on May 5, 1920, Shaukat Ali stated, "I tell you that to kill and to be killed in the way of God are both satyagraha. To lay down our lives in the way of God for righteousness and to destroy the life of the tyrant who stands in the way of righteousness, are both very great service to God. But we have promised to co-operate with Mr. Gandhi who is with us. . . . If this fails, the Mussalmans will decide what to do."[39]

We must assume that Gandhi realized that the basic Muslim view of violence differed from his own. Did he think that the experience of working together would modify the Muslim opinion and bring it into closer harmony with his own? Or, as is more likely, did he simply accept the limited possibilities, taking the practical approach? He seemed to recognize his own utilitarianism. Peter Hardy quotes him as saying, "I have been telling Maulana Shaukat Ali all along that I was helping to save his cow [i.e., the caliphate] because I hoped to save my cow thereby."[40]

There is no need to go into the details of the Mappila Rebellion and the suffering that it entailed for both Hindus and Muslims. The events came like a pail of cold water on the flame of Muslim–Hindu harmony. The Mappilas not only turned violently against their British overlords, but also against the landowning Hindu establishment in a six-month uprising beginning August 20, 1921. Hindu leaders shocked by the Mappila militance drew back from what had been initially regarded as a joint effort. The Mappila sense of betrayal was a major factor in the anti-Hindu nature of the rebellion in its latter stages. As some Hindus even aided British forces, Mappilas responded with killings, arson, robberies, and forced conversion. While the rebellion did not begin as a communal outbreak it ended as one. After six months the Mappilas were severely repressed, and suffered most with 2,266 slain, 252 executed, 502 sentenced to life imprisonment, thousands jailed in different parts of India, and many exiled to the Andaman Islands.[41] The fact that the Mappilas later rose like a phoenix from the ashes to become a changed community that has become positively and dynamically involved in societal development is a marvel of Indian Muslim history. At the close of the rebellion though, they were stunned and silent. There were others, however, who were not silent.

Some of them were Muslims. The cultured and educated northern leaders of Indian Muslims felt trapped by the situation, damned if they did, and damned if they didn't. Hakim Ajmal Khan took the middle ground, as the majority of Muslims did, in his 1921 presidential address to the Congress Assembly in Ahmedabad. He said, "I cannot close without referring to the tragic events that are daily taking place in Malabar and the prolonged agonies of our unfortunate Moplah brethren." He blamed the government for provoking the disturbances and denounced the British "pacification," but he also condemned the forcible conversion of Hindus. "There will be no Muslim worthy of the name who will not condemn the entire un-Islamic act in the strongest possible terms."[42] But the opinion that Gandhi had to deal with directly was that of Hasrat Mohani (1878–1951), the pen name of Syed Fazlul Hasan. An Aligarh graduate, Urdu poet, fiery worker for the Freedom movement, advocate of a forceful approach, and critic of ahiṁsā, he found no fault in the essential Mappila approach. As to their attack on the Hindus he argued that it occurred because of Hindu support for the British.

Gandhi made frequent references to the Mappilas in his letters and speeches between 1921 and 1924. His reaction ranged from criticizing some Mappilas to blaming the British to pointing to Hindu failure to a bare recognition of possible responsibility on the part of the Non-cooperation movement. In a Madras speech in the middle of the rebellion he had said, "I would like you to swear before God that we shall not resort to violence for the freedom of our country or for settling quarrels between Hindus and Mussulmans . . . that in spite of the madness shown by some of our Moplah brethren we Hindus and Mussulmans shall remain united forever."[43] He repeated the phrase "Moplah madness" frequently, and he advised Hasrat Mohani not to defend their actions. But he also blamed the British saying, "They have punished the entire Moplah community for the madness of a few individuals and have incited Hindus by exaggerating the facts."[44] As for the Hindu responsibility he declared, "The Moplahs have sinned against God and have suffered grievously for it. Let the Hindus also remember that they have not allowed the opportunity for revenge to pass by."[45] He gave the following advice to Hindus: "We must do away with the communal spirit. The majority must therefore make a beginning and thus inspire the minorities with confidence. . . . Adjustment is possible only when the more powerful take the initiative without waiting for response from the weaker."[46]

In regard to the crucial question of whether there was responsibility on his own part, or on the part of the Non-cooperation movement or whether his theory was at fault, Gandhi was not very forthcoming. He acknowledged the critiques saying, "Many letters have been received by me, some from well-known friends telling me that I was responsible even for the alleged Moplah atrocities in fact, for all the riots which Hindus have or are said to have suffered since the Khilafat agitation."[47] Yet he felt that the significance of the Mappilas should not be overstated because they constitute a special case. Their response cannot undermine the validity or cause of nonviolence. He declared, "The Moplahs themselves had not been touched by the non-cooperation spirit. They are not like other Indians nor even like other Mussalmans. I am prepared to admit that the movement had an indirect effect upon them. The Moplah revolt was so different in kind that it did not affect the other parts of India."[48] A Muslim historian, I. H. Qureshi, gives a less sanguine perspective: "The Moplah rebellion confirmed Hindu fears and provided the first nail in the coffin of Hindu amity."[49]

THE CRITIQUE OF GANDHI'S HINDU ORIENTATION

It is not surprising that some Muslim suspicions regarding Gandhi and the movement that he led stemmed from his Hindu frame of reference. In this section I will examine the critique of his "Hindu-ness," noting the views of Muhammad Iqbal and Muhammad Ali Jinnah.

Gandhi's Hindu Frame Of Reference

Indian Muslims were in an everyday relationship with the adherents of other religions and there was no essential problem for them in the fact that Gandhi was a committed Hindu albeit in a reforming mode. In fact, as I have noted, part of his appeal was his serious attitude toward religion. Moreover, he was a Hindu who had repeatedly affirmed and demonstrated his respect for Islam and Muslims, and Muslims regarded him as one who could be trusted. That regard, however, could not entirely offset his public language that sometimes communicated the sense of an oncoming Hindu raj, nor his associations with the Hindu right. The fear was expressed by Mohamed Ali and others. There was a strong and growing feeling among many Indian Muslims that the progress of events was leading them into a position of "perpetual servitude" to the Hindu majority. Was it true that Gandhi was, in fact, the knowing or unwitting agent of Hindu communalism? The charges must have seemed virtually unbearable to Gandhiji who had steadily reached out to Muslims with what he called "the law of friendship." Yet Muslims felt danger, and for some Gandhi was implicated. When we examine the critiques we immediately note that the fear was not for the religion of Islam, but for the well-being of Muslims. If it had been fear for Islam, Gandhi's movement could never have gained the support of Muslim religious leaders as it did.

Nevertheless, there were elements in Gandhi's approach that raised concerns among Muslims, and some observers have recognized the legitimacy of their apprehension. Ajit Roy includes Mahatma Gandhi in the charge that for most Congress leaders "nationalism was practically blended with Hindu religious inspirations. Hindu religious idioms and images served to articulate the nationalist message."[50] Prabha Dixit lists support for the caste system, the popularization of Hindi, cow protection, and the idea of trusteeship of Hindu civilization as elements in Gandhi's own ideology.[51] The adulation of Gandhi's followers added to the problem. In the late 1930s the Wardha Scheme of Education had been worked out by a committee headed by Zakir Husain. Its requirements that included honoring the Congress flag, wearing khadi cloth, and singing the "*Bande Mataram*" were a sufficient stretch for some Muslims. But when in practice it also included the reverencing of the Mahatma's portrait, it was too much for many. More than the tendency of some to venerate Gandhi's person, more than his own habit of drawing on Hindu religious stories in his communication efforts, more provocative were his associations with the Hindu right that piled up indiscretions, led by the president of the Hindu Mahasabha, V. D. Savarkar, who in 1938 publicly declared, "Mr. Jinnah is quite correct in stating that the Congress has been, since its inception down to this day, a Hindu body."[52]

The critiques of Gandhi's Hindu-ness were led by Modernist Muslims rather than by Muslim theologians. The theologians had decided that a free and united India was best for Muslims. They approved of Gandhi as an ally against the British, behind Azad generally accepted his leadership, and adopted a noncritical approach.[53] Others, however, did not share their view.

Ishtiaq Qureshi, who joined Pakistan and became its minister of education, actually suggested that Gandhi was "infusing Hinduism" into Congress thinking.[54] Holding that what especially shocked the Muslim community was Gandhi's failure to throw his weight against such movements as *suddhi* and *sangatham*, he agrees with Mohamed Ali's view that this was the result of Gandhi's desire to retain Hindu popularity. Mohamed Ali's own outburst at the Muslim Conference in 1930 testified to his sense of outrage. The one-time close colleague of Gandhiji declared that the latter's movement "is not a covenant for complete independence of India but of making seventy million of Indian Muslims dependent on the Hindu Mahasabha."[55] In contrast, Sir Muhammad Iqbal's views constitute a gentle reproof.

The Opinion Of Sir Muhammad Iqbal: A Mild Critique

The most biting critiques of Gandhi's Hindu orientation came in connection with the Pakistan issue, but Muhammad Iqbal (1876–1938) had passed from the scene before that idea had fully flowered. In fact, Iqbal and Gandhi pay each other surprisingly little attention. On reflection the reasons become evident. On the one hand Iqbal's poetic line well describes them both:

> In servitude life is reduced to a tiny stream,
> In freedom it is like the boundless ocean.[56]

Yet Iqbal's first priority, the revitalization of Islam, was quite different from Gandhi's. Moreover, the poetic and philosophic aspects of Iqbal's multisided career overshadowed political involvements. His practical politics were largely confined to the Punjab scene, and he chose not to participate in the Khilafat movement that drew together Gandhi and other Muslim leaders. Gandhi respected Iqbal's love of India and his poetry, and in later years more than once quoted the *ghazal* line: "Religion does not teach us to bear ill will toward one another." Iqbal, in turn, recognized Gandhi's special role as "the apostle" of Indian nationhood, although he did not appreciate the hero-worship attached to it. Muhammad Daud Rahbar points out how Iqbal once refused to rise for Gandhiji at a meeting presided over by the viceroy on the grounds that such veneration was Islamically inappropriate.[57]

Iqbal's primary critique of Gandhi is associated with his own vision of a Muslim territory within northwest India where Muslims could freely develop their life along modern lines, a vision that in his perspective required separate electorates. He did not regard this approach as a conflict with his commitment to religious harmony. In his presidential address to the Allahabad Session of the All-India Muslim League on December 29, 1930, Iqbal made his famous proposal for such a territorial alignment in India (which later evolved into Pakistan):

> Communalism, in its higher aspect, then, is indispensable to the formation of a harmonious whole in a country like India . . . which instead of stifling the respective individualities of the component whole, affords them choice of fully working out the possibilities that may be latent in them . . . thus possessing full opportunity of development within the body politic of India.[58]

The issue he presented became concrete in connection with the negotiations of the Second Round Table Conference in London in 1931, and the British government's Communal Award in 1932. Iqbal, who was present at the former, opposed Gandhi's view that the Congress represented all the people of India and that in the future Indians should vote only "as Indians." With his view of a "higher" communalism, Iqbal could not and did not criticize Hindu self-consciousness, but rather Hindu unawareness of Muslim needs. Iqbal saw Gandhi's opposition to the Communal Award as a demand "for safeguarding the interests of Hindus." He declared, "If separate electorates for Untouchables means disintegration of the Hindus, the joint electorate will mean political death for the minorities. In my opinion, it has become clear from the attitude of Mahatma Gandhi that the minorities who are keen to maintain their separate identity should not abandon separate electorate."[59] In Iqbal's view Gandhi should have been attacking the Hindu oppression of the Untouchables more rigorously and not the protective award. But we must turn to Muhammad Ali Jinnah for the strongest critique of Gandhi's orientation.

The Stern Critique Of Mohammed Ali Jinnah

The vision and careers of Mohammed Ali Jinnah (1876–1948) and Gandhi intersected in ways that made their disagreement almost inevitable. Jinnah's critiques of Gandhi are levied at both personal and policy levels and in the later years they became very pungent. In summarizing their relationship Stanley Wolpert says that they were "always at odds with deep tensions and mistrust underlying its superficially polite manners, never friendly, never cordial."[60] Jinnah was loath to use the word *mahatma*. His utilization of *Mr.* Gandhi not only revealed his view of what was appropriate, but in public contexts it also tended to be deliberately provocative. Their personal distancing did not mean that they failed to appreciate each other's talent. In September

1944, when they met for talks at Bombay, Gandhi began with the words: "Well, Jinnah, you have mesmerized the Mussalmans," to which Jinnah responded, "And you have hypnotized the Hindus."[61]

Jinnah took deep issue with Gandhi's methodology. It was not so much ahimsā as the very idea of noncooperation that bothered him. He was a constitutionalist, looking for solutions through moderate legislative change. The notion of civil disobedience violated his legal sense of appropriate procedure. Whereas Gandhi sought swaraj in whatever form that might ultimately take through nonviolent noncooperation, Jinnah wanted self-government within the British commonwealth, attained by constitutional methods. At the Nagpur Congress assembly and at the Muslim League meeting in 1920 Jinnah's approach lost out in what is described as "the most bitterly humiliating experience of his public life."[62] Gandhi, with the support of the Ali brothers, declared the first nationwide satyagraha on August 1, 1920. Six months later Jinnah described Gandhi as a great man, but stated firmly that he did not believe in and could not support his program.

From that point Jinnah's relationship with Gandhi went downhill, as his conviction grew that the Congress did not really represent Muslims and would not provide the safeguards they needed. He parted ways with the Nationalist Muslims in the Congress, and Azad became his headache. Their mutual role reversals are striking, Azad starting as a community revivalist but ending as a proponent of unity; Jinnah beginning from the latter and ending as the advocate of a separate homeland for the Muslims. Declining a peace overture from Azad in 1940, Jinnah sent him this telegram:

> I have received your telegram. I cannot reciprocate confidence. I refuse to discuss with you by correspondence or otherwise as you have completely forfeited the confidence of Muslim India. Cannot you realize that you are made a Muslim show-boy Congress President to give it colour that it is national and deceive foreign countries? You represent neither Muslims nor Hindus. The Congress is a Hindu body. If you have any self-respect, resign at once.[63]

Azad, who was never known to answer attacks, did not respond.

Jinnah's critique of Gandhi became forthright. In an extemporary speech at the annual meeting of the Muslim League in 1938, Jinnah charged Gandhi with turning the Congress into a Hindu body. Gandhi's own Hinduness is behind it.

> Who is the genius behind it? Mr. Gandhi. I have no hesitation in saying that it is Mr. Gandhi who is destroying the ideal with which the Congress was

started. He is the one man responsible for turning the Congress into an instrument for the revival of Hinduism. His ideal is to revive the Hindu religion and establish Hindu Raj in this Country and he is using Congress to
fulfil this object.[64]

Jinnah repeated this vehement charge at the time of the Quit India agitation in 1942. I will leave aside the question of whether this insightful leader
fully believed the indictment himself or whether it was a form of rhetoric related to his political agenda, but he was consistent in his attack. At the conclusion of the Bombay talks in 1944 he declared to Gandhi, "You do not
accept that the Muslims of India are a nation. . . . You do not accept that the
Muslims have an inherent right of determination." Gandhi's conclusion was:
"Mr. Jinnah is sincere, but I think he is suffering from hallucination when he
imagines that an unnatural division of India could bring either happiness or
prosperity to the people concerned."[65] So Jinnah and Gandhi parted ways,
and India in turn was parted.

THE CRITIQUE OF GANDHI'S PRIORITIES AND STYLE

The connection between priorities and style may not seem immediately obvious, but they come together in this final category of Indian Muslim critiques
of Gandhi. The stylistic element has to do with Gandhi's decision making in
matters that were perceived as deeply affecting the future of Muslims in India.
Gandhi's tendency to arbitrariness is well-known; it represented an exasperat-
ing quality for his Congress colleagues and others. He would refer major decisions to an "inner voice" that only he could hear, and the voice led him to
unpredictable actions. Yet he himself did not at the time doubt their necessity,
timing, or utility. When his self-willed approach took him in the direction of
modifying fundamental principles involving Muslim interests, however, it
inevitably became the object of critiques.

A notable example of such a critique came when Gandhi arbitrarily can-
celled the Civil Disobedience movement on February 12, 1922. It did not
matter that he took the action out of a well-founded conviction that people
were not yet ready for mass nonviolent action. The Mappila Rebellion, the
Chauri Chaura massacre, and other incidents signalled to him that he had to
make the decision to cancel. The Muslim reaction was one of ill-concealed
dismay. What mattered most to Muslims was the feeling that the principle of
mutual consultation was lost. Only two years previously 118 leading 'ulama

had subscribed to the fatwa enjoining Muslim participation in the Non-cooperation movement as a religious duty. In Islamic theory only they had the right to revoke that call. Whether Gandhi understood the point or not, he certainly ignored it. "Gandhiji who was not only not an *alim* but also not a Muslim called it off without taking the consent of the ulama."[66] The Jamiyat I Ulama called a special meeting to reconsider its entire stand on nonviolence, and Maulana Abdul Bari who spoke more strongly in private simply said, "There is general depression all over."[67]

More important than style, however, were the underlying issues. For Muslims one matter loomed most prominently: the question of the final, the ultimate priority in the Freedom movement. We have met that issue already in the friendly critique of Gandhi's close colleague Ansari. It was crucially important for all Muslims. The question was clear. Was the first goal the achievement of Muslim–Hindu harmony, or was it the achievement of independence? The two goals were functionally linked, but they could be and were distinguished. There is no doubt of Gandhi's original priority. From the beginning of his association with the Freedom movement he had made it clear that its first concern must be the attainment of Hindu–Muslim understanding and harmony. Without that, independence could not be attained, indeed, would not be worth attaining. If the adoption of right means is important because means are ends in the making, so also the achievement of right relations is critical because they provide the essential basis for the life to come. Muslims sensed the high significance of Gandhiji's initiative. In fact, we may even say that they thrilled to it. The Khilafat movement came along in a convenient way to underline the principle. Muslims also understood the proleptic significance of Gandhi's stance: if his priority was maintained, mutually acceptable solutions to Muslim concerns could and would be found before the advent of free India, and Muslim fears would cease.

But it was not so maintained. Gandhi upheld the concern, but reversed the priority, giving precedence to the achievement of independence over the goal of Hindu–Muslim unity. Muslims might have made their peace with a nonconsultative style, but they were less able to accept this fundamental shift in policy. The change, which was in part the result of the upsurge of communal disharmony in the late 1920s, became evident after 1930. Gandhiji himself was aware of the change he was making and its implication. As usual blaming himself, he felt that the present approach was not working and needed to be given a rest. Muslims such as the Ali brothers expressed their distress over the decision in embittered language. Ansari, representing Gandhi's distraught friends, gently suggested that the Congress and Gandhi were drifting from the goal of communal harmony, and thereby they were in danger of losing the Muslim heart. He said, "Perhaps you were not very confident of yourselves, or perhaps you felt that you could not succeed in bringing about a communal settlement by means of conferences. Whatever the causes that is how it strikes me and many others."[68] Gandhi's reply to this reproof did not give the assurance needed. He said,

> My views are just as strong as they were on the necessity of this unity. But I have come to the conclusion that this is the time for real lovers of unity to sit still and simply pray showing in their individual action what a living unity of hearts can mean. Do you not meet in your practice with boils which grow worse with teasing? The more you tease it the worse it becomes. It needs a rest cure.[69]

He expressed his belief that "if we have true freedom we will shed communal fear. The Hindu and Muslim will cease to fear one another."[70]

Nationalist Muslims, though unhappy, did not abandon Gandhi or the freedom struggle, even though the shift in priorities created space for the advocates of the idea that Muslims could only be safeguarded in a distinct homeland. Nevertheless, they believed that Gandhi had made a fatal choice.[71] Whether justified or not, the perceived reluctance of Congress and Hindu leaders to deal further with Muslim aspirations, especially after 1937, eventually threw Muslim sympathies into the direction of the proposal for Pakistan.

CONCLUSION

I have argued in this chapter that there were Muslim critiques of Gandhi, some cogent and well intended, some passionate and ill-founded. I organized the critiques into four categories: the friendly disagreements of close colleagues, the critique of ahiṁsā, the critique of Gandhi's Hindu orientation, and the critique of his reformulation of priorities, recognizing that the material might well be presented in other ways. We cannot end without noting that almost all the "critics" wrapped their remarks in the blanket of appreciation for Gandhi, for his deep friendship with Muslims, and for his concern for their needs. The overall Muslim approbation of Gandhi exceeds and outlasts the critiques.

S. Abid Husain (1896–1978), philosopher, educator, author, and junior colleague of Gandhi, described him as "the great one." He regretted that their preoccupation with politics had prevented Muslims from participating in Gandhi's constructive welfare work for the masses. He believed that it was only Gandhi who fully understood the importance of Muslim integration in the Indian nation.[72] Above all, he was overwhelmed by Gandhi's affection for Muslims that became so strikingly clear in the Calcutta conflict of 1940. Abid Husain declared, "In Calcutta and Noakhali the fire of hatred was put out with the miraculous power of love by Mahatma Gandhi":[73] He had put into words what many thought.

When the post-Partition turmoil enveloped Delhi, Gandhi went on a six-day fast (January 12–18, 1948) two weeks before his assassination. Abul Kalam Azad went to Gandhi to ascertain Gandhi's terms for breaking the fast, and then Azad addressed a Delhi crowd of about three hundred thousand people to communicate those terms. Without exception they had to do with Muslim needs: the evacuation of mosques by non-Muslims, freedom of worship and religious festivals, full safety and freedom of movement, the lifting of economic boycotts, and full discretion for Muslim evacuees "to come home" if they so desired.[74] Considering events such as these, and Gandhi's entire career of service, Zakir Husain (1897–1969), colleague, scholar, and president of India, pointed very simply to what he considered to be the essence of the matter: "It is part of our national temperament, and inheritance from the great leader of our liberation movement, Mahatma Gandhi, that power should be used only for moral purposes."[75]

It is appreciation rather than critique that represents the final word of Indian Muslims on Mahatma Gandhi.

Notes

1. Quoted in P. C. Chaudhury, *Gandhi and His Contemporaries* (New Delhi: Sterling, 1972), 136.

2. Stanley Wolpert, *Jinnah of Pakistan* (New York: Oxford, 1984), 7.

3. Space limitation precludes dealing with such diverse yet important and representative figures as the Agha Khan, Mahmud al-Hasan, Abdul Bari, Yakub Hasan, Zafar Ali Khan, Zakir Husain, and others.

4. Mushirul Hasan, *A Nationalist Conscience* (New Delhi: Manohar, 1987), 93.

5. M. Zaidi, ed., *Congress Presidential Addresses* (New Delhi: Indian Institute of Applied Political Research, 1989), 4:295, 306.

6. Hasan, *A Nationalist Conscience*, 56f.

7. Ibid., 56f.

8. Ibid.

9. Ibid., 215; letter to Gandhi, n.d.

10. Ibid., 152.

11. Chaudhury, *Gandhi*, 56.

12. Ibid., 159f.

13. Mushir U. Haq, *Muslim Politics in India* (Meerut: Meenakshi Prakashan, 1976), 53.

14. Quoted in S. P. Bakshi, *Abul Kalam Azad: The Secular Leader* (New Delhi: Anmol, 1991), 26.

15. Ravinder Kumar, ed., *Selected Works of Maulana Abul Kalam Azad* (New Delhi: Atlantic, 1991), 2:37.

16. Mushirul Hasan, "Secular and Communitarian Representation of Indian Nationalism: Ideology and Praxis of Azad and Mohamed Ali," in Mushirul Hasan, ed., *Islam and Indian Nationalism* (New Delhi: Manohar, 1991), 77.

17. Cf. Haq's treatment of Azad's "religion," in *Muslim Politics*, 72–87. For his theology of unity, see Roland E. Miller, "Modern Indian Muslim Responses," in *Modern Indian Responses to Religious Pluralism*, ed. Harold Coward (Albany: State University of New York Press, 1987), 234–256.

18. Zaidi, *Addresses*, 5:31.

19. Kumar, *Selected Works*, 2:163.

20. Ibid., 1:32.

21. Abul Kalam Azad, *The Tarjuman al-Qur'ān*, vol. 1, *Sūrat-ul-Fātihā*, trans. Syed Abdul Latif (Bombay: Asia, 1962), xiv.

22. Kumar, *Selected Works*, 7:8.

23. Mushirul Hasan, "Azad and Mohamed Ali," in *Islam and India Nationalism*, ed. Mushiral Hasan (New Delhi: Manohar, 1991), 85.

24. Ibid., 87.

25. Saleem Kidwai, "Mohammed Ali, a Forgotten Patriot," in *Muslims and India's Freedom Movement*, ed. B. K. Ahluwalia and S. Ahluwalia (New Delhi: Heritage, 1985), 178.

26. Judith Brown, *Gandhi's Rise to Power: Indian Politics, 1915–1922* (Cambridge: Cambridge University Press, 1972), 331, fn. 1.

27. Zaidi, *Addresses*, 4:132–135.

28. Ibid., 4:136.

29. Ibid., 4:137.

30. Ibid., 4:138.

31. Hasan, *A Nationalist Conscience*, 69.

32. Interview with Professor K. A. Jaleel, Feroke, Kerala, 25 November 2000.

33. Cf. statistics in Roland E. Miller, *The Mappila Muslims of Kerala*, rev. ed. (Madras: Orient Longman, 1992), 317 and appendices. For a sum-

mary article, cf. Miller, "Mappila," *Encyclopaedia of Islam*, 2nd ed., 6:458–466.

34. Cf. Roland E. Miller, "Trialogue: The Context of Hindu–Christian Dialogue in Kerala," in *Hindu–Christian Dialogue*, ed. Harold Coward, (Maryknoll, N.Y.: Orbis Books, 1989), 47–63.

35. *Malabar*, meaning "place of the hills," was the ancient generic term for southwest coastal India. Under the British the name was used to signify an administrative district in the Madras Presidency. United with Travancore–Cochin it became the State of Kerala in 1957, but the name lingers on.

36. Cf. Madhavan Nair, *Malabar Kalāpum* ("Malabar Rebellion" Malayalam) (Manjeri: K. Kalyani Amma, 1971), 82.

37. *The Collected Works of Mahatma Gandhi* (Delhi: The Director, Publications Division, 1965), 17:177–180. Hereafter cited as *CW*.

38. Gail Minault, *The Khilafat Movement* (New York: Columbia University Press, 1982), 179.

39. Quoted in G. Krishna, "The Khilafat Movement," *Journal of the Royal Asiatic Society* (1968): 49.

40. Peter Hardy, *The Muslims of British India* (Cambridge: Cambridge University Press, 1972), 196.

41. Miller, *Mappila Muslims*, 49. The whole rebellion is examined on pages 126 to 154.

42. Zaidi, *Addresses*, 4:20f.

43. *CW*, 21:135; speech dated September 16, 1921.

44. Ibid., 22:201.

45. Ibid., 23:514.

46. Ibid., 23:152.

47. Ibid., 24:136.

48. Ibid., 23:3.

49. I. H. Qureshi, *Ulama in Politics* (1972; reprint, Delhi: Renaissance Publishing House, 1985), 260.

50. Ajit Roy, "RSS and Its Cultural Ideological Roots," in *Religion, State, and Politics in India*, ed. Moin Shakir (Delhi: Ajanta Publications, 1989), 209.

51. Ibid., 70.

52. Haq, *Muslim Politics*, 135.

53. Cf. Hardy, *Muslims*, 243–346, for the surprising political views of the Jam'iyyat al-'ulama-i Hind. For Mahumud al-Hasan's definitive fatwa on the subject of Muslim cooperation with Hindus, see A. A. Engineer, "The Ulema and the Freedom Struggle," in *The Role of Minorities in the Freedom Struggle*, ed. A. A. Engineer (Delhi: Ajanta Books International, 1986), 1–15.

54. Qureshi, *Ulama*, 317.

55. Hasan, *A Nationalist Conscience*, 173.

56. Quoted in Muhammad Sadiq, *A History of Urdu Literature* (London: Oxford University Press, 1964), 383.

57. Muhammad Daud Rahbar, "Glimpses of the Man," in *Iqbal*, ed. Hafeez Malik (New York: Columbia University Press, 1971), 42.

58. C. H. Philips, ed., *The Evolution of India and Pakistan: 1858–1947* (London: Oxford University Press, 1962), 4:239.

59. Iqbal's comments on Gandhi's 1932 correspondence with Ramsay MacDonald are reported by Masud-ul-Hasan in *Life of Iqbal, Book 1* (Lahore: Ferozoons, 1978), 312. For Iqbal communalism "in its better aspect" equates culture, cf. 270f.

60. Wolpert, *Jinnah of Pakistan*, 38.

61. K. H. Kurshid, *Memories of Jinnah*, ed. Khalid Hasan (Karachi: Oxford University Press, 1990), 29.

62. Wolpert, *Jinnah of Pakistan*, 70.

63. Kumar, *Selected Works*, 1:161.

64. Wolpert, *Jinnah of Pakistan*, 166.

65. Ibid., 234ff.

66. Haq, *Muslim Politics*, 157.

67. Minault, *Khilafat*, 185.

68. Hasan, *A Nationalist Conscience*, 213.

69. Ibid., 213f., fn. 10.

70. Ibid., 176.

71. M. C. Chagla, a Muslim minister of education in India, expressed the grievance when he said that his one criticism of Gandhi was that he "gave all importance to the communalists instead of the Muslim nationalists." Quoted in Rama Kundu, "Common Civil Code," in Shakir, *Religion*, 209.

72. S. Abid Husain, *The Destiny of Indian Muslims* (Bombay: Asia Publishing House, 1965), 234.

73. Ibid., 118.

74. Kumar, *Selected Works*, 3:125.

75. Chaudhury, *Gandhi*, 234.

10

Gandhi and the Hindi-Urdu Question

Daud Rahbar

Introduction

Three languages had enjoyed the favor of the ruling class in the centuries of Muslim dynasties: Arabic, Persian, and Urdu. All three were written in the Arabic script, the script of the Muslim holy book, the Qur'an. Urdu evolved as a language from the interaction of Arabic and Persian with the vernaculars of northern India. While Persian was the court language of the Mughuls, Urdu became the lingua franca of the area. Although not all Indian Muslims were Urdu speakers, and not all Urdu speakers were Muslims, the language came to hold a special significance for the Muslim community and its future in free India was a matter of great concern for its members.

The original meaning of the word *Urdu* is army encampment. Its pronunciation varies in different languages. It is the same word as the English word *horde*. In Turkey of today it is spelled Ordu and means army. The military headquarters of the Mughul Empire in Delhi in the time of Shah Jehan (1628–1666) was called Urdu-I-Mu'alla (the exalted army camp). The name *Urdu* for the language suggests that the development had something to do with the daily contact between the Turk and Afghan soldiers and the native Indian shopkeepers at the marketplace of the army encampment, resulting in the assimilation of Arabic and Persian vocabulary by vernacular languages. John B. Gilchrist (1759–1841), the first president of Fort William College at Calcutta, whom I shall consider in more detail later, invented the name *Hindustani* to cover the various forms of this linguistic development. In its heavily Sanskritized form it became known as "Hindi."

Right up to the end of the British raj in 1947 most of the educated
Hindus in northern India were able to read Urdu in the Arabic script with the
same ease with which people like me today can read English. Thousands of
Hindu authors produced with felicity books and pamphlets in Urdu on all
kinds of subjects in the nineteenth and twentieth centuries. The more influential newspapers representing Hindu interests in northern India were in
Urdu (or English). Hundreds of Hindu poets produced poetry in Urdu and
were invited to recite their poetry in the popular symposia of poetry known
as *musha'aras*. The dialogues and songs of the most popular cinematic films
also were in Urdu.

However, as the Freedom movement developed, Hindu stewards of education and politics were bothered by the force of momentum of Muslim culture and were now eager to replace Urdu written in the Arabic script with
Hindi written in the Devanagari script, the script of Sanskrit. *Devanagari*
means the script of the city of gods. The "two languages" called "Hindi" and
"Urdu" were by now almost completely identical in grammatical structure.
The difference between them included:

1. That of script. Devanagari for Hindi and Arabic script for Urdu.

2. That of vocabulary. For Hindi preference of words coming from
   Sanskrit and Prakrits (native vernaculars). For Urdu preference of
   words borrowed from Arabic and Persian.

The desire of Hindu leaders to see Hindi replace Urdu in national life is understandable. Their zeal in this matter was motivated by the spirit of vindica-
tion. "Let us de-Muslimize our culture, purify it and restore our pride in the
glorious achievements of pre-Muslim times." This was the mood of the
Hindu leaders in the day of struggle for independence.

Thus what should be the national language of independent India after
the end of the British raj was a hot question in the first half of the twentieth
century in India. The question anxiously preoccupied the elite of the Muslim
and Hindu communities. By "national language" was meant not lingua franca
but an official language to be preferred for government transactions, law
courts, educational institutions, and broadcasting. The question has its roots
in a thousand years' history of the Hindu community's encounter and coexis-
tence with the militant Muslim minority on the subcontinent. However,
within the scope of this chapter I can only briefly mention the background of
the British period.

BACKGROUND OF THE HINDI-URDU CONFLICT

Arabic, the language of the Qur'an, had one advantage over Sanskrit. It was the language of a people who immediately after the death of the Prophet sent out missionaries to all the countries they conquered. These missionaries set up schools everywhere for the teaching of Arabic. Arabic quickly rose to the position of an international language. Sanskrit, on the other hand, was the sacred language of the religious community that had no interest in converting foreign nations to the Hindu faith. Within India it remained the language of high society. The contents of the canonical scriptures of the Vedas were chanted in Sanskrit by the priests at religious ceremonies but their meanings were not understood by common folk. No translations of the Vedas into any of the spoken languages of India existed before the twentieth century. Production of Sanskrit literature discontinued after the eleventh century. Sanskrit now could not compete successfully with Arabic and Persian.

Arabic came to the Indus Valley with the Arab invaders in A.D. 713. The Arabs were no strangers to the populations of the west coast of India. Their trade relations with this part of India had existed from ancient times. In the four centuries of Arab rule in Sindh, Arabic was learned not only by Sindhi converts to Islam, but by other natives as well out of interests economic and cultural. In the period of the Ghaznavid kingdom instruction of Arabic went on also in the mosques of the Punjab (1001–1186). When non-Arab Muslim conquests of India began (circa A.D. 1000), Persian, written in the Arabic script was used by the governments of Iran, Khorasan, Turkestan, and northern India for international communication and for service as the lingua franca around these countries. During the Ghaznavid rule of the Punjab, and later in the three centuries of the Sultanate of Delhi (1206–1526), instruction in Arabic was available in India as part of religious education. In these two periods instruction of Persian went on too, though on a smaller scale. A class of Persian-knowing natives was needed to assist the administration.

At first high-caste Hindus were reluctant to learn Arabic and Persian. One class of Hindus, however, seized the opportunity of employment in the governments. They belonged to the caste known as "Kayasth." The *Hindustani Dictionary* of J. T. Platts gives us this meaning of the word: literally, incorporate; name of a mixed tribe or caste of Hindus (sprung from a Kshatriya father and a Sudra mother); the writer caste; a man of that caste, a writer, scribe, clerk. With the passage of time, Hindus of other castes too learned Persian and developed a taste for exotic delicacies of Persian poetry and ornate rhymed Persian prose.

In his excellent book *Adabiyat-i-Farsi men Hindu'on ka Hissa* (The Participation of Hindus in the Production of Persian Literature), Professor Sayyid Abdullah of the Punjab University of Lahore traces four periods of Hindu authorship of Persian literature in India:

> Four periods of Hindu authorship of Persian literature are traceable. The first period commences during the reign of Moghul Emperor Akbar. Due to lack of proficiency the number of works produced in this period is rather small. The second period begins with the accession of [Akbar's son] Jehangir and extends into the early years, or one should say, up to the middle of the reign of Shahjehan. In this period Hindus translated their religious books into Persian. The third period begins with the reign of Aurangzeb Alamgir and ends with the decline of the Moghuls. This is the best period of Hindu works in Persian. In it countless fine works were produced by Hindu authors in the fields of historiography, literary essays, poetry, music, prosody, ethics, lexicons, mathematics, etc. Also translations [from native languages']. . . . As a matter of fact historiography, accounting, mathematics and the writing of stylish prose required for official correspondence were the special skills of Hindu employees in government offices. Their duties were writing of chronicles, drafting of official letters, ledger keeping and composing of manuals of government regulations. Some of these functions became hereditary. Holders of such offices trained their children in their own special disciplines to make them eligible for those offices. That is how historiography, well-composed prose and accountancy became hereditary specializations in certain [Hindu] families."[1]

Professor Sayyid Abdullah's list of Hindu authors in Persian includes authors in the period of decline of the Moghuls and the growing power of the East India Company. Preeminent among these is Raja Ram Mohan Roy of Bengal (1772–1833). He learned to read the Qur'an in Arabic and could write in Persian with great felicity. He was basically a reformer of the Hindu religion and founded the Brahmo Samaj in Calcutta, a religious society of Vedantic Hinduism. He was sent to London by the Moghul King Akbar Shah II as ambassador. He died in Bristol in 1833.

Persian remained the language of the Moghul court for more than two centuries (1526–1761). By the end of the seventeenth century Urdu had become highly Persianized, rich in vocabulary and refined enough for graces of courtly address. Shah-i-Alam II who was enthroned in 1761 wrote poetry in Urdu and was a patron of Urdu poets. So was Bahadur Shah II, the last Moghul king (1837–1857).

Appreciation of Urdu poetry now became fashionable and the Hindu cultivators of high culture were diverted from Persian to Urdu literature, especially poetry. This switch was easy because they were already fully literate in the Arabic script. Persian, however, still enjoyed the status of state language in the country. The East India Company used it for communication with the Muslim, Hindu, and Sikh princedoms of the country. Neither English nor any other language of India could be regarded capable of replacing Persian.

The responsibilities of the directors of the East India Company became bigger after the British conquest of Bengal in 1757. Their deliberations on the need of understanding the ways of native Indian society became earnest. Warren Hastings was appointed governor of Bengal in 1772 and his position was elevated to that of governor-general two years later (1774–1785). He was made aware of the importance of Persian, which was still the official language of the Moghul government. In 1780 he laid the foundation stone of Madrasah-i-Aliya (The Grand School) for the study and teaching of Arabic and Persian.

Some time before the end of his ten years as governor-general he received proposals for the promotion of Oriental studies from Dr. John Gilchrist, a medical doctor who came to India in 1782 for medical practice. After a short period of employment as assistant surgeon in the service of the East India Company, he became interested in learning the most widely spoken language of the country, namely, Urdu, to which the English people had already given the name *Hindustani*, the language of Hindustan.

Hastings received the proposals of Dr. Gilchrist with enthusiasm but soon resigned (1785) and returned to England. Sir John MacPherson who was appointed acting governor-general also supported Dr. Gilchrist's proposal soon after taking charge of his office. He provided funds for John Gilchrist who was given the assignment to visit the more important centers of high culture in India and study Oriental literature. Dr. Gilchrist spent many years in Faizabad, Lucknow, Delhi, and other cities studying Urdu and Hindi in depth. In 1786 he published part I of a lexicon entitled *A Dictionary, English and Hindoostanee* and published part II of it in 1790. In 1796 he published *A Grammar of Hindoostani Language*. He returned to Calcutta to settle down there in 1799 and opened his own *madrasah* (school) for the teaching of Hindustani to Englishmen.

In December 1798 Lord Wellesley arrived in Calcutta as governor-general. He announced the plans of founding Fort William College in Calcutta and ordered that all the English officials employed by the company take courses in Indian languages at this college. The college was inaugurated on May 4, 1800. Dr. Gilchrist was appointed professor there and lectured for four years, combining his teaching duties with the writing of a number of books.

Hitherto most of the Urdu literature was poetry. During his four years of service at the college Dr. Gilchrist engaged a number of capable writers to produce works in simple Urdu prose fit for the study of Urdu by English employees of the company. Before the publication of these works, prose literature in Urdu was scarce and was almost exclusively on religious subjects. Of the works produced under Gilchrist's direction *Bagh-o-Bahar* of Mir Amman Dihlavi and *Tota Kahani* of Haidar Bakhsh Haidari are classic works. The production and publication of books in Urdu and Persian by Fort William College continued for a half-century after the departure of Dr. Gilchrist. It was facilitated by the invention of type for the printing of Urdu and Persian books in 1778. The inventor was Sir Charles Wilkins.

Fort William College was closed in 1854. By stimulating the writing of original works in simple Urdu prose, and translations of Arabic, Persian, and Sanskrit classics into simple Urdu, the college popularized Urdu. As a result, Urdu became suitable for replacing Persian as the official language of the government of the East India Company. The administration of the college did not exclude from its program the publication of works in Hindi in the Devanagari script, but in this line the output was relatively small.

In 1834 Thomas Macaulay was made a member of the governor-general's council and assumed the duties of president of the Committee of Public Instruction in Calcutta where he served for three years. He vigorously put his views on education before the court of the East India Company. Being himself a superb essayist in English he had an ardent desire to see the younger generations of India get acquainted with and appreciate the best of English literature.

Owing to the momentum from Moghul times, the teaching of Persian had prevailed in the existing network of educational institutions in northern India. In the hope of replacing it, a new network of "district" schools was set up. Macaulay hoped that some time in the future English would be the medium of instruction in higher levels of education. But for the immediate future, it was decided that the media of instruction were to be the vernacular languages. Among these, Urdu was foremost. By now it had a fairly regulated standardized grammar and a considerable variety of literature in print, and was spoken and understood by lots of people in the urban centers of culture in northern India. About the same time, in 1835, Urdu replaced Persian as the official language of the company's government in northern India.

Muslims of India and Pakistan are grateful for what Fort William College did for Urdu literature but they believe that the trouble of rivalry between Urdu and Hindi was stirred up by the publication of a few books in Hindi prose (in the Devanagari script) by this college.

The outcome of the revolt of Muslims and Hindus known as the Mutiny of 1857 changed the dynamics of politics radically. The titular King Bahadur Shah who took part in the revolt was sent into exile in Rangoon. The Moghul throne was overthrown. The Muslim aristocracy of northern India was chastised by the victorious English government ruthlessly and for the next quarter-century Hindus enjoyed the favors of the government.

The mediator between the Muslims and the English people was Sir Sayyid Ahmad Khan (1817–1898). He founded the Mohammadan Anglo-Oriental School in 1875 in Aligarh and Mohammadan Anglo-Oriental College in the same town in 1877. It is here that after a century's reluctance Muslim families began to send their sons to get an education that combined the study of English, Western sciences, and British history along with the history of India, the history of Islam, and Arabic and Persian literature. Until 1921 this college remained affiliated with the Allahabad University. Then it grew to be a full-fledged university and was named the Muslim University.

Sir Sayyid Ahmad Khan did for the Muslims in India what Raj Ram Mohan Roy did for the Hindus. Each of them helped his own religious community in its adjustment to the British raj. The role of Mahatma Gandhi was different. He aspired to being a mediator between the Hindus and the Muslims. His efforts at mediation, however, were hampered by the question of a national language of a United Free India.

The political leaders on both sides were untrained in scientific study of historical linguistics and therefore were unable to be objective in their understanding of the origin of Hindi and Urdu. Even the scholars on both sides were biased in this period of political tension. The echo of statements of Hindu leaders (including Mahatma Gandhi) was that Hindi already existed. The Muslims adopted it for their literary works, used the Arabic alphabet for it, and stuffed it with Arabic and Persian vocabulary. The Muslim leaders retorted, saying that Urdu is a blend of underdeveloped vernaculars of north India which got groomed, refined, and enriched by Muslim poets and prose writers who chose to write it in the Arabic script. The Hindi of seven centuries ago, they said, was of the *ap bharansh* kind. This word means "a vernacular without a regular standardised grammar." The Hindi of the twentieth century, they said, was invented at the Fort William College of Calcutta by Hindu authors serving on its faculty who in their prose works shunned the use of Arabic and Persian words and used instead words derived from Sanskrit, and moreover used the Devanagari characters instead of Arabic characters.

Dipping into the results of serious research on this issue by scholars of both communities will take too much space here and is not necessary for our discussion of things political. The political leaders were not interested in academic opinions at that time anyway. Their minds were made up. Knowledge of historical grammars of a number of north Indian vernaculars would be required for any objective understanding of the relation between Hindi and Urdu. Sir George Grierson's monumental *Linguistic Survey of India* identifies a vast number of dialects spoken in India. At the beginning of volume 2 of his survey he has the following announcement:

Subject to subsequent revision, the following is the proposed list of eleven volumes for the Linguistic Survey of India.

Vol. I.   Introductory
Vol. II.   Mon-Khmer and Tai families.
Vol. III.   Part I.   Tibeto-Burman languages of Tibet and North Assam.
             Part II.   Bodo, Naga, and Kachin groups of the Tibeto-Burman
             languages.
             Part III. Kuki-Chin and Burma groups of the Tibeto-Burman
             languages
Vol. IV.   Dravido-Munda languages.
Vol. V.   Indo-Aryan languages, Eastern group.
             Part I.   Bengali and Assamese.
             Part II.   Bihari and Oriya.
Vol. VI.   Indo-Aryan languages, Mediate group (Eastern Hindi).
Vol. VII.   Indo-Aryan languages, Southern group (Marathi).
Vol. VIII.   Indo-Aryan languages, North-Western group (Sindhi, Lahnda,
             Kashmiri, and the 'Non-Sanskritic' languages).
Vol. IX.   Indo-Aryan languages, Central group.
             Part I.   Western Hindi and Panjabi.
             Part II.   Rajasthani and Gujarati.
             Part III. Himalayan languages.
Vol. X.   Eranian family.
Vol. XI.   "Gipsy" languages and supplement.[2]

THE FIRST EPISODE OF HINDI-URDU CONFLICT

In his book entitled *The Muslims of British India*, Peter Hardy gives us the following account of this episode.

A concern in the United Provinces, which the Aligarh leadership could share both with the smaller Muslim *zamindars* and with minor but literate Muslim government employees, was the fate of Urdu as the language of the lower courts and the lower administration. The centuries of Muslim rule in the upper provinces had left Urdu, with its Arabic script and Persianised and

Arabicised vocabulary, as the *lingua franca*. In the eighteen-sixties a movement in favour of Hindi, written in the Devanagari script and with a vocabulary drawn more from Sanskrit, started from Benares. The argument was that Urdu was the language of an urban minority, and that its use for most purposes of legal and official contact with the Indian population discriminated against Hindus in favour of Muslims. British officials were inclined to see the demand for Hindi in the North-Western Provinces and Awadh as a ploy by Bengalis to gain employment there, as they would find it easier to work in Devanagari, but this was an exaggeration; Babu Shiv Prasad, a Hindu member of Sir Saiyid Ahmad Khan's Scientific Society from the North-Western Provinces, demanded that the proceedings of the Society be conducted in Hindi and published a periodical to further the cause of Hindi. A number of memorials were received by the Hunter Education Commission in favour of Hindi from both the upper provinces and the Panjab.

Although in the eighteen-seventies Hindi was adopted as the language of the lower courts, first in Bihar and then in the Central Provinces, British officials in the upper provinces resisted the demand, partly on the ground that Urdu was the vernacular at least in Awadh, and partly because they did not wish to cause Muslim disaffection. Moreover, recent research has suggested that, as a subject of study in the schools of the North-Western Provinces and Awadh, Urdu had gained ground relative to Hindi. In 1860–1, 11,490 boys were studying Urdu in government schools and in 1873, 48,229, a percentage increase of over 219. The equivalent figures for Hindi were 69,134 and 85,820, a percentage increase of rather over twenty-four. In the Panjab the British themselves had been largely responsible for promoting Urdu as the language of day-to-day dealings with the "native" population.

In 1900, however, without consulting Muslim opinion, but after receiving in March 1899 a Hindu deputation to press for the change, the Lieutenant-Governor of the United Provinces, Sir Anthony MacDonnell, issued orders permitting the optional use of the Devanagari script in court documents and requiring a knowledge of both scripts by court officials. Although these orders did not enforce the use of Hindi in place of Urdu, but merely permitted it, they provoked a strong Muslim agitation led by Muhsin al-Mulk (1837–1907) and Wiqar al-Mulk (1841–1917) of Aligarh, who founded an Urdu Defence Association. Sir Anthony MacDonnell, who feared too much official reliance upon Muslims and played off Hindus against them, intervened to force Muhsin al-Mulk to choose between the presidency of the Urdu Defence Association and the secretaryship of the Muhammadan Anglo-Oriental College at Aligarh, by threatening withdrawal of government financial support for the college. Muhsin al-Mulk resigned the presidency, but after MacDonnell's departure from the United Provinces organized the Anjuman-i-Taraqqi-i-Urdu in 1903, as an adjunct of the Muhammadan Educational Conference. Muslim fears of a relative loss of ground of Urdu to Hindi proved justified. In 1891 twenty-four Hindi newspapers had an estimated circulation of about 8,000 whereas sixty-eight

Urdu newspapers had a circulation of over 16,000. In 1911 eighty-six Hindi newspapers had a circulation of over 77,000, about 1,000 more than the 116 Urdu newspapers.[3]

CHRONOLOGY OF GANDHI'S ROLE
IN THE POLITICS OF NATIONAL LANGUAGE

1893–1915	Most of these years he lived in South Africa. Later, when back in India he recalled with satisfaction his ability to use the Hindustani language as a facility in his contact with the pluralistic Indian community of South Africa.[4]
March 1919	He presided over the session of the Hindi Sahitya Sammelan (Hindi Fellowship Conference) (CW 90:255).
1925	He accepted the term *Hindustani* for the national language, to replace his erstwhile use of the term Hindi for it. This was in consequence of the following resolution passed by the Indian National Congress at its Cawnpore Session: "This Congress resolves that the proceedings of the Congress, A.I.C.C. and the Congress Working Committee shall ordinarily be conducted in Hindustani" (CW 75:251–253; 81:97).
1935	He presided over the session of the Hindi Sahitya Sammelan the second time (CW 90:255).
1936	He participated in the Nagpur Session of the Akhil Bharatiya Sahitya Parishad (All-India Fellowship Assembly). Here he confused, and in fact, offended, Dr. Abdul Haq, secretary of the Society for Promotion of Urdu, by saying, "The national language is *Hindi athava Hindustani* (Hindi or Hindustani) (CW 62:383–384).
Perhaps 1941	He founded the Rashtra Bhasha Prachar Samiti (National Language Society) at Wardha (CW 78:343–344).
May 2, 1942	He founded the Hindustani Prachar Sabha (Society for the Propagation of Hindustani) at Wardha (CW 78:343–344).
October 8, 1945:	He resigned from his membership of the Standing Committee of the Hindi Sahitya Sammelan.[5]

1947 (shortly before August 15):	He predicted publicly "that Hindi in Devanagari script can never become the national language of India" (*CW* 88:417). Needless to say this prediction proved to be wrong. The Lok Sabha (National Assembly) passed a resolution in November 1949 declaring Hindi in Devanagari script as the national language.

The subject index to *The Collected Works of Mahatma Gandhi* gives us references to nearly three hundred pronouncements by Gandhi relating to the question of national language. They fall into the following categories:

I. Statements in Favour of Hindi as the National Language
    Examples: "The key to speediest achievement of swaraj lies in . . . the spread of Hindi as the national language" (*CW* 17:370).
    "Hindi alone can become the common language of the educated people of India."[6]

II. Statements Expressing Gandhi's Wish to Propagate Hindi in South India
    Examples: "My appeal to you is that you should give your mind to the spread of Hindi" (in a speech in Mysore; *CW* 34:209–210).
    "It is necessary that you should learn Hindi" (From a speech in Bangalore).[7]

III. Statements Recommending that Hindustani Be Recognised as the National Language
    Examples: "The national language of India can be no other than Hindustani" (*CW* 88:351).
    "In the end the national language has to be Hindustani. (*CW* 86:55).
    "I have said it time and time again, and I repeat it, that Hindustani alone can become the common language of all Indians. Neither Hindi nor Urdu can take its place."[8]

IV. Statements That Tell the Dravidians of South India to Learn Hindustani
    Example: "I want a pledge from you here and now . . . that you will all learn Hindustani" (from a speech at a prayer meeting in Madras).[9]

V. Statements Defining Hindustani
    Examples: "[A] natural fusion of the two [i.e., Hindi and Urdu] becoming a common interprovincial speech called Hindustani. Then the equation would not be Hindustani = Hindi + Urdu but Hindustani = Hindi = Urdu" (*CW* 75:280).

"It is generally agreed that that medium should be Hindustani—a re-
sultant of Hindi and Urdu, neither highly Sanskritised nor highly Persianised or Arabianised" (*CW* 28:119–120).

VI.   Conciliatory Statements
       Example: "[I]f the Hindus and the Muslims or rather people of all re-
       ligions are friends, they must accept a common language evolved from
       Hindi and Urdu."[10]

VII.   Statements Recommending the Learning of Both the Devanagari
       Script and the Urdu Script by All the People of India
       Examples: "If I could have my way, I would make the learning of De-
       vanagari script and the Urdu script, in addition to the established
       provincial script, compulsory in all the provinces" (*CW* 28:121–122).
       "It is our duty to learn both the scripts. Then alone can we honestly
       serve the country in a humble way."[11]

VIII. Statements Recognising the Importance of Urdu
       Example: "I had made it clear at Indore that Hindi did not mean ex-
       clusion of Urdu. . . . [W]e include Urdu-knowing people in taking ac-
       count of the supporters of the national language. Therefore the
       national language = Hindi + Urdu."[12]

IX.   Statements That Confused or Alienated Muslim Lovers of Urdu
       (Note: The explanatory comments at the end of each statement are
       mine.)

       1. "A correspondent writes to ask why I object to English being
           used, but not to Urdu. The Muslims and the English are the same
           to us since we are friends of all. The correspondent's complaint
           arises out of ignorance. Not only do I not object to Urdu being
           used, I am its advocate. It is a provincial language like Punjabi,
           Marathi, Gujarati, Bengali and Oriya" (*CW* 90:254–255).
       Comment: This statement was made after Independence, on Decem-
       ber 18, 1947. It is for the first time that Gandhi gives to Urdu the sta-
       tus of a provincial and not an interprovincial language.

       2. "I have been saying that there should be a single national language,
           and that this should be Hindi. This, I hear, has created some mis-
           understanding among Muslims. Some of them imagine that, in ad-
           vocating Hindi, I ignore the claims of Urdu. By Hindi I mean the
           language spoken by Hindus and Muslims in North India and writ-

ten in Nagari and Urdu scripts. I am in no way ill-disposed to the Urdu language. In my view, the two languages are one; they have a common structure and idiom, except for the difference in respect of the use of Sanskrit and Persian words" (*CW* 14:80).

Comment: Urdu-loving Muslims would object to this definition of Hindi.

3. "Equally important is the question of a national or all-India language. It can never be English. English is undoubtedly the language of the rulers and of international commerce. But Hindi-Hindustani alone can be our national language. At present it has two forms. In order to understand both the forms of the national language, viz., Hindi and Urdu, and for their natural synthesis we must learn the Devanagari and Persian scripts" (*CW* 79:24–25).

Comment: Urdu-loving Muslims would object to the hyphen between Hindi and Hindustani.

4. "And then for all-India intercourse we need, from among the Indian stock, a language which the largest number of people already know and understand and which the others can easily pick up. This language is indisputably Hindi. It is spoken and understood by both Hindus and Muslims of the North. It is called Urdu when it is written in the Urdu character. The Congress, in its famous resolution passed at the Cawnpore session in 1925, called this all-India speech Hindustani. And since that time, in theory, at least, Hindustani has been the Rashtrabhasha. I say 'in theory' because even Congressmen have not practiced it as they should have" (*CW* 75:157).

Comment: That Hindi is called Urdu when it is written in the Urdu script is a statement that would sound coercive to champions of Urdu.

5. "But is Urdu a language distinct from Hindi as, say, Bengali is from Marathi? Is not Urdu a direct descendant of Hindi, written in the Persian character with a tendency to borrow new words from Persian and Arabic rather than Sanskrit? If there was no estrangement between the two communities, such a phenomenon would have been welcomed. And when the animosities have died out, as they will one day, our descendants will laugh at our quarrels and will be proud of the common Hindustani speech which will be a mixture of words indifferently borrowed from many lan-

guages according to the tastes and equipment of its multitude of writers and speakers" (*CW* 75:279).

Comment: Partisans of Urdu would not agree that Urdu was "a direct descendant of Hindi."

6. "Even the South Indian languages—Tamil, Telugu, Malayalam, Kannada—are full of Sanskrit words and, if there was just a little fervour and love of the country in us, we should not hesitate to decide to write all the languages derived from Sanskrit as also the Southern group in the Devanagari script" (*CW* 75:244).

Comment: Urdu lovers would be troubled by this bias in favor of Devanagari.

7. "The first note of opposition was sounded when I attempted to use Hindi as a term synonymous with Hindustani. Again it was an attempt in the right direction. But I had lost caste by then and every act of mine had begun to be suspect" (*CW* 74:6).

Comment: He owns his responsibility for bringing confusion to the situation and is self-righteous at the same time.

8. "Then why insist on 'Hindi or Hindustani' and why not simply say 'Hindustani,' the writer may say. For one simple reason that it would be impertinent for me, a newcomer, to ask an association of 25 years' standing to alter its name when the need for it is not clearly proved. The new Parishad is an offspring of the older Association and wants to cater both for the Muslims and Hindus of the North who speak the common mother tongue, it does not matter whether it is called Hindi or Hindustani. For me either word has the same connotation. But I would not quarrel with those who would use the word 'Hindi' if they mean the same speech as I do" (*CW* 62:384).

Comment: This statement was made at the Nagpur Session of Akhil Bharatiya Sahitya Parishad in 1936. Here he is upholding his formula of Hindi athava Hindustani, preferring it to the straightforward formula of simply Hindustani as the national language. The reason he gives for the preference is his loyalty to Hindi Sahitya Sammelan (Hindi Fellowship Conference).

9. "There are obvious limitations. A common script for all India is a distant ideal. A common script for all those who speak the Indo-Sanskrit languages, including the Southern stock, is a practical ideal, if we can but shed our provincialisms" (*CW* 28:120).

Comment: This is inconsistent with his oft-repeated recommendation that both the Devanagari and the Urdu script be learned by all the citizens of India.

10. "The Hindu–Muslim madness no doubt stands in the way of a thorough reform. But before the acceptance of Devanagari script becomes a universal fact in India, Hindu India has got to be converted to the idea of one script for all the languages derived from Sanskrit and the Dravidian stock" (*CW* 34:168).

Comment: He is forgetting his own message that both the scripts should be learned by all.

11. "[T]housands of Hindus even today write in the Urdu script and some even do not know the Devanagari script. In the end, when Hindus and Muslims will have ceased to regard each other with distrust, when the causes for such distrust have disappeared, the script which has greater range and is more popular will be more widely used and thus become the national script. In the intervening period, Hindus and Muslims who desire to write their petitions in the Urdu script should be free to do so and these should be accepted at all Government offices" (*CW* 34:25).

Comment: He is hinting at the prospect that in the end Devanagari will prevail.

12. "Once we forget the Hindi-Urdu controversy, we shall realize that for Muslims throughout India Urdu is the lingua franca. This proves that since Moghul times, Hindi or Urdu was well on its way to becoming the national language of India. Even today, there is no language to rival Hindi in this respect. The question of national language becomes quite easy of solution once we give up the Hindi-Urdu controversy. Hindus will have to learn some Persian words while Muslims will have to learn some Sanskrit words. This exchange will enrich and strengthen the Islamic language and provide a very fruitful means for bringing Hindus and Muslims closer together. In fact we have to work so hard for dispelling the present fascination for the English language that we must not raise the Hindi-Urdu controversy. Nor must we fight over the script" (*CW* 14:295).

Comment: There is equivocity in the statement "since Moghul times, Hindi or Urdu was well on its way to becoming the national language of India." The statement has a strong bias in favor of Hindi.

13. "Should both the scripts and the styles be learned by national workers and Congressmen only or by all? My answer to this question is
that all Indians should become Congressmen, and thus everybody
should learn both the styles and the scripts" (*CW* 14:344–345).
Comment: In this statement by "both the scripts" is meant both the
Devanagari and the Urdu scripts. And by "both styles" is meant both
the Sanskritized style and the Persianized style. That all Indians should
become Congressmen to solve all the problems would sound coercive
to most Muslims.

14. "I don't want Hindi to die nor Urdu to be banished. What I wish
is that both should become useful to us. The law of saryagrapha
says that one can clap with one hand. It may not produce sound,
but what of that? If you stretch one hand, the other will follow au-
tomatically. Haq Saheb had said something in Nagpur, which I
could not then understand. I did not accept his 'Hindi *alias* Urdu.'
It would have been better if I had accepted his point. He came for
friendship, but was met with opposition and turned almost an
enemy. But I have no enemy. Then, how can Haq Saheb be one?
That is why today we are again on the same platform. An all-India
literary conference was held at Nagpur, but it was its first and last
session. We had gathered to come closer, but were divided. What
was the use of such a gathering? It was a literary conference of all
India not only Hindustani and so my speech on the occasion was
full of Sanskrit words. If I were again required to speak before such
a gathering, I should speak the same language" (*CW* 78:179).
Comment: The date of this statement, made at a session of the Hindustani Prachar Sabha (Society for the Propagation of Hindustani) is
February 27, 1945. In this speech he tries to befriend a preeminent
champion of Urdu, Dr. Moulavi Abdul Haq, honorary secretary of Anjuman-e-Taraqqi-e-Urdu (Society for the Promotion of Urdu). He recalls with regret having offended Dr. Abdul Haq in 1936 at a session
of Akhil Bharatiya Sahitya Parishad by proposing the formula Hindi
athava Hindustani. He regrets also that at that Assembly he had failed
to understand Dr. Abdul Haq's prudent formula of *Hindi ya'ni Urdu*
(Hindi alias Urdu).

A united India with a single national language was Gandhi's dream.
However, the limitations of his linguistic aptitude were at play in his thinking
about the national language question. He admits these limitations: "Gujarati

being my mother tongue, naturally, I have love for it. But everyone knows how imperfect my Gujarati is. My grammar is weak, my spelling indifferent. What need I say about my Hindi, Urdu and Hindustani? Yet I have allowed myself to be the president of the Hindustani Prachar Sabha" (84:274). The only language in which he could speak and write with command was English. He was not an avid reader of literature of any language. Here and there in his speeches and writings he mentions with admiration Hindu poets such as Tulsidas, Surdas, Tukaram, and Kabir (*CW* 28:21; 38:230). His acquaintance with great Persian and Urdu poets was nil. His longtime associations with the Hindi Sahitya Sammelan were known to the Muslim leaders.

On the Muslim side the counterpart of the Hindi Sahitya Sammelan was Anjuman-e-Taraqqi-e-Urdu (Society for the Promotion of Urdu). Founded in 1903, it began to develop into an institution of tremendous accomplishment and influence in 1912 when Dr. Moulavi Abdul-Haq (1870–1961) took charge as its honorary secretary.

Affectionately remembered by the Urdu lovers of India and Pakistan as "Baba-e-Urdu" (Grandpa Urdu), he was like Gandhi, a man of phenomenal drive, energy, and dedication to his cause. He lived a life of celibacy that enabled him to devote himself fully to the service of Urdu. More has been written in Urdu on his life and work than on the life of any other Indian Muslim leader of the twentieth century. His life is by now a legend. Unfortunately, no biography of him has been written in English.

Born in the town of Hapur in the district of Meerut, he graduated from the Mohammedan Anglo-Oriental College of Aligarh in 1894. The founder of that college, which later grew to become the Muslim University of Aligarh, was Sir Sayyid Ahmad Khan. Abdul Haq was one of his most favorite disciples.

After his graduation Abdul Haq chose to make Hyderabad, Deccan, the base of his career. Hyderabad was the largest of the native princedoms within British India. It was ruled by His Exalted Highness the Nizam. To the Muslims of British India it represented a beloved remnant of the Moghul Empire. The Nizam was looked upon by the Muslims as a benefactor of Muslim organizations.

During his employment as muhtamim (director) of education in Aurangabad in the Nizam's government, Dr. Abdul Haq was elected Secretary of Anjuman-e-Taraqqi-e-Urdu. This society was supported by a grant from the Nizam's government. The medium of instruction for most of the subjects in the universities of British India was English. Dr. Abdul Haq wished that the administration of the university in Hyderabad would introduce Urdu as the medium to replace English. His friend, Sir Ross Masud, grandson of Sir Sayyid Ahmad Khan, supported the idea and the dream became a reality. The need of Urdu books in all the subjects necessitated creation of a Darut-Tarjama (translation bureau). This activity in Hyderabad was a new chapter in the progress of Urdu in the country.

Dr. Abdul Haq edited *Urdu*, a scholarly quarterly journal, and *Hamari Zaban*, a fortnightly organ of the Anjuman. He assembled a team of collaborators to prepare the first English–Urdu dictionary, which he edited and published in 1937. Some of his colleagues in Hyderabad called him the "Dr. Samuel Johnson of India." His work included editing a number of classical Urdu texts, guiding research work, organizing Urdu conferences, and traveling to all parts of India to help fellow Muslims in their efforts to provide instruction in Urdu. In 1936, by invitation, he attended the Nagpur session of the Akhil Bharatiya Sahitya Parishad. The organizers of the assembly told the public that its purpose was to bring together the literati of all communities for deliberation on how to enrich the literature of the nation in all the languages.

The atmosphere of this assembly made Dr. Abdul Haq uncomfortable. To him it seemed a predominantly Hindu event, true to the highly Sanskritized name of the organization. Here in his dialogue with Gandhi he protested against the latter's equivocal formula of Hindi athava Hindustani for the national language. When asked what he meant by it, Gandhi answered, "Hindi which at some time in the future will become Hindustani."

Alarmed by the anti-Urdu mood of Hindu leadership at this assembly, Dr. Abdul Haq decided to move the office of his Anjuman from distant Hyderabad to Delhi for close and ready contact with the leaders of all communities. So he took retirement from his professorship at Hyderabad and moved to Delhi in 1938.

In 1947 the office of the Anjuman in Delhi was plundered. Abul Kalam Azad who was minister for education, advised Dr. Abdul Haq to leave India and make Pakistan the home of the Anjuman. The government of India allowed Dr. Abdul Haq to move the library of the Anjuman to Pakistan. The Anjuman's office was now established in Karachi. Today there are two Anjumans with the same name, the Anjuman-e-Taraqqi-e-Urdu of Pakistan and the Anjuman-e-Taraqqi-e-Urdu of India, with its office in Aligarh.

In Pakistan the clash of Urdu was no more with Hindi but with Bengali. The Hindi-Urdu conflict was one of the causes of the partition of India in 1947. The Urdu-Bengali conflict was one of the causes of severance of East Pakistan from West Pakistan in 1971 and the creation of Bangla Desh.

In the debates over the question of national language Dr. Abdul Haq was the spokesman for the defenders of Urdu. In several of his presidential addresses given at Urdu conferences before and after Independence he spoke about his mistrust of Gandhi's intentions regarding the national language. Here is an extract from one of his speeches:

> In the beginning the Anjuman carried on its work quietly. Its goal was propagation and progress of Urdu and enrichment and expansion of Urdu literature. It stayed away from any action of opposition to Hindi or any other language. But when its work was interfered with it became necessary to get ready with defenses.
>
> Here I must mention that episode which marks the beginning of an entirely new phase in the life of the Anjuman. In 1935 Mr. Kanhayya Lal Munshi came to see me in Hyderabad and said to me, "We wish to found a new Association in the hope of participation by the literati of every language, enabling us to get acquainted with the literature of each other. We would like you to be a member of its Working Committee." Since the matter was literary, I consented. In 1936 the Session of this Association was held in Nagpur, with Gandhiji presiding. The Association was named Akhil Bharatiya Sahitya Parishad (All-India Fellowship Assembly). The question was raised here as to what should be the language of proceedings of the Parishad. When the question was put to me, I answered, "Hindustani should be the language." Gandhiji asked, "What is the reason for calling it Hindustani?" I answered, "Because the Resolution of the Indian National Congress says so. Moreover, Article 21 of the Constitution of the Congress is clear on this issue." Gandhiji said, "That Resolution is not explicit on the connotation of the name." I said, "Sir, if the connotation is going to be a new one after every decade how will things work?" Gandhiji was in favour of Hindi. When the pitch of the dialogue rose, Gandhiji tried another trick and proposed a new language with a new name: Hindi-Hindustani. I enquired, "What do you mean by Hindi?" He answered, "It is that language which is in the books but not in the common parlance." Then I asked, "What do you mean by Hindustani?" He replied, "That language which is in the common parlance but not in the books." Then I asked, "What then is this new thing you call Hindi-Hindustani?" He answered, "That language which some time in the future will become Hindustani." I said, "Hindustani is already here. Why wait half-a-century for its materializing." Now he snapped at me, saying, "I cannot disown Hindi." I retorted, "If you cannot disown Hindi, why should we give up Urdu?" To this, he reacted with words least expected of him. He said, "Muslims can hold on to Urdu. It is a language of religious value for them. It is written in the script of the Qur'an. It was propagated by Muslim kings." After this statement from him, I resigned from my membership of the Working Committee of the Parishad. Our eyes were opened by this experience."[13]

Dr. Abdul Haq's report of the Nagpur meeting received countrywide publicity through the Urdu press, particularly "the revelation" that at this meeting Gandhi had tactlessly spoken of Urdu as "the language of the Muslims, written in the script of the Qur'an." Serious damage was done by this to the possibility of reconciliation between Hindus and Muslims.

An enlightened but unrenowned Muslim woman by the name of Sultana Hayat took the initiative to do something about it. She came from a family known for its Nationalist commitment. She approached Gandhi to verify if he had really uttered those insensitive words about Urdu in Nagpur. In a lengthy article she gives an account of her efforts to persuade Mahatma Gandhi and Dr. Abdul Haq to meet and work out a compromise.[14] Here is a quotation from her article:

> Even in my mind the sentence [attributed to Mahatmaji] rankled like a thorn. . . . In August 1941 I was blessed with the opportunity to be in the presence of Bapu [i.e., Mahatmaji]. . . . I said to him, "You are the leader of the entire Indian nation. What then made you say that Urdu is the language of the Muslims?" Bapu's face flushed with surprise and emotion. [It being Monday, his weekday of fast of speech] he conveyed his answer in writing, as follows: "The truth is that I never uttered those words."[15]

Sultana Hayat goes on to tell us that she was advised by Gandhi to verify his denial by turning to the testimony of a number of eminent leaders who had attended the meeting of the Parishad at Nagpur. Following his advice, she took the question to Dr. Zakir Husain, Dr. Abid Husain, Rajindar Babu, Kaka Kalekar, Jawaharlal, and Manshoorwalaji. All of them, she tells us, denied that Mahatmaji ever uttered such a sentence.[16]

On whose side is the truth in this story? Emotions on both sides disallow a unanimous answer to this question.

NOTES

1. Sayyid Abdullah, *Adabiyat-I-Farsi men Hinduon ka Hissa* (Delhi: Anjuman-e-Taraqqi-e-Urdu, 1942), 254–255.

2. Sir George A. Grierson, *The Linguistic Survey of India* (Calcutta: Office of the Superintendent of Government Printing), 2:2.

3. Peter Hardy, *The Muslims of British India* (Cambridge: Cambridge University Press, 1972), 142–144.

4. *The Collected Works of Mahatma Gandhi* (Delhi: Government of India, 1971), 29:212. Hereafter cited in the text parenthetically as *CW* followed by volume and page(s).

5. Ibid., 81:33–34, 332. The date of his resignation indicated in 82:9, is July 25, 1945.

6. Ibid., 13:419. Other statements of this category can be found in 1:179, 181; 10:56; 14:121, 123, 193, 294, 301; 31:222; 42:318; 75:279.

7. Ibid., 35:196. Other statements of this category can be found in 34:551; 42:319; 15:80; 15:159.

8. Ibid., 87:123. Other statements of this category can be found in 84:3, 412, 424, 273; 83:40, 55, 92; 79:171; 75:72–74, 280; 90:255; 87:123; 82:362; 28:119–121, 399; 20:530; 17:97; 16:220; 33:62–63; 19:314; 88:420.

9. Ibid., 83:18. Other statements of this category can be found in 21:405; 83:40, 53, 60, 96.

10. Ibid., 89:248. Other statements of this category can be found in 34:169; 38:330; 42:114; 90:255.

11. Ibid., 82:99. Other statements of this category can be found in 81:97; 89:249; 88:467–468; 83:40, 96; 82:99, 362; 13:4, 420; 19:59.

12. Ibid., 79:397. Other statements of this category can be found in 75:403; 82:46; 84:273.

13. Abdul Haq, *Khutbat-e-Abdul Haq* (Karachi: Anjuman-e-Taraqqi-e-Urdu, 1952), 503–505.

14. Hayat, Begam Sultanah, *"Maulana" Abdu'l-Haq Sahib, Urdu aur Mahatma Gandhiji* (Delhi: Urdu Abad, 1992), 19–49.

15. Ibid., 20.

16. Ibid., 22, 46.

Conclusion:
A Debate for Our Times

Julius Lipner

The horrific events of September 11, 2001, in the United States, with special reference to the destruction of the twin towers of the World Trade Center and the resulting vast loss of life, show us that Gandhi's relevance for our time continues to be acute. There seems to be general agreement that the attack on the twin towers was especially symbolic. But symbolic of what, one may ask. Not of "the clash of civilizations," even though this is a favorite description (or at least unspoken presupposition) among politicians and commentators. I doubt if most of the victims of the destroyed towers and the bereaved families would wish their loss to be associated with the technological prowess of thrusting skyscrapers, global capitalism, and their attendant military might as the symbols of the cherished values of their lives.

No. The civilization they would wish to stand for would be expressed through the everyday freedoms they took for granted: the freedom to expect security of life and limb; the freedom to vote for a polity that allowed equal respect for and by the other as a human being; irrespective of differences of color, gender, creed, and lifestyle, but within the rule of law; the freedom to work and to care for loved ones and the wider community with the fruits of one's labor; and the freedom to build a society on this basis. One did not need to work in the World Trade Center for that.

On the other hand, the perpetrators of this crime did not stand for a civilization. It is hardly civilized not only to be deliberately uncaring about the loss of innocent life but also to encompass this in the pursuit of one's own ends, however legitimate one may claim these to be. Certainly this action cannot be derived from any form of Islamic civilization. As Muslim leaders and politicians the world over were quick to point out, the values of Islam do not condone the wanton destruction of innocent life, nor indeed the willed killing of noncombatants even in what is perceived to be a just war.

The events of September 11 pointed, in spectacular fashion, to a clash of moral codes that focus on the role of violence in the deliberation of means and ends—not only physical violence, but violence in other forms: social, political, economic, psychological. This is *the* debate for our times. And a salient crux of this debate must be the life and thought of Mohandas Karamchand Gandhi (1869–1948), alias the "*mahåtmå*," the "great-souled one," that is, the one who lives by the spirit.

This life straddled the intensification of apartheid in South Africa, two world wars, and the dismantling of colonial rule in India as the culmination of Nationalist movements that ended in the partition of the country. It was terminated by a bullet to the heart.[1] Gandhi's life, words, and death articulated the issue of violence as a moral concern in all its major aspects. This is why the discussion begun in this book is so important: It does not take Gandhi at face value. It does him the honor of constructively inquiring into serious critiques that held his beliefs and actions concerning the role of violence and nonviolence in our lives to account.

In this concluding chapter, then, my task is not one of accretion: to add a further (Indian) critique of the Mahatma, however informative and important such as project might be. I shall adopt a different register, and attempt to draw the strands of the discussion together to allow them to converge reflectively on an issue critical not only for Gandhi but also for the increasingly global age in which we live. On the basis of the insights of the preceding chapters, my task is to educe a theoria that might generate a praxis of integrity.

What Gandhi helped us see, and what the critiques of this book help draw out, is the various modes and agencies of violence in our lives, and its scope and moral complexity. Gandhi gave no reductive definition of *violence*, some schoolboy description whose neat contrary could be termed "nonviolence." He was sagacious enough to realize that violence and nonviolence come in different guises and that they exist symbiotically.

His was a dialectical understanding of nonviolence, an understanding that grew out of his encounters with and scrutinies of violence. Both violence and nonviolence are polymorphic. That is why he used not one word, but several context-specific terms to describe his goal, for example, *ahiṁsā* or *noninjury*, where the apparently negative particle "non," reflecting its roots in Jaina tradition, refers not only to the absence of ill will toward the other but also to a positive disposition of benevolence,[2] or satyagraha, literally "truth-grasp," namely, not only one's hold on truth but also, perhaps more important, truth's hold on oneself, or again *noncooperation*, or even, *civil disobedience*. These were among the terms he used to describe his pluriform strategy of nonviolence.

It was, in fact, a strategy to articulate and possess the reality of truth in our lives. Truth, for Gandhi, in the human condition, is also polymorphic, and the polymorphism of truth is but the obverse, kaleidoscope-like, of the polymorphism of nonviolence. Amid life's bewildering complexities, the implementation of this strategy must often give rise to no more than the uncertainties of trial and error. Here we have the serious intent, I believe, underlying the apparently flippant use of *experiments* in the title of his early but quite unfinished attempt at systematic autobiography, *The Story of my Experiments with Truth* (the first volume of which was published in 1927).

In this chapter I will focus on Gandhi's politics of nonviolence as the means to articulate his understanding of truth. Ironically, as some of the critiques in this book indicate, Gandhi sometimes failed to appreciate that what he regarded as a course of nonviolence could be perceived by others as a form of violence. The dialectics of non-violence sometimes shade into moral ambivalence. I will consider this in due course.

It is in terms of the overriding theme of this book then, namely, the dialectics of nonviolence, that I will respond to the discussions in it, under the following headings: nonviolence and theories of violence, and nonviolence, identity, and pluralism. These are not the only headings, of course, under which the material of this book may be interpreted. But I hope they will be useful for us to deal in some depth with the substantial issues involved, notwithstanding the unequal length of my treatment of each.

NONVIOLENCE AND THEORIES OF VIOLENCE

As many of his critics saw, Gandhi regarded nonviolence in its various modes as "an exclusive ideology and strategy" (chapter 4), "a creed" (chapter 9). Indeed, it was an article of faith, an inherent feature of his integration of religion, social concern, and politics. Gandhi's starting point, then, was a stumbling block for many. For a number of his sympathetic critics discussed in this book, including Nehru, and members of the Muslim and Sikh communities, though nonviolence was appreciated as an intrinsic value, it could not be regarded as an absolute end-in-itself, incapable of being relativized under any circumstances.

In other words, though some believed that there are circumstances in which the use of violence has inherent limits, they also argued that there are situations in which the application of nonviolence cannot be enforced, or indeed, may not be endorsed. Here distinctions were made: distinctions concerning forms, fields and objects of violence, for example, the social and economic injustices of caste discriminations and untouchability. Thus although Ambedkar, who played such a crucial leadership role in initiating action that led to making the centuries-old practice of untouchability an unconstitutional and punishable offense (chapter 2), showed admirable restraint in inducing his followers to refrain from physical violence on occasion, he did not shrink from recommending another form of violence in response: that of burning, abrogating, or subjecting to extreme government censure the revered scriptures of a great many Hindus that seemed to support caste discrimination and untouchability. These were sentiments that caused serious offense to many of his compatriots, and prescribed a course of action that Gandhi could not endorse. True to his lights, Gandhi's reply was to argue that such passages were interpolations or not part of the true Hindu canon. Gandhi wished to retain the scriptures, but to reinterpret them. Their truth-value was not to be shunned, but like a rough diamond they were to be properly cut and faceted for their light to shine through.

Muslims too were unable to follow Gandhi's ideology of exclusive nonviolence. They were prepared to embrace nonviolence as a limited strategy or policy, not as an absolute moral imperative. In opposition to Gandhi, the Muslim religious scholar Abdul Kalam Azad (1888–1958) was, like Jawaharlal Nehru, Vallabhai Patel, and others, prepared to support the British war effort during World War II if the British promised freedom for India in return. And the journalist and political leader Mohamed Ali (1878–1931) stated, "I believe that war is a great evil, but I also believe that . . . [w]hen war is forced on Muslims . . . then as a Musalman and follower of the Last of the Prophets I may not shrink but must give the enemy battle on his own ground and beat him with his own weapons. . . . [But] when persecution ceases . . . warfare must cease. These are the limits of violence in Islam" (see chapter 9). For the Muslims it was the Prophet Muhammad who acted as the exemplar for the proper use of force.

Gandhi was not completely unnuanced, of course, in his advocacy of (physical) nonviolence. "Sickened by the Nazis" persecution of the Jews, he declared, "If ever there could be justifiable war in the name of and for humanity, war against Germany to prevent the wanton persecution of a whole race would be completely justified." "Still," he said, "I do not believe in war." He proposed "a calm and determined stand offered by unarmed men and women possessing the strength of suffering given to them by Jehovah." "That," he said, "would convert [the Germans] to an appreciation of human dignity."

While Winston Churchill summoned his countrymen to "blood, toil, tears and sweat," Gandhi, hoping to find in the English a people brave enough to put his theory to the ultimate test, proposed another course. "Invite Hitler and Mussolini to take what they want," he wrote to the English at the height of the Blitz. "Let them take possession of your beautiful island. . . . You will give all this, but neither your minds nor your souls."[3]

We know that, in the case of the Holocaust, there was a display of "unarmed men and women possessing the strength of suffering" given to them by their belief in Jehovah. Yet this did not result in the conversion of the Nazis to an appreciation of human dignity. For a populist who could sway not only the variegated components of the immense population of India but also the privileged as well as the disadvantaged of people in other lands,[4] Gandhi could seem to be extraordinarily out of touch with reality, if not insensitive, in his personal search for truth. (I will return to this concern.) The point here is that even those who valued the principles of his stance on nonviolence as a legitimate course of action morally saw the need to relativize these principles in certain circumstances. As we can see from the implications, historical and otherwise, of the extract quoted above, they appear to have a point.

This is different from saying that recourse to a strategy of nonviolence is a legitimate pragmatic device in the pursuit of some larger objective. As some of the discussions in this book indicate, this was often the basis on which people and groups were willing to collaborate with Gandhi. This in itself does not seem to be morally reprehensible, but it is not the same thing as adopting strategies of nonviolence, even as an intermediate political or social device, on intrinsically moral grounds as a preferred means to an end. In fact, many of Gandhi's cooperators went along with his strategy of nonviolence on a number of important issues on the grounds of both pragmatic expediency and moral approval. But because they perceived a distinction between the two, they were prepared on occasion to abandon the strategy if it seemed inappropriate at the time, either politically or morally, for the end they had in mind.

This is an important distinction that often comes into view in the analyses undertaken in this volume. But Gandhi seems unwilling or unable to acknowledge it. For him, nonviolence was politically apt precisely because it was a moral absolute. And it was a moral absolute because it was rooted in human nature. It is an expression of the human constitution. It is how human beings can be true to themselves: *Nonviolence is the law of our species as violence is the law of the brute*. Nehru interprets Gandhi by saying that the Spirit lies dormant in the brute, and he knows no law but that of physical might. The dignity of man requires obedience to a higher law—to the strength of the Spirit (see chapter 1).

It must be said that even though the principle of nonviolence was morally nonnegotiable for Gandhi for the reason stated this does not mean that he did not also appreciate its pragmatic value in the various political liaisons he made. As Miller notes, we must assume that Gandhi realized that the basic Muslim view of violence differed from his own and took a practical approach. He recognized his own utilitarianism. As he told Maulana Shaukat Ali, "[A]ll along I was helping to save your cow [i.e., the caliphate] because I hoped to save my cow thereby" (see chapter 9). On their different levels then, pragmatism and moral intransigence can be compatible courses it seems, but their ongoing compatibility in any instance demands continuous scrutiny.

But even from the standpoint of faith, namely, a particular interpretation of and its continuing justification by experience, Gandhi faced implacable challenges. This is where Minor's and Neufeldt's chapters (4 and 6, respectively) become particularly interesting. For their subjects—Sri Aurobindo and Veer Savarkar respectively—saw Gandhi's ideology of nonviolence as positively immoral. It was not that nonviolence could be immoral in certain situations—this is a common enough position to maintain—it was that it was immoral as an ideology, as an absolute end-in-itself. But both Aurobindo and Savarkar held their views for different reasons.

As Minor points out, Aurobindo had always endorsed the use of violence as a means to an end. All that had changed, when he turned his back on active politics and sought contemplative refuge in his ashram in Pondicherry, was the philosophical articulation and defense of his position. Like Gandhi, but unlike Nehru for instance, Aurobindo had a concept of religion that was all-embracing. For Nehru—heir to secularist–humanist tendencies of the nineteenth-century West which sought to corral religious commitment and its expression in private space in contrast to the public, civic domain of an egalitarian polity—religion and politics were to be kept apart. Hence Nehru's revealing description of satyagraha as "a most *civilized* form of warfare" (chapter 1). In other words, it was not necessarily the only moral option.

Nehru kept tripping up on Gandhi's insistence that one's political motivation and its public display must be a manifestation of one's religious commitment. But for Gandhi, the pursuit of nonviolence was the pursuit of Truth. This is why he sought nonviolence with religious zeal. Gandhi once said that Truth is God (not God is Truth). In this respect, what he wanted by the life he lived, was to see "God" face to face, in utter transparency. This is why there could be no sectioning of truth, into private and public space. As in the case of his struggles with his sexuality, which were also an expression of his pursuit of truth, truth here too could have no "private parts."[5] So, if one went to the root of the matter for Gandhi, it was religion that made one tick, not politics. This is why Gandhi's politics of nonviolence, rooted supposedly in the human constitution, was essentially a religious affair and as such nonnegotiable.

Aurobindo too absorbed politics into religion, his religion, that is, of Integral Yoga. According to Integral Yoga, Reality comprises two dimensions: Pure Being and Becoming. Pure Being is, in fact, an undifferentiated, never-changing unity, while Becoming is represented by our phenomenal world of differentiation and change. Both are integral parts of Reality, and neither must be sacrificed to the other. This makes our multilayered world of Becoming a place of ultimate meaning whose various processes tend inherently to evolve into higher and higher forms of Consciousness. Integral Yoga is the personal acceleration of the evolutionary process that is the Becoming of the All and it is the goal of the integral yogin to realize this and in this realization to facilitate not only the evolutionary transformation of the multilayered self (spirit, psyche, and body), but also the evolution of the universe (see chapter 4).

In this scheme, violence and nonviolence both have a necessary part to play: neither can be dispensed with. In certain circumstances, nonviolence can be espoused for pragmatic reasons, but never as an absolute end-in-itself, for this would be to seek to displace the ineluctable place of violence in the evolutionary process and to thwart the inherent law of the universe. As Minor noted: When ego and the assertion of individuality and separateness ("egoism") hinders, or at least does not promote, the evolutionary process which is the intention of the universe, it becomes the content of evil in Aurobindo's viewpoint (chapter 4). In short, in his advocacy of nonviolence as a moral absolute, Gandhi was acting ignorantly and egoistically, and eventually, unavailingly.

Aurobindo based his view on what he regarded was unsuitable authentic "yogic" experience. But as we saw, Gandhi claimed too, more modestly perhaps, to base his own conviction of the absolute moral imperative of nonviolence on personal experience (his "experiments" with truth). This is why there seems to be a point where one's morality—the morality of violence and nonviolence included—seems to be an anti-foundational "response of faith" to an interpretive and constructed world. This does not mean that one interpretation is as good as any other. There is an important role for consensus, for the application of reason and logic within an agreed framework of rationality, for accountability to oneself and the wider group, and for the determination of acceptable social and moral values in which the unprivileged, defenseless, suffering, and vulnerable must be reckoned with, in any interpretation of reality. It is not the case that "anything goes" based on one's claim for experience. For the experience itself, as a construing of the world, calls for justification. But it shows the importance and necessity of the role of "construal" in its ongoing dialectic with "legitimation."[6] Gandhi's stance on the moral status of nonviolence was a construal, not an absolute given, just as Aurobindo's was.

Although Savarkar, like Aurobindo, saw Gandhi as a significant (but also) misguided adversary in the struggle for India's independence, Savarkar's disagreement with Gandhi was different (chapter 6). Aurobindo—the philosopher of the integral dialectic—based part of his view, if you will, on a major strand running through Hindu tradition: the martial code (dharma) of the warrior or Kshatriya. This was a dharma of the acceptable use of violence in the safeguarding of one's society, lifestyle, and territory. Anyone knowledgeable about the history of Hinduism will know how salient this strand has been historically and textually. But since Aurobindo claimed to see the whole picture, the part could not be privileged over the whole in the quest for independence. Violence, or nonviolence for that matter, could have only strategic value.[7]

Savarkar, for his part, may be regarded as taking his stand squarely on Kshatriya–dharma as the normative criterion for patriotic ends. Arguably his was a warrior code that showed crucial discontinuities with that of the past in its exclusivist implications not only for a determination of patriotism and Hindu identity, but also for a recommended morality. The Kshatriya–dharma of much of past Hindu tradition was constructed—perforce—by processes of racial, cultural, caste, social, and political amalgamation and assimilation. A cursory study of Indian history testifies to this. Hindus are survivors par excellence. But Savarkar was not interested in studying Indian history. He was intent on reinventing it, because he wished to invent a nation—a Hindu nation, based on its inherent property of *hindutva* or "Hinduness."

It is not necessary for our purposes to go into what hindutva means for Savarkar. Neufeldt gives a careful analysis in chapter 6. Rather, I am interested in Savarkar's ideology of violence vis-à-vis Gandhi's position. For Savarkar, violence—physical and military force—is necessary in human affairs not only as an occasional strategic ploy, but because it is the law of human nature, at least in its present condition. For it is the implementation of violence that can enable human groups to create the agents—a common purpose, a common past and future, a shared culture, a national identity—that can best fulfill their destiny. Thus he turned on its head Gandhi's rationale for nonviolence as a moral absolute, that nonviolence is the law of our species as violence is the law of the brute, by declaring precisely the opposite: As Sarvakar saw it, nations which, other things being equal, are superior in military strength are bound to survive, flourish, and dominate while those which are militarily weak shall be politically subjected or cease to exist at all.

Violence was essential for survival, since the law of the jungle prevailed. And the latest lesson from history that endorsed this reading was the way the British rulers of India had seized and maintained power: by first using and then brandishing the ultimate threat of force. The Jallianwalla Bagh massacre of 1919 in which General Dyer and his soldiers had slaughtered hundreds of unarmed Indians, men, women, and children near the sacred precincts of the Golden Temple, was still fresh in people's minds.[8] The violent events of human history, then, which Gandhi interpreted as a violation of the basic law of human nature and a summons to the human race to come to its senses and adopt nonviolence as a moral imperative, Savarkar interpreted as an endorsement of the law of violence for the higher end of fulfilling human and national destiny. In this reckoning, Gandhi's monomaniacal principle of absolute nonviolence is immoral and anti-human, and is not only devoid of saintliness, but is, in fact monomaniacal senselessness. Once more we come up against two contending dyads of construal and legitimation.

We turn now to those critics who saw Gandhi's construals of nonviolence—the implementation of satyagraha and ahiṁsā in such actions as noncooperation, civil disobedience, and fasting—as expressions, in fact, of harmful coercion. From the discussions at hand, these were Annie Besant (chapter 3), Rabindranath Tagore (chapter 5), and C. F. Andrews (chapter 7). Both Besant and Andrews were foreigners, in fact British, who had temporarily made India their home. Besant did not particularly care for Gandhi, whereas Andrews was devoted to him. Nevertheless, both envisaged an India set free from the trappings of colonial rule, yet still retaining in one way or another a strong "British connection."

Andrews, as we shall see, was the more politically radical and psychologically sensitive. Besant, for her part, sought a "free" India that belonged to a federation of dominions with Britain as their head; her "Home Rule" movement was meant to give India self-government within the Empire on colonial lines. As Dixon shows, Besant's political goals were framed in terms of her commitment to Theosophy, a religious movement founded in New York in 1875 which she had helped implant among the Western-educated in India. Although Theosophy sought "universal brotherhood" among a "family of nations" evolving through mutual cooperation, it was neither socially egalitarian nor politically democratic. As Dixon demonstrated in chapter 3, Besant was no democrat, and her understanding of authority and hierarchy was shaped by her belief in the occult hierarchy of Theosophy. This was a hierarchy at whose higher levels were spirit–sages who gave secret messages of guidance (to which Besant and a few others had direct access) for the development of the human race. Those in the know were to be the spiritual leaders of the rest. In the light of such elitist thinking, Besant's political solution was always a restoration of power to those most able (in her estimation) to make use of it, and throughout Besant's voluminous writings, that invariably meant an appeal to an "India" that was Aryan, Hindu, Brahman, middle class, and educated.

This is where Gandhi and Besant could not agree: Not on the basis of articulating politics out of a religious vision—they were in agreement here—but because Besant's politics and religion would neither encompass nor appeal to the people at large. Gandhi longed to belong to the masses. In his view, any secrecy hinders the real spirit of democracy. As to Gandhi's own democratic credentials, I will pause to look into this under the next heading. But whatever else one may say of Gandhi, he was a consummate populist who saw through the inadequacies of Besant's occultist elitism where his own political goals were concerned. But on a higher level, occultism also militated against that transparency required for the pursuit of Truth. Once again, Gandhi's politics and religion were of a piece with one another.

Thus the clash between Besant and Gandhi was a clash not only of means but also of ends. From 1916 onward claims Dixon (chapter 3), Besant continually pointed up the supposed contrasts between her own peaceful, reformist, law-abiding, and constitutional activities and the violence, disorder, and revolutionary activities of Gandhi and his followers. Gandhi's movement was a form of "mass action," and in Besant's opinion, India's "ignorant masses" were unfit to participate in and envisage India's "spiritual mission to humanity."

There is a profound question here, one that Gandhi detected very early in his dealings with Besant. It concerns the capacity, role, and understanding of people at large in using what are generally agreed to be elevated means to further "noble" collective ends: a country's "spiritual mission to humanity," or a nonviolent society, or national destiny. Ultimately, it boils down to a question of shrewd insight, trust, and an element of genuine risk. Does one take the people into one's confidence or not? Does one seek to identify with the people, including the poor, the ignorant, the disenfranchised, the dispossessed? Gandhi, the canny politician and impossible idealist, was willing to throw in his lot with "the masses"; Besant, the prophet of universal brotherhood, could not—she remained an outsider.

Andrews, unlike Besant, was in favor of complete political independence for India. Thus he did not side with many Indian Christians who were alarmed at the prospect of losing the privileges that came with British rule (chapter 7). The wished-for continuing connection with Britain would be through a dialogue of faiths, a sharing of the benefits of progress and modernity. It is here that some of his major disagreements with Gandhi arose.

A dialogue of faiths would come about, Andrews believed, on the basis of the perception of proper human equality between those involved, which entailed the abolition not only of untouchability but of the socioeconomic structures of caste itself. Tinkering or tampering with the system wouldn't do. To Andrews, caste was every bit as bad as white racism. As several places in this book have shown, Gandhi wanted to clean up or purge aspects of caste, including what was for him the unconscionable phenomenon of untouchability, but as in the case of the scriptures offensive to Ambedkar, he was committed to an idealized form of *varnashrama* or caste-dharma. For not only would caste in an ideal form be a marker of Hindu identity, its (regulated) multilayered manifestations were an expression of human nature. In Gandhi's view, once caste is purged of its impurities, it will be a bulwark of Hinduism and an institution whose roots are embedded deep in human nature (chapter 7). Here Gandhi the Nationalist could not rise above his commitment to a particular Hindu way of life. But for Andrews, this was in effect, to condone a form of inhumanity, a form of violent enslavement that could not really give India the full freedom Gandhi craved.

Further, Andrews often shared with Tagore a hesitancy about Gandhi's degree of militancy. When Gandhi decided on the policy of noncooperation after the Amritsar massacre, Tagore disapproved. Rukmani, in chapter 5, goes into the reasons for this. Tagore, who had returned from abroad, was disturbed by the "oppressive atmosphere" of the land. The power Gandhi was gathering through his seemingly nonviolent protests was in danger of getting out of hand. The deployment of force is in itself neutral, and sometimes it is necessary. But the accumulation of force carries an inherent danger. The danger inherent in all force grows stronger when it is likely to gain success, for then it becomes temptation, argued Tagore.

As Tagore, Andrews and others saw, this temptation expresses itself in two ways: (1) exteriorly, it encourages the wielders of the accumulated force to violate the rights or at least the sensitivities of others; and (2) interiorly, it encourages the wielders to act blindly and self-righteously.

1. Both Tagore and Andrews were pained at Gandhi's endorsement of the burning of foreign cloth; such noncooperation measures found no favor

with internationalists such as Tagore and Andrews. Andrews felt keenly for the poor Lancashire mill hands who would suffer as a result of this movement. Tagore, for his part, deplored the call to students to quit schools and colleges. This was a step against progress and modernity and would isolate and harm India in an increasingly interactive world. In short, a measure of critical detachment from Gandhi's Nationalist agenda, which both Tagore and Andrews had acquired from different sources and for different reasons, prompted each of them to adjudge aspects of Gandhi's program of nonviolence as the sinister harbingers of forms of psychological hurt and social distress.

Gandhi refused to acknowledge this or, rather, felt compelled to choose a course of the lesser evil. For Andrews Gandhi's lighting a pile of beautiful and delicate fabrics shocked him intensely destroying in the fire the noble handiwork of one's brothers and sisters abroad. But Gandhi replied that he saw nothing wrong in making it a sin to wear cloth that has meant India's degradation and slavery. Often enough interpreting the complex dialectics of violence and nonviolence gives rise to grim ambiguities of moral ambivalence.

2. But Gandhi's belief in nonviolence was prey to another inherent problem. Andrews joined Tagore in warning of the danger of self-righteousness in campaigns of nonviolent resistance. The accumulation of power tends to go to one's head, resulting in a form of blindness or worse. Again and again we seem to come up against this charge in the course of this book: Gandhi's apparent arbitrariness, his abrupt changes of policy without prior notice, his intransigent attention to his "inner voice" without consulting friends and others. I will return to this in the next section. As Tagore and Andrews saw, it is a heavy burden to walk around with such tags as *Mahatma* attached to one. The danger is they may actually be perceived to be true, and, as we shall now see, this can cause serious rifts of misunderstanding between their bearers and those they seek so assiduously to succor.

NONVIOLENCE, IDENTITY, AND PLURALISM

As this volume shows, Gandhi's struggle by and through nonviolence was also a struggle for self and identity. This was an internal no less than an external struggle. On the level of the individual, Gandhi's notion of the self was dualist. This was derived from Jaina and Vaishnava thought, in the case of the latter with special reference to the *Bhagavad Gita*. In other words, each individual has a spiritual, immortal, unchanging core to their being—their deepest and truest Self—which underlies the ever-changing interactions internally of the various levels of mind and body, and externally with other selves and the world. It is the human condition that the psychophysical or empirical self—also called the *jiva*—exists in a state of internal disorder, subject to unruly passions, inordinate desires, and a clouded mind. It is this internal disorder that gives rise to the disorder in our relationships with others, often expressed in the different forms of violence. The goal is to create harmony within the jiva, and concomitant order in our external dealings. This is a kind of pilgrimage to the center of our beings—the inner Self or *âtman*—which is the source of true peace, compassion, order and love. This is where Truth or "God" resides.

Thus the psychophysical self is the locus of ignorance, disorder, and suffering. It must be brought under control by a strict code of mental and physical ascetic practice. This will work externally toward an approximation of harmony in the world. Thus Gandhi's regimen of ascetic discipline, his subjugation of the body by recourse to dietary restrictions and other bodily practices, so often the cause of derision and criticism, was not undertaken for aesthetic or ethical reasons; it was an expression of religious belief. The psychophysical self was a "lower" self in more ways than one. It must be made to reflect the serene purity of the higher Self. Its worldly transactions of conjugality and commensality then, which could so easily foment its internal disorders, were not conducive toward this end. They were a tainted expression of the human condition, and must be relegated to a lower order of human morality and strictly monitored.[9]

This aspect of Gandhi's religious philosophy gave rise to serious misunderstanding, not least with Andrews who understood Gandhi to say that if he ate a particular diet he would gain spiritually. "I simply can't understand that," he complained. After all, his mentor, Bishop Westcott was a meat eater but still a truly spiritual man. Gandhi's answer was revealing: "Hard cases make bad law. You can't preach to the generality of people asking them to eat what they like, and yet continue to believe that they are pure."

Andrews, as a Christian, subscribed to a religious philosophy that was less sharply dualist than Gandhi's, drawing as it did on the doctrine of the Incarnation, namely, God's enfleshment in a human body, as Jesus. This is why, though he was a celibate himself, he affirmed the goodness of marriage and decried Gandhi's own view of celibacy as a "slur on marriage." The human body, for Gandhi, was, said Andrews, an evil, not a good. Only by complete severance from this body can perfect deliverance be found. For reasons given above, this was precisely Gandhi's position. He wrote in *Hindu Dharma*,

"Hinduism is undoubtedly a religion of renunciation of the flesh so that the spirit may be set free. It is no part of a Hindu's duty to dine with his son. . . . Hinduism does not regard a married state as by any means essential for salvation. Marriage is a 'fall' even as birth is a 'fall.' Salvation is freedom from birth and hence death also" (chapter 7). Andrews saw these personal and social strictures endorsed by Gandhi as a form of misplaced hurt on the individual and on human relationships.

It is important to grasp the essentials of Gandhi's personal religious philosophy to understand how he went on to develop it socially and politically. For it is the basis of his critique of modern, that is, Western, civilization, and its social and political structures, such as colonialism, the concept of the nation–state, the technologization of culture, militarized might with its ingenious weaponry of mass destruction, global capitalism, urban industrialization, sexual permissiveness and other forms of hedonism, and consumerism. For Gandhi these features of modernity tended seriously to damage human nature and its potential for true growth. Naturally, not all of these aspects could be considered in this book. But we have a sufficient basis for understanding the nature of Gandhi's critique and of some of the objections that it faced.

There can be no doubt that the essentials of Gandhi's approach were shaped, as indicated above, by features of traditional Indian thought. A. Parel, in his fine introduction to his edition of Gandhi's "seminal work" *Hind Swaraj*, shows in addition the Western influences that reinforced and developed the intellectual content of this approach.[10]

This arsenal of ideas helped Gandhi tackle issues of national identity and pluralism in the religious and ethnic mix that constituted the subcontinent.[11] There is another element: his early, formative influence in South Africa. Other Nationalist-minded Hindus of the later second half of the nineteenth century, such as Vivekananda, built their Nationalist aspirations by widening localized bases. They started off, impassioned, from the limited perspective of a particular place, toured various parts of the country, and only then acquired a larger vision of their nation-in-the-making. With Gandhi it was different: "In the first place, it was in South Africa, not in India, that he first acquired his vision of Indian nationalism. . . . His idea of nationalism does not start with the locality and then gradually extend itself to the province and then finally to the nation. Quite the reverse. He was first an Indian, then a Gujarati, and only then a Kathiavadi. And South Africa has a lot to do with this."[12] To some extent this explains his apparent insensitivity to budding aspirations of religious, cultural, and/or ethnic identity, especially in the subcontinent, or to put it another way, his tendency to sit lightly on occasion to the demands of democratic procedures of consultation and attentiveness to self-affirmations of identity on the part of others. But only to some extent.

He also had quite a bit of the assimilativeness of the Hindu in him—the a priori impulse to recognize the other in terms of predetermined and predeterminative categories of sense and sensibility. And this impulse was heightened by his masked and somewhat uncritical allegiance to one of its most classical expressions historically: the philosophy of Advaita or nondualism, which, baldly put, states that differentiation is provisional and is to be sublated ultimately into an underlying unchanging, nondifferentiated, ineluctable One that is identical with the deeper Self of the individual.

Gandhi's broad allegiance to this view is insufficiently recognized in studies of his thought and action.[13] But it is the hidden rationale that enables such statements as the following to be made: "Satyagraha implies that the individual carries within himself or herself the burden of social failings, and that one reads from social developments as from a mirror the history of one's own thought and practices." Thus could Gandhi agonize repeatedly when he felt unable to explain or remedy the fracturedness of some situation, namely, its "violent" *dvaitic* (divisive) state: "There must be something terribly lacking in my ahiṁsā and faith which is responsible for all this."[14] For such a fractured state, as unregenerately dvaitic or split, was indeed a fall from grace, from its true condition of wholeness, which was a reflection of the perfect *Advaita* (nondual) underlying all. As an individual who pursued the advaitic goal (or Truth: *satya*) holistically and selflessly in mind, body, and spirit, he had remedial access, especially by suffering and asceticism, to others in their dvaitic brokenness. In this context, self-suffering was not an isolated act. S. K. Saxena paraphrases Gandhi's position: "[T]o suffer is to fraternize. True, the ego here ceases to serve as a foothold. But the loss is at once a release; and the 'sufferer' feels anchored and enriched in his realized identity with others. . . . [S]o far as we are really identical in being, when anyone is purified through prayerful suffering the good in others too tends freely to surface."[15]

We are now ready to consider with greater insight, perhaps, Gandhi's attempts at forging national identity or integration. And a good example is his seemingly inept assimilation of the Sikhs (and others) into the Hindu fold as demonstrated so vividly by Nikky Singh (chapter 8), or his apparently inapt conflations of Hindi and Urdu in trying to create a national language, as discussed with such erudition by Daud Rahbar (chapter 10).

Both Singh and Rahbar point to Gandhi's compulsion to assimilate, to unify. Singh focuses her analysis on an important literary exchange between Gandhi and the Sikh Shromani Gurdwara Prabhandak Committee in 1924, which is a turning point in the Gandhi–Sikh relationship and a vital opening for our understanding of the rupture between the Mahatma and the Sikhs, a rupture whose impact is still felt on the Indian subcontinent today. At heart, the exchange has to do with the nature of the burgeoning (Sikh) Akali movement. In short, who are the Sikhs? What is their place in (Gandhi's) nationalist agenda?

In her discussion, Singh notes how the Sikhs were developing a strong sense of identity politically and religiously by 1924. Yet Gandhi was reluctant to recognize this. In Singh's view, Gandhi is an inclusivist for whom Hindus, Buddhists, Jains, and Sikhs all flow into the vast ocean of Hinduism. (chapter 8). This is a remarkable metaphor, remarkable because it is often used in advaitic contexts. Point by point, Singh takes us through the Sikh delineation of their own separateness: once Gandhi recognized this, the Sikhs would be prepared to act in concert with him. But Gandhi remains obdurate. His belief about the Sikh Gurus is that they were all deeply religious teachers and reformers, that they were all Hindus. Gandhi did not regard Sikhism as a religion distinct from Hinduism but saw it as part of Hinduism and reformation. Thus Gandhi's reluctance to acknowledge Sikh aspirations for identity (aspirations, which at the time, were also part of a new world order of postmodernism) were ideological on several fronts: political, religious, but also, as this book has tried to show, metaphysical. And the moral is, I suppose, that an imposed metaphysics in the name of unity, when married to politics, can also be consequential, and give rise to the hurt of nonrecognition and divisiveness.

Rahbar argues that the contestation between Hindu and Muslim politicians in the first half of the twentieth century about the relative merits of Hindi and Urdu as a national language also concerned issues of cultural and national identity. As the Freedom movement developed, Hindu stewards of education and politics were bothered by the force of momentum of Muslim culture and were now eager to replace Urdu with Hindi. The "two languages" called Hindi and Urdu were almost completely identical in grammatical structure, with Hindi being written in Devanagari script and Urdu in the Arabic script. (see chapter 10). The other main difference between the two was Hindi's preference for borrowing words from Sanskrit and local vernaculars, and Urdu's preference for using terms taken from Arabic and Persian.

As indicated by Rahbar, Gandhi's position on the issue of a national language tended to be confused, if not conflicting. Throughout there seemed to be no consistent demarcation in his mind between Hindi, Urdu and Hindustani (see chapter 10). There was a porosity of boundaries here, an amorphousness, that appears disconcerting. I suggest that Gandhi was not trying consciously to dissemble or scheme; rather, the advaitic impulse was at work, seeking to submerge if not dissolve difference in a more encompassing unity. This can give offense, appearing to belittle valued and perhaps needed markers of identity, and it can readily be perceived as a disempowering rather than an enabling approach. What Gandhi's critics sought in this respect was not a sense of national identity that obliterated difference, but one that affirmed and then integrated difference in a higher unity of consensus—an identity-in-difference, if you will, in the context of an egalitarian polity, rather than an identity-sans-difference. This is an arduous task, and requires strategies of negotiation rather more complex than at times Gandhi seemed willing or able to offer.

So, in the course of his agonistic career, Gandhi had bitter lessons to learn too. What impresses is the enduring integrity in his chosen arena of his unremitting efforts to experiment with Truth. And for the light they throw on this heroic engagement, we must be grateful to the contributions of this book.

NOTES

1. See Louis Fischer, *The Life of Mahatma Gandhi* (London: Granada, 1982), 13.

2. Sanskritic terms, preceded by the particle *a*, often carry an ambiguity. Thus *a-brahmana* and *a-dharma* can mean "not a Brahmin" (that is, a simple denial of identity) as also "anti-Brahmin," and "not dharmic" (that is, not pertaining to the code of proper conduct) as also "unacceptable behavior," respectively.

3. L. Collins and D. Lapierre, *Freedom at Midnight* (London: Collins, 1975), 58.

4. For example, in South Africa, and in England during his visit for the Round Table Conference in 1931. See Hussein Keshani's useful chronology in the appendix to this volume.

5. On Gandhi's sexuality, see Vinay Lal's remarkable piece "Nakedness, Nonviolence, and Brahmacharya: Gandhi's Experiments in Celibate Sexuality," *Journal of the History of Sexuality*, 9, no.1–2, 105–136.

6. A more apt dyad than its analogous counterpart of "faith" and "reason."

7. Consistent with his later religious philosophy, in his early assessment of Gandhi's notion of passive resistance, Aurobindo was willing to approve of passive resistance because, he believed, there was still time to experiment with it. Its value was its possibility of success, not its exclusive morality. Yet to use it in the wrong circumstances was actually to sin against the divinity within ourselves and the divinity in our motherland (see chapter 4).

8. See the appendix.

9. This does not mean that Gandhi did not strive to integrate and sublimate his bodily functions and sexuality into his spiritual or religious life. On his politics of sexuality as an attempt to engage with Truth, see Lal, "Nakedness." Also see Joseph Alter, "Celibacy, Sexuality, and the Transformation of Gender into Nationalism in North India," *Journal of Asian Studies*, 53, no. 1 (1994): 45–66; and, more particularly, Alter's *Gandhi's Body: Sex, Diet, and the Politics of Nationalism* (Philadelphia: University of Pennsylvania Press, 2000). What these works show is that for Gandhi, truth is not only theologized, politicized, and socialized, but it is also sexualized, or perhaps more correctly, transsexualized. "Having renounced sex, Gandhi had by no means abjured sexuality. . . . Where players at the finite game of sexuality view persons as the expressions of sexuality, Gandhi was interested in sexuality as the expression of persons" (Lal, "Nakedness," 136).

10. A. Parel, *M. K. Gandhi: Hind Swaraj and Other Writings* (Cambridge: Cambridge University Press, 1997). Parel examines a range of sources. We may single out Plato's *Apology*, which strengthened Gandhi in the belief "that there was an irrefragable moral link between the order in the soul and order in society. Of equal importance was the doctrine of the ultimacy of the inner conscience and the option to suffer harm rather than to inflict it" (xxxv); Leo Tolstoy, whose various works endorsed Gandhi's distinction between institutional religion and its underlying religious vision, with special reference to Christianity and the Sermon on the Mount. Tolstoy affirmed and developed the view that nonviolence was a moral absolute and that external changes in society that could truly benefit human beings could arise only if the appropriate internal changes occurred; and John Ruskin, who not only reinforced Gandhi's view that "the good of the individual is contained in the good of all," but also helped convince him about the special dignity of manual labour (xxiif).

11. Alter notes correctly that Gandhi's was a "program of militant nonviolence" ("Celibacy," 48).

12. Parel, *M. K. Gandhi*, xxi.

13. But see S. K. Saxena, "The Fabric of Self-Suffering: A Study in Gandhi," *Religious Studies*, 12, no. 2 (1976): 239–247; and J. T. F. Jordens, *Gandhi's Religion: A Homespun Shawl* (New York: St Martin's, 1998), esp. chaps. 3 and 6.

14. Lal, "Nakedness," 133, 134.

15. Saxena uses Gandhi's discipline of periodic fasting to make these general points ("The Fabric of Self-Suffering," 240–241).

Appendix

Chronology of Gandhi, His Critics, and the Independence Movement

Hussein Keshani

1875	The Theosophical Society is founded in New York by Helena Blavatsky and Henry Olcott, who relocate to India four years later.
1876	Queen Victoria is proclaimed empress of India.
1879	Sri Aurobindo Ghose moves to England as a young boy and studies there.
1882	The Theosophical Society establishes its headquarters in Adyar near Madras (now Chennai). The society initially avoids involvement in Indian political and social reform.
1885	The Indian National Congress first convenes under the direction of A. O. Hume, a former Indian civil servant and Theosophist.
1891	Mohandas K. Gandhi travels from India to study law in Britain.
1892	Aurobindo joins London-based Indian student society called Lotus and Dagger that advocated the overthrow of British rule in India. He fails to enter the Indian Civil Service.
1893	Aurobindo secures an appointment to the Baroda Service and returns to India. He begins to study Sanskrit, Indian religions, and the Upanishads in particular. Aurobindo begins writing the series "New Lamps for Old" for Bombay's *Indu Prakash*, attacking Congress's leadership.
	Annie Besant publishes her autobiography, prior to leaving Britain for India.
	Gandhi leaves India for South Africa, where he later arranges protests against discrimination toward Indians and develops the

	experimental Phoenix community, refining his ideas on nonviolent resistance.
1896	Famine in India due, in part, to drought. The plague reaches Bombay and Pune. Congress blames British taxation policies and administrative extravagance.
1898	Famine in India due, in part, to drought lasts until 1900.
1899	Gandhi rejects membership in the Theosophical Society because of its interest in the occult and its secrecy, but he continues to respect its values of universal brotherhood and religious tolerance. V. D. Savarkar establishes the revolutionary organization Mitra Mela known later as Abhinava Bharat (1904).
1902	Aurobindo first attends a session of the Indian National Congress in Ahmedabad. He meets with the activist Bal Gangadhar Tilak of Maharashtra, and aligns with the Extremists, joining a secret society endorsing armed revolution against the British.
1904	Prompted by his brother, Aurobindo establishes the Bengali newspaper *Yugantar (Jugantar)* advocating revolution and guerrilla warfare. His brother proposes to establish an order of sannyasis to prepare the nation for revolution.
1905	Bengal is partitioned along religious lines provoking great discontent in the region. Aurobindo begins writing for the Bombay Extremist English journal *Bande Mataram.* Two years later, he publishes the series later known as "The Doctrine of Passive Resistance," using the *Bhagavad Gita* to justify violence.
1906	Aurobindo moves to Calcutta, Bengal, and helps form within Congress the Nationalists, who favored Indian self-reliance and British boycotts. Gandhi recalls that this is when he first becomes aware of his inner voice as a living force. Gandhi takes the vow of *brahmacarya* (sexual moderation or abstinence). Savarkar goes to England on the Shivaji scholarship established by Shyamji Krisnavarma to train young men in the theory of violent revolution. He resides at India House and initiates the Free India Society.

	Mohammadan Educational Conference in Dacca lifts ban on political discussions.
1907	Following the Nationalists' inability to take control of Congress at the Surat session, Aurobindo orders to "break" the Congress and criticizes its leader, Gopal Gokhale, heavily.
1908	Aurobindo is imprisoned for one year in connection with the Alipore Conspiracy Case; he immerses himself in the practice of Yoga.
	Besant publishes the pamphlet *The Future Socialism*, arguing for an aristocratic socialism rather than a democratic one.
	Gandhi publishes *Hind Swaraj*.
1909	Savarkar and Gandhi share a public platform. They disagree over interpreting the *Gita* and the *Ramayana* as endorsing armed struggle.
	Sir William Curzon-Wyllie is assassinated by a follower of Savarkar, Madan Lal Dhingra.
1910	Aurobindo retires to Pondicherry in French India and pursues yogic thought and practice. Despite repeated requests to lead Congress in the following years, he abandons Indian politics altogether.
	Besant calls for an ideal state based on a modern reinterpretation of the caste system in a lecture in Banglore.
	Savarkar is arrested in London and sent to Bombay under suspicion for his revolutionary activities and for participating in the assassination of A. M. T. Jackson, the British collector of Nasik. He is convicted and imprisoned in the Andamans Islands.
1911	Ottoman power is threatened by the Italian attack on Tripoli and the Balkan wars, enhancing pan-Islamic sentiment and mobilizing Indian Muslim sentiment for Turkey.
	Plans to shift British India's capital from Calcutta to New Delhi are announced.
	Besant reorganizes occult school in Theophical Society, instituting an oath demanding complete loyalty.
1913	Besant claims to have met with the Rishi Agastya in the Theosophical Society's Great White Lodge in Shamballa and is instructed to "claim India's place among the Nations."

	Tagore wins the Nobel Prize for literature. He sends encouragement to Gandhi with C. F. Andrews and W. W. Pearson who visited his South African experiments. Andrews first meets Gandhi in South Africa, beginning a lifelong friendship. Subsequent private correspondence shows differing views on caste and Gandhi's non-cooperation policies in response to the Amritsar massacre. Azad calls for the support of the Ottoman caliph and Muhammad Ali Ansari leads an Indian Muslim Red Crescent medical mission to Turkey. The Muslim League issues a call for Muslim self-government.
1914	World War I breaks out and the Ottoman government allies with Germany. Besant launches the English weekly *The Commonweal* aiming for Hindu religious reform, Indian self-government under British rule, and better British–Indian understanding. She unsuccessfully attempts to form an Indian party in the British parliament. Besant buys and converts the *Madras Standard* into the *New India*, achieving a circulation of ten thousand. Besant's disciple establishes in Bombay *Young India*. Gandhi leaves South Africa for India, shutting down the Phoenix ashram. Tagore offers to temporarily accommodate the Phoenix inmates at Santiniketan.
1915	Gandhi spends six days with Tagore at Satiniketan recommending reforms. Besant proposes the formation of an All-India Home Rule League resulting in the establishment of two separate leagues based in Poona and Adyar. Gandhi challenges Besant's agenda at the opening ceremonies for Benares Hindu University, formerly the Central Hindu College, souring relations between the two. The Hindu Mahasabha is founded to promote cow protection, Hindi, and caste reform.
1916	Jawaharlal Nehru first meets Gandhi at the Lucknow Congress. Initially pro-Congress, M. A. Jinnah helps develop the Lucknow Pact tentatively integrating the Congress and the Muslim

	League by agreeing on separate electorates and Muslim representation; a high point in amity. The Montagu–Chelmsford Reforms of 1918 later reaffirm separate electorates.
1917	Gandhi launches satyagraha in India for the first time in Champaran, Bihar, to protest the exploitation of peasants by British indigo planters.
	Besant and colleagues are imprisoned at Ootacamund for violating the Press Act of 1910. Gandhi calls for the deployment of satyagraha on Besant's behalf. Besant elected president of the Indian National Congress.
1918	Gandhi attends viceroy's war conference at Delhi and favors the recruitment of Indians to fight in World War I. He leads the strike of Ahmedabad mill hands and employs fasting as a means of protest for the first time in India
1919	The All-India Khilafat Committee forms with Gandhi's support, stimulating joint Hindu–Muslim agitation in India on behalf of the Ottoman caliph. Gandhi presides over All-India Khilafat Conference at Delhi.
	The Rowlatt Acts are made law, extending wartime restrictions on Indian civil liberties. Gandhi mobilizes an all-India mass protest to protest the Rowlatt Acts.
	Tagore writes an open letter proclaiming Gandhi a great leader. Besant urges the Theosophical Society not to support satyagraha. In Amritsar, individuals in a crowd protesting the Rowlatt Acts are killed, the infamous Amritsar masacre of April 13.
	Tagore resigns his knighthood to protest the Amritsar massacre.
	To alleviate tensions, Great Britain formally declares on August 20 that its goal in India is responsible government in the Government of India Act.
	Gandhi assumes editorship of the English weekly *Young India* and the Gujarati weekly *Navajivan*.
1920	Congress adopts Gandhi's program of nonviolent noncooperation, which he claims will achieve swaraj in one year.
	The Treaty of Sevres dismembers the Ottoman Empire, agitating Indian Muslims now intent on supporting Gandhi's Noncooperation movement.

	The Jami Millia is founded in New Delhi, breaking from Aligarh University and becoming the Muslim intellectual base for a unified India.
	The Nagpur Congress meeting results in Gandhi's declaration of the first nationwide satyagraha. Although the Ali brothers support Gandhi, Jinnah privately criticizes Gandhi in a letter for introducing illegal and divisive strategies.
	One hundred eighteen 'ulama endorse a fatwa enjoining Muslim participation in the Non-cooperation movement as a religious duty.
	Gandhi is elected president of the All-India Home Rule League.
1921	Tagore establishes his international university Visvabharati at Santiniketan.
	Gandhi publishes his autobiography, *The Story of My Experiments with Truth.*
	Tagore delivers speech, *Satyer Ahvan* (The Call of Truth) at the Calcutta University Institute, his most explicit criticism of Gandhi's Non-cooperation movement due to the potential for unrestrained mob violence. Gandhi responds with his article "The Great Sentinel." Gandhi visits Tagore in Calcutta to seek his support.
	Gandhi adopts loincloth and homespun cotton. He presides over the burning of foreign-made clothes. Andrews privately questions Gandhi's campaign to burn foreign cloth and his increasing self-righteousness. He later questions Gandhi's emphasis on the adoption of khaddar and the spinning wheel as a religious duty.
	Due in part to the Khilafat agitation, the Mappila Muslims of Kerala violently turn on the British and Hindu landowners, resulting in their harsh suppression. Gandhi condemns Mappila violence and the responses of Hindus and the British. Critics argue Gandhi shares responsibility due to his participation in the Khilafat movement.
	The Ali brothers are jailed, deflating the Khilafat movement.
1922	Hakim Ajmal Khan and Ansari issue a joint manifesto urging Indian Muslims to follow Gandhi.
	Gandhi abruptly withdraws support for the Khilafat movement and suspends Civil Disobedience movement after a village mob

	in Chauri Chaura burned down the local police station. Muslim leaders are annoyed by his lack of consultation.
	Tagore writes the novel *Muktadara* (Free Current), indirectly criticizing Gandhi.
	The editors of the *Madras Christian College Magazine* criticize Gandhi as an "apostle of lawlessness."
1923	Kemal Ataturk exiles the Turkish Ottoman sultan and later abolishes the caliphate, weakening the basis of Muslim–Hindu mutual support in India. Besant begins organizing a convention of moderates to develop The Commonwealth of India Bill, advocating self-rule, a village system of government, and a restricted franchise.
	The Hindu Mahasabha is revived with Pandit Malaviya and later Lajpat Rai at its head.
	Savarkar publishes *Hindutva*, which establishes the ideology of the Hindu Mahasabha.
	Mohammad Ali delivers a presidential address to Congress stating his own belief that violence in self-defense is valid despite his agreement to abide by Gandhi's policy of nonviolence.
1924	Gandhi launches his only satyagraha in the cause of Untouchables to protest the denial of the use of public roads by Untouchables at Vaikam.
	Khan cautions Gandhi for overreacting to Hindu–Muslim violence at Kohat, North-West Frontier Province.
1925	Tagore writes an article in the *Modern Review* criticizing Gandhi's emphasis on home spinning of cotton. Gandhi publishes a response in *Young India*, "The Poet and the Charkhā."
	Gandhi engages unsuccessfully in a three-hour debate with Vaikam pundits on the issue of untouchability. Gandhi accepts the divinity of the Hindu shastras and the law of karma and reincarnation.
1926	Besant publishes *India—Bond or Free?* in Britain to garner support for The Commonwealth of India Bill in Britain. The book explicitly criticizes Gandhi's Non-cooperation movement.
	Ansari resigns from the Muslim League and the Khilafat Committee to promote secular politics.

| 1927 | Tagore criticizes Gandhi's defense of *varnasrama dharma* (caste law) in "The Shudra Habit," *Modern Review*.

Dr. Bhim Ras Ambedkar leads two satyagrahas at Mahad to gain the rights for Untouchables to drink water from the Chawdar tank. A copy of the *Manusmriti* is burned, alienating Ambedkar from caste Hindus but violence is avoided. In *Young India*, Gandhi later commends the restraint of the Untouchables.

Britain forms the Simon Commission with no Indian representative to investigate constitutional reform in India. |
|------|------|
| 1928 | The *Nehru Report* responds to the Simon Commission, calling for dominion status and joint electorates without provisions for minorities. Muslims oppose the report.

Gandhi credits Besant with bridging religion and politics and stimulating Indian nationalism in a speech in Ahmedabad celebrating Besant's birthday. |
| 1929 | Andrews publishes *Mahatma Gandhi's Ideas*, which includes a public critique of Gandhi's early support for recruiting Indians to fight in World War I and his views on celibacy.

Responding to the *Nehru Report*, Jinnah unsuccesfully calls for protection of the Muslim minority in his proposed "Fourteen Points."

Azad and Ansari found the All-India Nationalist Muslim Conference to rally Indian Muslims. |
| 1930 | The British government calls a Round Table Conference in London on India's future constitution. Ambedkar and D. B. R. Srinivasan are selected to represent the Untouchables. They unite with Muslims and Sikhs to seek separate electorates. Congress and Gandhi do not attend.

Ansari writes to Gandhi stressing the importance of Sikh–Hindu–Muslim harmony above independence

Mohammad Ali reverses his pro-Gandhi stance and publicly criticizes Gandhi as trying to make Indian Muslims subservient to the Hindu Mahasabha at the Muslim Conference.

Gandhi leads Salt march in Gujarat to protest British monopolization of salt production.

Tagore questions the new tactics in letters to the *Manchester Guardian* and *The Spectator*. |

1931	Gandhi announces the Gandhi–Irwin pact with the British viceroy, halting the Civil Disobedience campaign without consulting others, which greatly distresses Nehru.
	Gandhi and Ambedkar first meet privately in Bombay and disagree on whether to establish separate electorates for Untouchables. The Second Round Table Conference is called with Gandhi attending on behalf of Congess. Gandhi and Ambedkar publicly clash on the issues of separate electorates and who represents the Untouchables.
	Upon returning to India, Gandhi is imprisoned and Congress is outlawed.
	New Delhi becomes the country's capital.
1932	British Prime Minister Ramsay MacDonald announces the Communal Award, stating separate electorates were to be incorporated into India's new constitution.
	In protest, Gandhi launches his fast until death resulting in the Yeravda Poona Pact granting more assembly seats for the Untouchables but eliminating separate electorates.
	Gandhi initiates a two-year anti-untouchability campaign.
	Andrews publishes *What I Owe to Christ*. Andrews privately criticizes Gandhi's "fast-unto-death" to nullify the Communal Award as a willful act of suicide.
1933	Gandhi founds English and Hindi weekly paper *Harijan*, the Harijan Sevak Sangh organization, and the Harijan Fund. The inaugaral issue of *Harijan* includes both Ambedkar and Gandhi's diverging views on caste. Gandhi undertakes a twenty-one-day fast against untouchability.
	An Untouchability Abolition Bill put forward by Ambedkar is not passed by the Legislative Assembly.
1934	An earthquake devastates Bihar and is interpreted by Gandhi as a divine chastisement for his work with the Harijans, to Tagore and Nehru's distress.
	Tagore successfully seeks funding from Gandhi for the Viswabharati University.
	Ansari helps Gandhi reestablish the Swaraj Party.
	Gandhi resigns from Congress and Nehru succeeds him.

1936	Ambedkar publishes *The Annihilation of Caste*, prompting Gandhi to reply in the *Harijan*. One year later, Ambedkar continues this significant exchange with his essay, "A Reply to the Mahatma." Ambedkar announces he is leaving the Hindu religion, prompting others to join him. Buddhism is eventually decided to be the religion of conversion.
1937	World War II breaks out. The Government of India Act based on the Round Table discussions is passed, approving the goal of Indian independence and guaranteeing Muslim representation. Nehru is conceptually alienated from Gandhi at this point and privately expesses his disagreement to Gandhi. Tagore requests Gandhi to become a life trustee for Viswabharati University, but he is declined. Andrews privately disagrees with Gandhi's disapproval of conversion. The Congress sweeps the elections. The Muslim League wins only 109 of 482 reserved seats, prompting Jinnah to begin mobilizing the Muslim grass roots.
1938	Jinnah speaks to the Muslim League accusing Gandhi of compromising the principles of Congress and establishing a Hindu raj.
1939	Savarkar calls for compulsory military training at universities, colleges, and schools at the twenty-first Mahasabha session in Calcutta.
1940	Jinnah refuses Azad's offer to reconcile with Congress since he believes it to be a Hindu body. The Muslim League passes its Pakistan Resolution based on the concept that Indian Muslims were a distinct people in need of a homeland. A Civil Disobedience campaign is launched in India demanding self-rule in exchange for supporting Britain's war effort in World War II.
1942	The British institute the Cripps Mission proposal for an interim government during World War II to be followed by full independence. Gandhi launches the Quit India movement to demand immediate independence, resulting in British repression,

	the imprisonment of Congress leaders and supporters, and the outlawing of the Indian National Congress.
1943	Famines occur in Bengal due, in part, to rice price speculation.
1944	Jinnah meets Gandhi at the Bombay talks and scorns his refusal to accept Muslim self-rule.
	The Japanese invade India along the Burmese border but are repelled. Gandhi is released from jail.
1945	Ambedkar publishes his most vigorous critique of Gandhi in *What Congress and Gandhi Have Done to the Untouchables*.
	Gandhi privately doubts his ability to change Hindu attitudes on untouchability and publicly invites educated Harijans to participate in politics.
	The Muslim League sweeps the Muslim seats in the elections for India's provincial and central assemblies.
1946	Ambedkar organizes massive satyagraha demonstrations before the state legislatures at Pune, Nagpur, Lucknow, and Kanpur to highlight the cause of the Untouchables.
	Congress sweeps Scheduled Caste seats in the election.
	Jinnah calls for "direct action" to secure Muslim independence. Subsequent Hindu–Muslim unrest in Calcutta results in many deaths.
1947	Congress accepts the proposal for partition of British India into Pakistan and modern India. British parliament approves Indian Independence Act, favoring the partition of India. India's first cabinet is formed with the inclusion of Ambedkar on Gandhi's recommendation. Nehru becomes India's first prime minister.
1948	Gandhi is assassinated by a member of the Mahasabha. Untouchability is made illegal in India.

Contributors

Robert D. Baird, Professor Emeritus of the History of Religions at the University of Iowa, has taught both undergraduates and graduates at Iowa for thirty-five years. During the period 1995–2000 he served as director of Iowa's School of Religion. He presently holds the Goodwin–Philpot Eminent Chair in Religion at Auburn University. He teaches Asian religions with special competence in Indian religions. His research focuses on methodology, modern Indian religious thought, and religion and law in modern India. His major works are *Category Formation and the History of Religions* (Mouton, 1971); with Alford Bloom, *Indian and Far Eastern Religious Traditions* (Harper and Row, 1971); and *Essays in the History of Religions*, Toronto Studies in Religion, vol. 11 (Peter Lang, 1991). He is editor and contributor to *Methodological Issues in Religious Studies* (New Horizons, 1975); *Religion in Modern India* (Manohar, 1981, 1991, 1995); and *Religion and Law in Independent India* (Manohar, 1993). In addition, he has published numerous articles in professional journals and as chapters in scholarly books. He has done frequent fieldwork in India and the Far East.

Harold Coward is professor of history and director of the Centre for Studies in Religion and Society at the University of Victoria, British Columbia, and fellow of the Royal Society of Canada. His main fields are Hinduism, Hindu–Christian relations, comparative religion, psychology of religion, and environmental ethics. He has directed numerous research projects and published widely. His publications include *Jung and Eastern Thought* (1985); *Derrida and Eastern Philosophy* (1990, 1991); *Philosophy of the Grammarians* (1990); *Population, Consumption, and the Environment: Religious and Secular Responses* (1995); *Yoga and Western Psychology* (2002) and *T. R. V. Murti* (2003). He is also the editor of the *Hindu–Christian Studies Bulletin*.

Joy Dixon is assistant professor of history at the University of British Columbia, where she teaches British history and the history of gender and sexuality. Her book *Divine Feminine: Theosophy and Feminism in England* appeared in 2001. She is currently working on a new project: exploring the relationships between religion, science, and sexuality in modern Britain.

Timothy Gorringe is St. Luke's Professor of Theological Studies at Exeter University, England. He has taught in Oxford and St. Andrews, and worked in India for seven years. His most recent publications include *The Education of Desire* (SCM, 2001) and *Karl Barth: Against Hegemony* (Oxford University Press, 1999).

Hussein Keshani is a student of the art and architectural traditions of South Asia, focusing on the Muslim courts from the twelfth to the nineteenth centuries. His Master's thesis was entitled "Building Nizamuddin: A Delhi Sultanate Dargah and its Surrounding Buildings" (Victoria, B.C.: University of Victoria, 2000), and he is currently working on a doctoral thesis dealing with the history of the eighteenth-century Bara Imambara of Lucknow.

Julius Lipner is reader in Hinduism and the comparative study of religion at the divinity faculty at the University of Cambridge. Of Indo–Czech origin, he was born and brought up in India. He received his Ph.D. from King's College, University of London, and then taught briefly at the University of Birmingham, joining Cambridge in 1975. He has lectured and written widely, and his books include *Hindus: Their Religious Beliefs and Practices* (1994, 1998) and *Brahmabandhab Upadhyay: Life and Thought of a Revolutionary* (1999, 2001), which was adjudged Best Book 1997–1999 by the Society for Hindu–Christian Studies. At present he is completing an annotated English translation (with substantial introduction) of Bankimchandra Chatterjee's nineteenth-century Nationalist novel *Anandamath*. Dr. Lipner travels regularly to India to meet family and friends and undertake research.

Roland E. Miller, Professor Emeritus of the University of Regina, received his Ph.D. in Islamic studies from the Hartford Seminary Foundation, and spent twenty-three years in India. Thereafter he became a professor at the University of Regina, chair of its Religious Studies Department, and academic dean of Luther College. He was the founding director of the Islamic Studies Program at Luther Seminary, St. Paul, Minnesota. His major field is Indian Islam, with additional interests in India Studies and Missiology. He has authored or coauthored six books, fourteen book chapters, numerous journal and encyclopaedia articles, and has edited other works. Three of his major volumes are *The Mappila Muslims of Kerala*, 2nd rev. ed. (1992); *Muslim Friends: Their Faith and Feeling* (1996), and, as editor, *Christian-Muslim Dialogue: Theological and Practical Issues* (1998).

Robert N. Minor is professor of religious studies at the University of Kansas. He received his Ph.D. from the University of Iowa in 1975. His research is primarily on modern Indian thought and its relationships to traditional thought and contemporary institutions. He is the author of five books, the most recent *The Religious, the Spiritual, and the Secular: Auroville and Secular India* (1999), and articles on modern Indian thought and the *Bhagavad Gita*.

Ronald Neufeldt is professor of religious studies at the University of Calgary. He received his Ph.D. in the history of religion from the University of Iowa in 1977. He works primarily in Indian religious traditions, with particular emphasis on the Hindu renaissance and religion and law in modern India. In addition to various articles, he has published *F. Max Müller and the Rig Veda* and he edited *Karma and Rebirth: Post Classical Developments*.

Daud Rahbar, Professor Emeritus of Comparative Religion, Boston University, received his Ph.D. from Cambridge University in 1953. His doctoral dissertation was published by E. J. Brill of Leyden in 1960, under the title *God of Justice: A Study in the Ethical Doctrine of the Qūr'ān*. The State University of New York Press published his annotated English translation of the *Urdu Letters of Mirzā Asadu'llāh Khān Ghālib* in 1987. He is author of a number of books in Urdu. He has taught at universities in England, Canada, Turkey, and the United States. He taught in the Department of Religion of Boston University from 1968 to 1991. He now resides in Florida and is engaged in writing a book entitled the *Faith of Individuals*.

T. S. Rukmani is currently professor and chair in Hindu studies at Concordia University, Montreal, Quebec, Canada, and was previously the first chair in Hindu studies and Indian philosophy at the University of Durban–Westville, South Africa, from 1993 to 1995. She holds Ph.D. and D.Litt. degrees from the University of Delhi, where her last assignment was as principal, Miranda House, University of Delhi. She is a Sanskritist by training and her areas of specialization are religious and theological issues in Hinduism, reform movements in India, women's studies, Gandhian studies, Indian philosophy (in particular Advaita Vedanta, Samkhya, and Yoga), and the Upanishads. She is the author of ten books and a number of papers in journals. Her latest books are *The Yogavarttika of Vijnanabhikshu* in four volumes and *The Yogasutrabhasyavivarana of Sankara* in two volumes (2001).

Nikky-Guninder Kaur Singh is professor and chair of the Department of Religious Studies at Colby College in Waterville, Maine. Her interests focus on poetics and feminist issues. Singh has published extensively in the field of Sikhism, including *The Feminine Principle in the Sikh Vision of the Transcendent* (Cambridge: Cambridge University Press, 1993), *The Name of My Beloved: Verses of the Sikh Gurus* (San Francisco: HarperCollins, 1995), and *Sikhism* (New York, 1993; Japanese translation, Tokyo, 1994).

Index

Index prepared by Angela Andersen with assistance from Hussein Keshani